THE ULTIMATE ENCYCLOPEDIA OF
SMALL PETS
AND PETCARE

The essential family reference guide to caring for the most popular pet species and breeds, including small mammals, birds, herptiles, invertebrates, and fish

DAVID ALDERTON

southwater

This edition is published by Southwater

Southwater is an imprint of
Anness Publishing Limited
Hermes House
88–89 Blackfriars Road
London SE1 8HA
www.southwaterbooks.com; info@anness.com

© Anness Publishing Limited 2001, 2005

UK agent: The Manning Partnership tel. 01225 478444

UK distributor: Grantham Book Services tel. 01476 541080

N. American agent/distibutor: National Book Network tel. 301 459 3366

Australian agent/distributor: Pan Macmillan Australia tel. 1300 135 113

New Zealand agent/distributor: David Bateman Ltd tel. (09) 415 7664

Publisher Joanna Lorenz
Managing editor Judith Simons
Project editor Sarah Ainley
Copy editor Susie Behar
Designer Michael Morey
Special photography John Daniels
Illustrator Julian Baker
Editorial reader Jonathan Marshall
Production controller Steve Lang
Indexer Helen Snaith

DISCLAIMER
The author and publishers have made every effort to ensure that all advice given in
this book is accurate and safe, but they cannot accept liability for any injury, damage or
loss to persons or property resulting from the keeping of any of the featured pets.

CONTENTS

INTRODUCTION

Pet-keeping is something that appeals to people of all ages, and is an activity which can literally change your life. Scientific research has now confirmed that having a pet can prove to be highly beneficial for both our physical and mental health. In an ever-more stressful world, pets provide a relaxing focus set apart from daily worries. Watching fish glide around in their aquarium is an activity which will lead to a measurable decrease in blood pressure, while the fascination of looking after a stick insect can not only trigger a child's interest in the natural world, but also helps to encourage the development of a sense of responsibility at an early age.

While dogs and cats are not ideally suited in many respects to city life, especially if you are out all day, the range of pets covered in this book means that you should be able to find the ideal choice for you, whatever your surroundings, whether your home is an apartment or a house with a large garden. Not only are there the obvious choices, such as small mammals, birds and fish, but also reptiles, amphibians and invertebrates, which have increased rapidly in popularity as pets over recent years.

◆ OPPOSITE
Beautiful and bizarre, the panther chameleon is just one of the many reptiles that are now being kept and bred successfully in domestic surroundings.

◆ LEFT
The White's treefrog is one of the most popular pet amphibians. It will thrive in a planted enclosure and can be tamed sufficiently to feed from the hand.

Making a choice

Choosing a pet can be difficult in the first instance, because much depends on what it is you are wanting from the new addition to your household. If you are looking for a cuddly companion, then one of the members of the small mammal group will be an obvious starting point. But there are significant differences between these creatures. In terms of everyday care, they can be split into two groups. There are those that are kept permanently in the home, such as hamsters, gerbils, chinchillas and mice, while others, such as rabbits, guinea pigs and chipmunks, can be housed outdoors in suitable enclosures throughout the year.

It is also important to think about the expected lifespan of your potential pet. Generally, with the exception of the chinchilla, small mammals are relatively short-lived. Their life expectancy ranges from two or three years in the case of hamsters, gerbils and mice through to six years or so for rabbits and guinea pigs.

◆ A B O V E
Pet tortoises have been known to live for over 160 years, but it is impossible to age them reliably as adults, unless their date of hatching is known.

Although small mammals are often regarded as children's pets, there is a considerable interest among enthusiasts of all ages in breeding them for show purposes. This helps to explain why there are so many established colour varieties in existence today.

The same applies in the case of the budgerigar, which is popular both as a pet and as an outdoor aviary occupant. If you have the space outdoors, the idea of constructing a planted aviary may be appealing, where a mixed collection of finches can be housed, at least during the summer, and these will hopefully breed here in due course. If you are seeking a talking companion to house indoors, a parrot is the unrivalled option; these birds may have a lifespan roughly equivalent to our own. It is relatively easy to obtain a young, handreared parrot chick these days, but bear in mind that these birds are naturally social and will require a lot of attention if they are not to become bored and destructive. Some parrots are also very noisy.

◆ BELOW
Although rabbits are often regarded as outdoor pets, they can be kept in the home, and can be house-trained to use a litter tray just like a cat.

It is among the herptiles – the reptiles and amphibians – that the pets with the longest lifespans are found, in the guise of tortoises. In the past, it was difficult to keep many species of herptile successfully, but now, thanks to an ever-evolving range of specialist equipment and foods, they can be maintained without difficulty. Some of these species look spectacular, and some can become very tame. Once established in their quarters, there is every likelihood that herptiles will breed successfully as well.

This also applies in the case of invertebrates, which are creatures without backbones. This group is more to be admired from a distance than handled directly. There are no competitive shows for this group, but exhibitions are held regularly, and enthusiasts at these shows will often have quality stock for sale.

Fish also offer considerable scope, either for the home aquarium or indeed for a garden pond. Few pets are easier to maintain than the humble

goldfish, both in terms of housing and feeding. There is also tremendous potential for creating freshwater and marine aquaria in a range of decorative styles, reflecting the habitats of the fish. Alternatively, you can opt for a general community tank, which is home to a wider variety of compatible, non-aggressive species.

This book has the advantage of allowing you to compare the requirements not just of these different groups, but of the individual creatures themselves. This will help to ensure that you make the right choice at the outset, and that you have the option to expand your interest as well.

◆ RIGHT
Rabbits are a good choice of pet for older children. They will not usually bite when being picked up, although they may scratch with their claws if they feel they are slipping out of your hold.

SMALL MAMMALS

The vast majority of small mammals that are popular as pets belong to the rodent family. The word "rodent" comes from the Latin word *rodere*, meaning "to gnaw", and describes the very sharp pair of chisel-shaped incisor teeth found in each jaw right at the front of the mouth. The shape and strength of these teeth is crucial to the survival of rodents as they enable them to crack seeds and nuts easily. Unlike our teeth, they continue growing throughout the rodent's life. This is essential to stop them from wearing down, which would prevent the rodent from eating.

Rabbits are not actually rodents, but are grouped instead with hares and pikas in a separate family known as lagomorphs. However, the structure of their teeth is very similar to that of rodents, except that they have a further tiny set of incisors each side of the main teeth at the front of the mouth.

Most rodents are relatively small in size, which makes them vulnerable to larger predators. As a result, they have keen senses to help them avoid detection. Their hearing is very acute, and they often communicate with each other using ultrasonic calls, which we are unable to hear because the frequencies are too high for our ears. They also have a very keen sense of smell. However, rodents generally have poor vision, since they spend much of their time hidden away in burrows during the day, emerging to forage for food at night.

✦ OPPOSITE
Guinea pigs are friendly rodents and they make excellent pets. They are suitable for housing either in outdoor accommodation or indoors in the home.

✦ LEFT
Rabbits come in a wide variety of sizes and colours. They are easy to care for, and an increasing number of owners are now keeping rabbits as indoor companions.

RABBITS

The rabbit is the most popular of all the small mammals kept as pets, thanks in part to its friendly nature. An ever-increasing range of breeds and colour varieties, many of which are likely to be on view at shows, has served to enhance their appeal both to breeders and pet-seekers. Rabbits have also proved to be very adaptable pets, with individuals settling well either in an outdoor hutch or as house-rabbits in the home.

INTRODUCTION

There are 25 different species of wild rabbit found around the world, but the ancestor of all today's domestic breeds is the Old World rabbit (*Oryctolagus cuniculus*), which was originally found in the Mediterranean region. At first, rabbits were kept as a source of food, in large outdoor enclosures. It is unclear when they were first brought to northern Europe; they may have been originally introduced by the invading Roman armies, but there is no evidence of an established wild population until after 1066.

Rabbits were originally valued for their fur and as a source of meat, and it was not until the late 1800s that they became popular with breeders as pets. By this stage, a number of the distinctive varieties were already established, and as a legacy from this era, the breeds today are often classified on the basis of fur or fancy, with the former group featuring those

which were originally kept for food. The advent of the killer viral disease myxomatosis in the 1950s altered the public's attitude to rabbit meat,

♦ ABOVE AND LEFT
The European wild rabbit, from which all of today's domestic breeds and varieties have been created. Domestication of the rabbit began thousands of years ago.

however, as the sight of sick and dying rabbits in the wild was very distressing.

As a result of changing perceptions, the rabbit has evolved into the most popular of all small animal pets, due to its friendly nature and attractive appearance. There are now more than 200 breeds in existence, some of which are very rare, while others are still being developed. One of the latest to be added to this list is the lionhead, a relatively small rabbit with a lion-like mane on its head. Unfortunately, some breeds have also become extinct, such as the angevin, which was the largest breed of rabbit ever known. Individuals were said to have a leg span of nearly 1.2 m (4 ft), and could weigh as much as 15 kg (33 lb).

Most breeds are short-coated, although the angora, which has been kept for centuries for its wool, is long-coated and needs special care to prevent its coat from becoming matted. Any rabbit that has an angora breed in its ancestry, such as the cashmere lop, must be groomed on a daily basis. Most other rabbits, however, do not need much grooming.

RABBITS AS PETS
All breeds of rabbit make appealing pets, although it is not a good idea to buy an adult rabbit without knowing its age. Start out with a youngster that is approximately nine or ten weeks old. At this age, the rabbit is fully

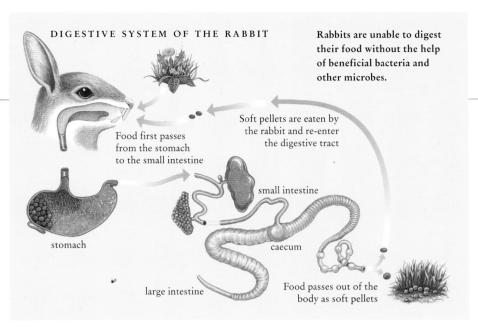

DIGESTIVE SYSTEM OF THE RABBIT

Rabbits are unable to digest their food without the help of beneficial bacteria and other microbes.

Food first passes from the stomach to the small intestine

Soft pellets are eaten by the rabbit and re-enter the digestive tract

small intestine

stomach

caecum

large intestine

Food passes out of the body as soft pellets

independent, but is still young enough to be tamed readily. Older rabbits that are not used to being handled are likely to be nervous and may never settle as pets. A rabbit will usually live for between six and eight years.

If, however, you are hoping to breed from your rabbit for show purposes, you will need to acquire older rabbits, although it may be better to start out with youngsters and wait for them to mature. It is generally better to start out with a doe (female) if you intend to breed rabbits for shows because, if necessary, you can arrange for her to be mated with

someone else's buck (male). However, most breeders are not keen to part with their best does.

Before buying any rabbit, always check its condition. The ears should be clean and clear of scabs, which can indicate an ear mite infestation. The eyes should be free from discharge, as should the nose. It is also important to part the lips so you can check the incisor teeth. If these are misaligned, you will have to have them trimmed back regularly throughout the rabbit's life. Check that the claws are not overgrown and that there are no sore patches on the underside of the hind legs. It is important to make sure that there is no sign of staining on the fur surrounding the vent, as this can indicate a digestive upset, which can be serious.

◆ ABOVE LEFT
Rabbits in the wild are very alert, since they face many dangers. The position of their eyes helps them to see well, while their tall ears detect and pinpoint the source of sounds accurately.

◆ BELOW
It is vital to consider size when choosing a rabbit. The larger breeds, such as the British giant, shown here with a Netherland dwarf, may be too big for younger children to handle easily.

◆ ABOVE
The sharp incisor teeth allow the rabbit to nibble plant matter, which is then ground up by molar teeth further back in the mouth.

A SELECTION OF SMALLER BREEDS

Rabbits today vary in size from the Flemish giant, which can tip the scales at 10 kg (22 lb) down to the tiny Netherland dwarf, which typically weighs about 900 g (2 lb). It is not just a matter of size, however, because breeds do differ significantly in temperament, and it is important to bear this in mind, especially if you are choosing a pet for a child. While the bigger breeds are generally placid, their size can make them difficult for a child to handle safely, and since rabbits are very susceptible to injury through falls, it is a better idea to choose a smaller breed for younger owners.

THE DUTCH
Although not as small as today's dwarf breeds, the Dutch, which weighs up to 2.5 kg (5½ lb), has long been a popular choice with rabbit enthusiasts. While pet owners enjoy its friendly nature, exhibitors are challenged by its highly distinctive coat markings.

The Dutch has a broad white area of fur encircling the front of the body, a half-coloured rear and white feet. The head and ears are coloured, with a distinctive white blaze extending down over the nose to the jaws. Dutch rabbits are currently bred in eight

colours. The dark shades, such as black or blue, are generally preferred to lighter shades, such as yellow. Rabbits with good fur markings can be identified while still hairless newborns, as the white areas can be recognized by their lighter pink skin coloration.

THE ENGLISH
The ever-popular English is the oldest of the fancy breeds, dating back as far as the early 1800s. It has a dark stripe running down its back to the base of the tail, with a variable pattern of spots on its sides, particularly on the hindquarters. There are several varieties, including black, blue and chocolate, plus a tortoiseshell. The ears are dark, as is the muzzle, with an area of dark fur usually encircling the eyes. The English is friendly, and the does usually make good mothers.

THE NETHERLAND DWARF
The breed known as the Netherland dwarf, which evolved from the Polish breed during the late 1800s, did not

◆ BELOW
The English rabbit is also known as the English butterfly because the dark fur around its nose resembles a butterfly's wings.

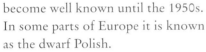

THE REX

The smooth, soft, sleek coat of the rex rabbit meant that it was originally very popular with furriers, but today, the rex has become a common sight at rabbit shows, and is now bred in a large range of colours and markings. The mini rex is a smaller version of the rex itself and, at only half its weight, tips the scales at up to 1.8 kg (4 lb). The rex's thin coat means that it needs snug winter quarters in temperate climates. Make sure that these rabbits have sufficient bedding on the floor of their hutch; the fur below the hocks on the hind legs may otherwise become thin, and this can be the cause of recurring soreness, which can prove troublesome to both you and your rabbit over the course of its lifetime.

become well known until the 1950s. In some parts of Europe it is known as the dwarf Polish.

The Netherland dwarf is the smallest of today's breeds. Now available in a huge range of colours, this breed has a characteristic compact nose and short ears. The breed is perhaps not always as friendly as others of a similar size.

DWARF LOP

This breed has grown in popularity over recent years, thanks to its gentle disposition. The appeal of the dwarf lop has been enhanced by its floppy ears, which hang down the sides of its head but do not touch the ground. The dwarf lop is a scaled-down version of the larger French lop, and was created during the 1950s in the Netherlands. Young dwarf lops are born with upright ears that start to trail down as they grow older. In turn, they have been bred to create the even smaller mini lop, which was first recognized for show purposes in 1994.

✦ **LEFT**
When deciding to buy a Netherland dwarf, inspect the teeth very carefully; these rabbits are vulnerable to malocclusion, and this will be a lifelong problem.

✦ **BELOW**
A fawn dwarf lop. Unlike some of the bigger lops, its ears are relatively short. The breed's friendly nature has made it very popular.

✦ **BOTTOM**
The fur of rex rabbits is short with a velvety feel as these rabbits lack the longer, coarse guard hairs seen in other breeds.

A SELECTION OF LARGER BREEDS

With the growing interest in keeping rabbits in the home, larger breeds have become very popular, and they can be given plenty of space to roam. Some of these rabbits are larger and heavier in size that a small dog. As an example, the British giant, closely-related to the Flemish giant, weighs up to 6.1 kg (15 lb). The breed originated from stock kept as long ago as the 1500s around the city of Ghent in Belgium.

FLEMISH GIANT

The traditional colour of the Flemish giant is steel grey, and it was the refusal of the British show authorities

✦ ABOVE
Large breeds of rabbit like this British giant are back in fashion, thanks to growing interest in keeping house-rabbits. The British giant is ideal for this purpose, but can be rather large for a small child to handle.

✦ LEFT
A white New Zealand rabbit. This breed is characterized partly by its relatively coarse, shaggy coat as well as its pink eyes. These rabbits have a steady temperament and make good pets.

to recognize this breed in other colours that originally triggered the development of the British giant strain in the 1930s. The Flemish giant is still better known internationally, and is also slightly heavier, averaging 7–8 kg (15½–17½ lb). These large rabbits are known to be friendly, with calm temperaments. As house-rabbits they will settle quickly into a domestic lifestyle, and can be trained to use a litter tray from an early age. Although the typical agouti-patterned form, resembling that of the wild rabbit, is commonly seen, a range of colours from pure white through to blue and black is available as well.

NEW ZEALAND VARIETIES

Several varieties of rabbit have their origins in New Zealand. The original white variety was created as a meat breed. It has a well-muscled body and relatively short ears, typically weighing up to 5.4 kg (12 lb). These rabbits grow very quickly and are capable of reaching almost half their adult weight by just ten weeks of age. They are

The similarity to a true hare can be seen in this Belgian hare, although it is a pure rabbit breed. These rabbits became immensely popular in the United States in the early 20th century.

an attractive silky texture, with individual hairs that are over 2.5 cm (1 in) long. The traditional colour is a pale shade of lavender. The black form was developed in 1919, followed by albinos and dark-eyed whites, and then the brown. One of the most recent additions to this group of friendly rabbits is the lilac, created during the 1980s. Recognizable by its white body and dark markings on the extremities, it is now becoming more common.

◆ BELOW
The Beveren has now been developed in a range of colours, but the attractive lavender variety, seen here, is the traditional form of the breed.

pure white in colour, with the pink eyes that confirm they are true albinos. Since the 1960s, two more colour forms have been developed – a black and a blue variety, both of which resemble the New Zealand in all respects apart from their coloration. Like the white New Zealand, the blue and black varieties are docile and placid. A smaller breed called the New Zealand red has also been developed in America. It is thought to be descended from crosses between Flemish giants and Belgian hares carried out in the early 1900s.

BELGIAN HARE

This slim, athletic, long-legged Belgian breed resembles a hare, but is nevertheless a rabbit. Its highly distinctive appearance caused a stir when it was first developed at the end of the 19th century. Early attempts at cross-breeding rabbits with hares

always proved futile, which confirms that the Belgian hare is in fact a pure rabbit. The coat is a deep chestnut colour with black shading. The long body means that it requires a tall hutch, to enable it to sit up on its hindquarters. It is active by nature, and this, coupled with its sleek appearance, makes it an attractive choice for a pet.

BEVEREN

The rabbit known as the Beveren also originates from Belgium, and was developed during the 1890s. Today, the breed is large, typically weighing up to 4.5 kg (10 lb), and has a distinctive mandolin-shaped body. The coat has

◆ B E L O W
Mount the hutch on legs to ensure the base
remains dry and to keep wild rabbits away from
your pet. Secure door fastenings are essential
to protect against foxes and other predators.

HOUSING IN THE GARDEN

Rabbits can be kept outdoors throughout the year, although they must have a snug, draught-proof area to retreat to when the weather is bad. As rabbits need to feel secure, the hutch should be divided into two connecting sections, one with a solid door, the other with a front made of wire mesh. Many pet shops sell hutches, or alternatively you can build one yourself. When choosing a hutch, make sure that it is high enough for the rabbit to be able to sit up to its full height and stand without difficulty. Ideally, the hutch is connected directly to a run, which allows your rabbit to run around and exercise freely without the need for supervision.

Position the rabbit hutch in a sheltered spot, out of the direction of prevailing winds. Avoid an area beneath trees, as branches may break off and damage the hutch. The run may extend off one of the sides or from the back of the hutch, with a broad, gently sloping ladder giving easy access in to and out of it. A door, which can be securely closed (and preferably locked), should always be incorporated into the hutch design.

If you decide to make your own hutch, choose good materials. Thick plywood should be used for the covered part, with good quality roofing felt providing a barrier on top to keep the interior dry. Place sliding trays inside to make cleaning easier. Put these in the rabbit's sleeping quarters and cover them with a layer of coarse shavings, with hay on top.

The run needs to have wire on its underside, unless it is placed on concrete slabs, such as a patio. This will prevent your rabbit from tunnelling out, or a predator, such as a fox, from getting in. Especially if the run is not connected to the hutch, place it in the shade: rabbits exposed to hot sun can die rapidly from heat stroke. Incorporate a sheltered area in the run to be safe.

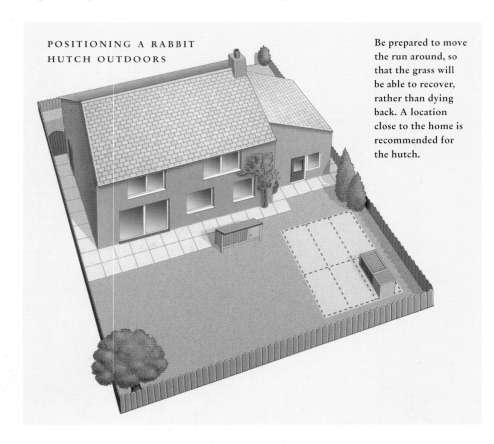

POSITIONING A RABBIT
HUTCH OUTDOORS

Be prepared to move the run around, so that the grass will be able to recover, rather than dying back. A location close to the home is recommended for the hutch.

Rabbit mix

Bran mash

Vitamin supplement and mineral blocks

Always wash the food beforehand and make sure it is fresh. Many rabbits develop serious diarrhoea when they are first put in an outdoor run, because they are not used to eating grass. The consequences can be fatal, so it is important to acclimatize the rabbit to grass before it goes outside.

A rabbit that is fed a commercial formulated food is unlikely to need any supplements to its diet. Treats available from pet stores can be offered occasionally, but watch out for signs that your rabbit is overweight: pet rabbits can become

obese, especially if they are fed a diet that is too concentrated. Aim to provide a balanced diet, matched to your pet's energy requirements. Rabbits kept outside need more food than those kept indoors. A neutered rabbit will also need less food.

Pet rabbits can be tamed to eat from the hand. Children need to be taught not to hold on to the food item for too long, however, because the rabbit will carry on nibbling and may then take a bite at their fingers.

◆ BELOW
A rabbit diet should consist of both fresh and dry foods. Make any dietary changes gradually to avoid digestive upsets.

Seed sticks

Rabbit biscuits

Carrots

Cabbage

Apples

GENERAL CARE

Rabbits can be nervous when they are first rehomed and it is important to get into the routine of picking up a young rabbit regularly so that it becomes accustomed to it. Always supervise a child attempting to pick up their pet for the first few weeks. Make sure that the child does not have bare arms as rabbits have sharp claws, which can cause painful scratches if they struggle. This applies especially in the case of young rabbits, whose claws are often especially needle-like. Although rabbits must never be picked up by their ears, holding these gently while supporting the body can quieten a rabbit that is proving difficult to restrain. Support the underside of the rabbit's body with one hand and use the other hand to hold its body, so that it will not leap

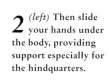

PICKING UP
A RABBIT
PROPERLY

1 *(left)* Gently restrain your rabbit by placing one hand on the side of its body and another under its hindquarters. Never pick a rabbit up by its ears.

2 *(left)* Then slide your hands under the body, providing support especially for the hindquarters.

◆ ABOVE
It helps to have a secure carrier so that you can move your rabbit safely from its hutch to the run.

out of your grasp. Once settled, rabbits rarely try to wriggle free, nor will they attempt to bite.

HYGIENE AND MAINTENANCE
You will need a suitable carrying container for your rabbit, particularly when you want to move it from its run back to its cage. Although you can use a strong cardboard box, a cat carrier will be more secure for longer journeys, such as trips to the vet.

Change the bedding in the rabbit's hutch at least once a week, and occasionally scrub out the hutch. Try to do this on a warm day, when the rabbit is in its run, which will allow the interior to dry quickly. You can use a special disinfectant recommended for this purpose. Check regularly on the back and undersides of the roof of the outdoor hutch for any leaks. A hole

◆ RIGHT
A large door forming part of the side of the run means that you will also be able to catch your rabbit easily when the time comes to return your pet to its hutch. The carrier itself will also be useful if you have to go to the vet.

in the roofing felt is the most likely reason, and this will need to be repaired before it becomes more serious. Do not treat the exterior woodwork of the hutch with a weather-proofing agent when the

rabbit is inside, as chemical fumes can be harmful. You should expect a well-maintained hutch to last for the rabbit's lifetime.

Gnawing of furniture and carpets can often be a problem inside the

house. Providing wooden blocks for your rabbit to gnaw on will help, or you can prepare dry crusts of wholemeal bread by roasting them in the oven. Allow the crusts to cool before offering them to your pet.

CLEANING OUT A RABBIT HUTCH

1 The hutch must be cleaned thoroughly at least once and possibly twice each week. A plastic dustpan and brush will be useful for this task, helping to remove the soiled bedding.

2 Having removed much of the soiled bedding, pull out the tray and tip the rest of the contents into a sack. This discarded material is ideal for composting.

3 When you decide to scrub out the interior, choose a sunny day when the rabbit is in its run, allowing the hutch to dry thoroughly before returning the rabbit here.

BREEDING

Rabbits have a justified reputation for being prolific breeders, and it is important not to let them breed without having planned what you are going to do with the offspring.

It is relatively straightforward to sex rabbits once they are mature, from about five months of age, when the testes of the buck have descended into the scrotum. Before this, a clear sign will be that the gap between the anal and genital openings will be longer in the case of the buck, compared to the doe. One of the reasons that rabbits breed freely is that does do not have a regular reproductive cycle resulting in ovulation. They are unusual among mammals, being "induced ovulators", which means that it is the stimulus of

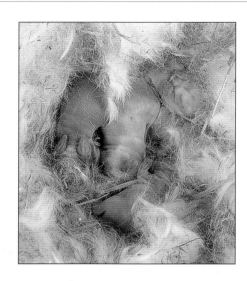

◆ BELOW
A Dutch rabbit with her young. In the case of this pure-bred breed, the pattern of markings is highly distinctive, with the white area on the face being called a blaze.

mating which triggers the release of eggs from the ovary. As a result, the likelihood of fertilization occurring is greatly increased.

It is not recommended to keep bucks together as they can fight viciously. Does are more likely to live in harmony in spacious surroundings, but it is not uncommon for bullying to occur, with a doe proving to be spiteful towards her companion.

MATING AND PREGNANCY

The larger breeds of rabbit can be much slower to mature than their smaller relatives. It may take up to nine months for giant breeds to become mature, which is twice as long as it takes in the Dutch, dwarf or rex breeds. The doe will be ready to mate when the skin around her genitals takes on a deep reddish hue, rather than pink. At this stage, she can be introduced to the buck, and mating is likely to occur soon afterwards. It may be better to leave the pair together for a couple of days to be sure, and then the doe can be transferred back to her quarters.

Assuming that she is pregnant, the doe will start to build a nest as the time for giving birth approaches, although in the first two weeks or so, she will not appear to put on any weight. This tends to occur towards the end of pregnancy, and her mobility is not unduly restricted in the early stages. The doe will benefit from being supplied with a kindling box, lined with clean hay, where she can give birth. Just beforehand, she will start to pluck her fur to form a nest for her offspring. Pregnancy in the rabbit lasts approximately 31 days. Although as many as 12 offspring may be born, a

✦ LEFT
A group of Dutch rabbits at 12 days old. Their
ears are still quite short at this stage, compared
with their bodies, which is a feature of all
young rabbits.

✦ BELOW
By 30 days old, the young rabbits are starting to
eat independently, and will soon be ready to be
weaned. They can be tamed easily at this stage
by being handled.

typical litter comprises six to nine
young, which are known as kittens.
At birth, they have no hair, although
dark fur markings, such as spots, will
appear as blotches on the skin, which
is otherwise pink. The kittens' ears are
short in relation to their body size.

Development is rapid, with fur
appearing after four days. The eyes
open just over a week after birth. It
is vital not to intrude into the nest,
because your scent may cause the
doe to abandon or even attack her
offspring. A problem is most likely
to be drawn to your attention by
repeated calls from the young if they
are not receiving enough food. The
doe may be suffering inflammation
of the mammary glands, known as
mastitis, which will require urgent
veterinary treatment.

HANDREARING

If you should have to handrear a litter
of young rabbits, you will need to feed
them on warm goat's milk, which is
the nearest natural substitute to that
of the doe. Use an eye dropper or a
small syringe as a feeding
tool, but always
disinfect this between
feeds. Unfortunately,
the task of hand-
rearing is made
difficult by
the fact
that the
doe
transfers
immunity to
her offspring via her
milk, and if this is denied to them,
they are likely to succumb to minor
infections. Young rabbits will normally
be fully weaned at nine weeks.

✦ ABOVE
Exhibition stock is usually rung in order to
identify the rabbits individually. The ring on
this rabbit cannot be removed without being
cut off, as the leg will have grown too large.

✦ LEFT
The patterning of rabbits such as the Dutch
does not vary as they grow older. These
particular individuals are now 60 days old.

GROOMING AND SHOWING

Most rabbits need very little by way of coat care, but the angora, with its soft, long coat, needs daily grooming to prevent the coat from becoming tangled and matted. If left, mats will need be to cut out of the fur. Breeds derived from the angora require similar care. Use special grooming combs, which are sold for cats and dogs. These have rotating teeth that help to tease the fur apart, rather than pulling on the strands of hair.

During the summer months, it is vital to examine the underparts of a rabbit regularly for fur soiled through a digestive upset. If bluebottle flies lay eggs in or near the soiled fur, the maggots will bore into the body through the skin, releasing potentially fatal toxic compounds into the blood. A rabbit with fly strike, as this condition is known, will need urgent veterinary treatment to remove all the maggots and treat the infected area; otherwise, the rabbit will die. It may be necessary to keep the rabbit indoors until the infection has healed, to reduce the chance of it recuring.

◆ LEFT
The grooming requirements of individual breeds differ significantly, and this is a factor that you need to consider when choosing a rabbit. The angora, seen here, is a particularly demanding breed in terms of its grooming needs.

◆ LEFT
Considerable care has to be given to show rabbits like this angora, so that they look at their best when being judged. Competition at rabbit show events is invariably fierce.

◆ BELOW LEFT
The result of all that hard work – an immaculate angora rabbit. If it is not groomed, the fur quickly becomes matted.

CLAW CLIPPING
A pet rabbit's claws can become overgrown quite easily. This is especially dangerous for a rabbit that lives in the home as it can become caught up by its claws in upholstery or floor coverings. You can clip the claws back yourself, although a steady hand is needed, and this is not a job for young children. If in any doubt, your vet will be able to do it for you. You will need a proper pair of claw clippers, rather than ordinary scissors, which are likely to cause the nail to fray and split instead of cutting it cleanly off.

If clipping the claws yourself, first locate the blood supply to the claw, visible as a reddish streak. This may be difficult to detect in rabbits with dark claws, and if this is the case, you will need veterinary experience to prevent the claw from being cut too short and starting to bleed as a consequence. Should you see blood when you are clipping the claws at home, press a damp piece of clean cotton wool (cotton ball) to the wound.

SHOWING RABBITS

Rabbit shows at local and regional level are listed in newspapers and specialist publications and, if you are interested in one particular variety of rabbits, there may be a breed club that you can join as well. Rabbits are rung for exhibition purposes at about two months of age, before the ankle joint becomes too big for the ring to pass over it. Rings are produced in various sizes for different breeds and it may be necessary to band the smaller breeds at a slightly younger age. The breeder's details and the year of the rabbit's birth are encoded on the ring, which will normally remain in place throughout its life. Check the ring occasionally, however, to check that it moves freely on the leg and is not causing the rabbit any discomfort. If the ring needs to be removed for any reason, ask your vet do this for you. Ringing is not the only way to mark rabbits for identification, however. In many countries, tattooing is preferred.

✦ ABOVE LEFT
At a show, it can appear as if the rabbits are being compared with each other to find the winner. However, in reality, they are being judged against the breed standard.

✦ ABOVE RIGHT
It is vital that show rabbits are used to being handled, so that when being judged, as here, they will not struggle but remain relaxed.

✦ RIGHT
Rabbits are kept in pens before and after judging. Vaccination, especially against the rabbit disease VHD, is very important for show rabbits.

GUINEA PIGS

Guinea pigs are unusual among rodents in that they lack a tail. It is possible that, in evolutionary terms, the tail was deemed unnecessary because of the guinea pig's reluctance to climb. Taming is straightforward, especially if they are obtained when young, as guinea pigs will not attempt to bite when being picked up, making them an ideal choice of pet for children. Guinea pigs are also highly popular as exhibition subjects.

INTRODUCTION

✦ BELOW
The agouti colour form approximates most closely to that of the wild guinea pig.

Guinea pigs are members of the rodent family, forming part of a group known as the caviomorphs. They originate from the Andean region of South America, and were probably first domesticated by the Incas over 750 years ago. The wild ancestors of the guinea pig look very different to the colourful varieties kept today. Their coats show greyish agouti patterning, not unlike that of a wild rabbit, and provide them with a good level of camouflage.

It was not until the 1700s that guinea pigs were first brought to Europe. There are a number of different explanations for their unusual name. It could be that they were brought from the area of Guianas, which became corrupted to "Guinea", or it may have been because the first ships that carried them across the Atlantic ocean visited Guinea, on the west coast of Africa, before sailing north to Europe. Alternatively, there could be a financial explanation – these

rodents soon became immensely sought-after as pets, and it could be a reflection of the high value initially placed upon them in England, where they could fetch the princely sum of one guinea. It is easier to see why they became known as pigs. This is not just a reflection of their

✦ LEFT
Camouflage is very important for the survival of guinea pigs in the wild, as they are surrounded by many potential predators.

✦ RIGHT
Young wild guinea pigs. Unlike many rodents, they are developed enough when born to move around freely.

While it is possible to keep pet rabbits and guinea pigs housed together, the rabbit may bully its smaller rodent companion. If you choose to have these pets sharing accommodation, make sure that the hutch is spacious, and select a smaller breed of rabbit, which is less likely to hurt the guinea pig if it accidentally jumps on top of it. Separate them at once if you notice signs of bullying.

Unlike some of the other rodent species, there is no unpleasant odour associated with guinea pigs.

corpulent body shape, but also of their "oinking" calls. Not surprisingly, therefore, males are known as boars while females are called sows.

Rather confusingly, guinea pigs are also sometimes known as cavies, which is a reflection of the name of the group to which they belong – the caviomorphs. This group is characterized by the arrangement of the muscles of their jaws, and also their long gestation period, compared with that of other rodents. As a result, although they have fewer young, their offspring are born in a relatively advanced state of development.

GUINEA PIGS AS PETS

Guinea pigs make ideal pets for children, particularly as they are small, easy to handle and will not attempt to bite when picked up. They can be housed either in the home or outside in a hutch throughout the year, even in temperate areas. Even so, as with rabbits, it is certainly not advisable to buy a guinea pig that has been kept in the relative warmth of a pet store, and then transfer it immediately to an outdoor hutch during the winter.

As household pets, however, guinea pigs are far shyer than rabbits. They can be handled easily since they do not bite, but they are likely to scurry away under furniture for long periods rather than being content to remain alongside you like a rabbit. Under normal circumstances, guinea pigs will live for about six years.

◆ BELOW

A typical guinea pig hutch. This can be lower in height than a rabbit hutch, but must still have a spacious interior.

◆ BELOW
A self black guinea pig. This individual is
showing reddish hairs in its coat, which would
spoil its exhibition potential; however, this will
not make it any less attractive to keep as a pet.

SMOOTH-COATED BREEDS

The smooth-coated guinea pigs are
nearer in appearance to their wild
ancestors than other varieties.
They are now sub-divided into two
categories – the self (single colour)
varieties, such as cream, chocolate
or black, and the patterned varieties,
such as the tortoiseshell.

SELF VARIETIES

The black is one of the most popular
members of the self group, thanks
to its glossy, sleek coat. For showing
purposes, it should be entirely black
in colour. Breeders regard any odd
white or even red hairs in its coat as a
serious show flaw. Even as they grow
older, these guinea pigs do not fade
in colour. The self chocolate is
another dark variety, the colour of
plain (semisweet) chocolate, with
similarly coloured dark eyes and ears.
Depth of coloration in the coat is
essential, as it is with all self-coloured
guinea pigs.

   As new colours have been
developed, some of the older varieties
have declined in numbers. One of
these is the self red, which is an
attractive shade of rich mahogany
with ruby-red eyes. The coloration of
the self golden can sometimes almost

◆ ABOVE
Agouti coloration arises from the
fact that there is a series of dark
and light bands running down the
hairs. Some forms of the agouti
have red eyes.

◆ LEFT
Light shades within the self
category are very popular. This is a
self beige, a dilute form of the self
chocolate. The depth of coloration
should be seen over its entire body.

verge on red, although the preferred
shade is ginger. The eyes in this case
are usually pink, although there is
also a rarer dark-eyed form.

Lighter shades in the self-coloured
group include the cream, and a darker
form that has a much yellower
appearance, known as the self buff.
The cream is sometimes known as
the "champagne cavy" to describe
the shade of colour required for show
stock, with paler coloration being
preferred. Self white guinea pigs are
often slightly smaller than other
colours, especially the true albino,
which is recognizable by its red rather
than dark eyes. The stipulation here
is for the coat colour to be pure
white, with no trace of a yellowish
hue. These white guinea pigs should
not be confused with the Himalayan
form, which is also pure white, but
is distinguishable by the darker
chocolate or black areas on the nose
and ears. The chocolate is the lighter
form of the two Himalayan varieties.

New self colours are still being
evolved as the demand for novelty
shades grows. The self blue – a
bluey shade of grey – which has
been developed in the United States,
marks a significant departure from
existing solid guinea pig colours.

PATTERNED VARIETIES

The tortoiseshell and white is a
striking example of a short-coated,
patterned guinea pig, with black,
white and red patches in its coat.
The Dutch form of the guinea pig
bears a strong resemblance in its
patterning to the rabbit of the same
name; the coloured and white areas
must be clearly defined for showing.
Darker colours, such as red or black,
are preferred, because these create
a more evident contrast in the coat,
but other colours are seen, even agouti
Dutch combinations. Agouti markings
result from light and dark banding
running down each individual hair.

The more recently developed
varieties include the Dalmatian,
so-called because its black and
white spotted patterning is
reminiscent of the dog breed, while
roans are distinguished by an even
distribution of coloured and white
areas throughout their coats. Roans
can be bred in various colours.

LONG-HAIRED AND REX COATS

ABYSSINIAN

For many years the Abyssinian and Peruvian breeds were the only long-haired guinea pigs recognized. The Abyssinian has a coat comprising a series of rosettes and ridges. The rosettes do not overlap but, where the hair extends out around the edge of the rosette to meet another rosette, a ridge is formed. There should ideally be four symmetrical rosettes running down the sides of the body, and a similar number along the back. In fact, the coat of the Abyssinian should not lie flat at any point over its entire body. The individual hairs themselves are quite short, measuring no more than 4 cm (1½ in) long.

As the wiry-haired coat of the Abyssinian is genetically dominant over short-coated cavies, if these are paired together, the offspring will have rosettes, but these are usually not as well defined as the rosettes seen in a true Abyssinian lineage. In this way, however, new self colours can be introduced to the Abyssinian breed. Even so, self reds and self blacks, as well as brindles, tortoiseshells and roans, are the most common colour forms of the Abyssinian because their

◆ TOP
A self red Abyssinian. This breed is characterized by the lie of its coat. In this particular case, the fur must be entirely red, displaying no trace of white hairs.

◆ ABOVE
Bi-colours exist in the case of the Abyssinian, as shown by this gold and white individual.

◆ BELOW
The rex mutation gives a coarser texture to the fur. This is a silver agouti example.

hair texture is often better. It can take up to 18 months for their coats to develop to their full extent.

PERUVIAN

Because of the Peruvian's demanding grooming requirements, it is not recommended as a pet, except for the most dedicated owner. The young are born with a short coat, but by adulthood it can reach 50 cm (20 in) or more in length. As the coat mats very easily, the Peruvian is not kept on hay, which can become entangled in the coat. Instead, the hay should be supplied in a hayrack.

SHELTIE

The sheltie is the long-haired form of the smooth-coated guinea pigs, and is instantly distinguishable from the Peruvian by its fur, which lies flat and is not swept forwards over its head, and the absence of a parting extending

◆ LEFT
Grey agouti and cream Abyssinian. The agouti
characteristic is shown by the dark and light
banding extending down the individual hairs,
creating a sparkling appearance.

CRESTED MUTATION

Another characteristic, linked with a
wide range of colours, is the crested
mutation. The crest itself should be
even in size and circular in shape,
being located just in front of the ears.
In the case of the English crested
mutation, the crest matches that of the
surrounding fur, but it is always white
in the case of the American crested.
When combined with the texel, the
crested has given rise to the form
known as the alpaca.

down the back. The satin
characteristic has been introduced to
these long-haired guinea pigs, and this
has ensured that their coats do not
lose their lustre as they grow older.
In other cases, the satin characteristic
highlights the natural gloss of the coat.

REX MUTATIONS

The rex mutation is a relatively new
variant, but has become very popular
both in Europe and North America,
where it is often described as a teddy.
The rex's fur is slightly curly and very
coarse to the touch. It is a recessive
mutation, so rex guinea pigs must
be paired together to produce rex
offspring. The rex has now been bred
in a very wide range of colours. It has
also been possible to combine it with
the sheltie to create the texel, which
has a curly but shorter coat than the
true sheltie. The merino is the result
of crosses between the rex and the
Peruvian guinea pigs.

◆ BELOW
The crested characteristic can be combined with
any colour. In the American form, seen here, it
is always white.

◆ BELOW
A family of tortoiseshell and
white rex guinea pigs. Note the
favoured white blaze extending
down the nose between the eyes.
Individual markings are variable.

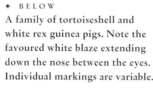

HOUSING IN HOME AND GARDEN

Guinea pigs are less destructive than some of the other rodent species, but it is to be expected that they will gnaw at woodwork within their hutch, often concentrating on one particular spot.

OUTDOOR HOUSING

Hutches outdoors should be divided into two sections – an outer area with a mesh front, and secure, snug sleeping quarters. Guinea pigs do not sit up like rabbits, so the hutch does not need to be especially tall. When you buy a hutch check that the doors are secure, and add combination locks to latches to deter dexterous foxes. It is also a good idea to oil the hinges every couple of months, enabling them to open smoothly and helping to prolong their lifespan.

Regularly check the roofing felt to ensure that the interior remains dry. A dense layer of hay will help to provide warm sleeping quarters, and will supplement the guinea pig's diet. If you are planning to construct the hutch yourself, you should give it

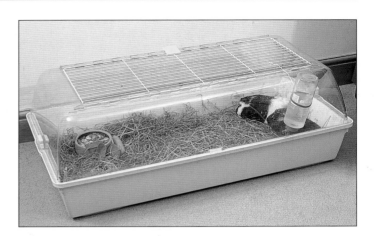

◆ RIGHT
An indoor enclosure for a guinea pig, complete with a water bottle. The base prevents bedding from being scattered in the room. Note the removable mesh lid, protecting the guinea pig from any dogs and cats also sharing your home.

secure legs, made of 5 cm (2 in) square timber, that stand at least 30 cm (1 ft) off the ground. The sides of the hutch can be constructed using tongue-and-groove timber, although thick marine plywood often proves to be more durable. The roof should slope from front to back, with an overhang at the back so that rainwater runs off readily, rather than down the back of the hutch where it would rot the wood.

Outdoor runs for guinea pigs are similar to rabbit runs, although, like hutches, they do not need to be as tall.

Pet stores usually stock a variety of runs, including ark-shaped designs, which have a dry section at one end where the guinea pig can retreat in bad weather, and rectangular runs, which also have a covered area. Check that you can reach right into the run to pick up the guinea pig, since guinea pigs can be very difficult to catch.

Position the run in a shady spot and remember to move it every week or so, to ensure that the area of grass beneath the sides of the run does not die back. Avoid using lawn that has recently been treated with weedkillers or potentially harmful chemicals. Place the run on level ground as a guinea pig may otherwise escape beneath one of the sides; you may not be aware of this danger if the grass is long. Fresh drinking water should always be available in the run.

INDOOR HOUSING

An indoor hutch should combine a cage with a plastic base and a wire mesh surround that prevents the guinea pig from clambering out. The base will ensure that bedding is not scattered out into the room. Wire mesh lids, which clip on to the hutch, prevent attacks from dogs and cats.

◆ LEFT
Outdoor guinea pig hutches need to be well constructed from durable materials, with a covering of heavy-duty roofing felt to keep the interior dry. You may need to reinforce the door fitments to keep your pet safe.

MAKING A GUINEA PIG HUTCH

1 Start by cutting all of the components to size. These may then be glued in place, using a non-toxic adhesive. Leave to dry.

2 Clamps will help to hold the glued surface to the adjacent area until it has dried. Holes can then be drilled as necessary.

3 Power tools will often simplify the assembly process. The screws themselves should fit snugly into the holes.

4 Here the sections are being assembled. The wooden supports are on the outside of the hutch, out of the guinea pig's reach.

5 The door hinges are an important part of the hutch. Do not economise here, as they may otherwise start rusting prematurely.

6 The assembled hutch, apart from the roof unit. Trim off any sharp edges of mesh on the door frame, so that they cannot injure your pet.

7 Apply the roofing felt. Note how the roof of the hutch is broader than the interior to ensure a better fit.

8 Fold over the roof felt at each of the corners, once the required length has been cut off the roll. Take care not to damage it at this stage.

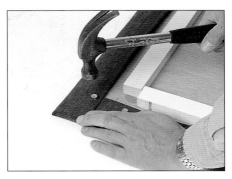

9 Broad-headed clout nails are needed to attach the roofing felt. Check that this is taut as otherwise it may be ripped off in a strong wind.

10 The roof section can then be fitted on top of the hutch. Screws fitted through the sides into the inner supports provide anchorage.

11 Bolts to keep the hutch door securely closed can be fitted next. These will make it difficult for a predator to reach the guinea pig.

12 *(right)* The cage must be kept off the ground, with legs being fitted to the base, along with supporting struts. This ensures that the interior will stay dry during bad weather. You may want to add sliding trays on the floor, so that it will be easier to clean the interior simply by pulling these out. They need to fit snugly over the floor area.

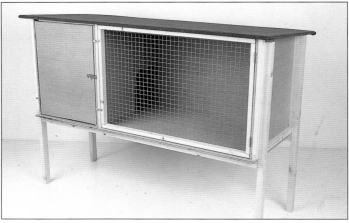

13 Treat the exterior sides, legs and underside of the hutch with a non-toxic wood preservative, and allow this to dry before placing the guinea pig into its new home.

FEEDING

◆ BELOW
A bottle brush will be required to clean the guinea pig's drinker at least once a week, preventing it becoming green on the sides as the result of algal growth.

Guinea pigs have an unusual metabolic quirk, shared with humans beings and marmosets but no other mammals. They are unable to manufacture Vitamin C from their food, and it must therefore be present in their diet if a deficiency is not to occur. As a result, complete foods for guinea pigs are supplemented with appropriate levels of this vital vitamin. Even if you are housing a rabbit and guinea pig together, it is very important to feed your guinea pig formulated food. A deficiency of Vitamin C causes a condition known as scurvy, resulting in dry, crusty skin and hair loss. Since

◆ BELOW
Guinea pigs need to be fed each day, with their dry food being provided in a heavy container that they cannot tip over easily. Change the drinking water at the same time.

scurvy can be confused with mite infestations, you should seek veterinary advice if the guinea pig shows these symptoms.

In addition to a prepared food, a guinea pig will readily eat a wide variety of greenstuff and vegetables. Broccoli and other brassicas, and spinach all contain relatively high levels of Vitamin C. Spinach is especially useful in the winter, when other sources of greenfood, such as dandelion leaves, are hard to find. Root vegetables, such as carrots, can also be offered regularly, particularly during the winter months.

Like rabbits, guinea pigs rely heavily on bacteria and protozoa in their large intestine to break down plant material, consuming their

◆ LEFT
Guinea pigs need a varied diet, and should not be offered dry food alone. They require a range of vegetables and other greenstuff if they are to remain in good health. Do not be surprised to find that they will nibble at bedding hay as well.

own droppings to obtain maximum nutritional benefit from their food. This means that you should not change your guinea pig's diet suddenly, but should make changes gradually, over a couple of weeks. It will not matter if you do not offer the same type of greenstuff each day, but it is harmful not to offer such foods for a period and then allow the guinea pig into a run where it will gorge itself on grass.

Always feed your guinea pig every day, and provide fresh water as well. It may help to provide the fresh food in a feeding bowl, rather than simply dropping it in the bedding where it can be harder to clear up and can possibly turn mouldy.

A range of treats is available for guinea pigs, but one addition to the diet traditionally favoured by guinea pig keepers is a bran mash. This is made by mixing bran with a little warm water and is especially valued during the winter months. Mix just enough to be eaten in a day, removing the food container when your pet has eaten and washing it out thoroughly.

There are a number of plants that are potentially poisonous for guinea pigs, and these should never be fed to your pet. Avoid bulbous plants, bracken and ragwort (*Senecio*). Among the more common garden weeds, both buttercups (*Ranunculus*) and convolvulus (*Convolvulus*) are toxic. The dangers posed by garden plants are usually listed in horticultural catalogues. Foxgloves (*Digitalis*) and lily-of-the-valley (*Convallaria*), as well as rhododendron (*Rhododendron*), should also be avoided.

Guinea pig mix

Bran mash

Broccoli

GENERAL CARE

It can be rather unnerving to hold a guinea pig for the first time as it may squeal as if in pain, and this can be especially alarming for a child. However, this shouldn't happen if you are gentle, and once your guinea pig is used to being handled regularly it will usually stop making this noise. Since guinea pigs do not bite instinctively, they can be picked up easily, although they will often try to avoid capture.

◆ LEFT
Starting out with a young guinea pig means that it will soon become used to being handled. Guinea pigs will not attempt to bite when picked up, but they will usually attempt to burrow deep into their bedding to avoid being caught.

HANDLING

To pick up your guinea pig, place your left hand in front of it as it runs around its hutch, with your right hand behind it. Use your right hand to restrain the guinea pig by placing your fingers around its body. If you are left-handed, it may be easier to reverse your grip. Having caught the rodent, slide your hand under its hindquarters, and lift it up out of its hutch. Once it is held in this way, the guinea pig will generally not struggle, but take care not to loosen your grip at this stage because if you do drop it accidentally it is likely to be seriously injured in the fall.

TRANSPORTING YOUR PET

Use a sturdy cardboard box or pet carrier for transporting your guinea pig. Check the flaps on the base of the box to ensure that it is strong enough. Reinforce the base with packaging tape, and, as a further precaution, support the box from

◆ LEFT
Transferring a guinea pig from its hutch to a carrier. Always support your pet's hindquarters from beneath, holding it gently but securely.

PICKING UP A GUINEA PIG

1 By scooping your hand under the guinea pig's body, you will stop your pet from being able to run away. Do not be alarmed if the guinea pig squeaks – this is its warning call to others.

2 As you start to lift the guinea pig off the ground, slide your other hand beneath its abdomen to provide support for its hindquarters. Take particular care if the guinea pig is pregnant.

beneath with your hands. If you place some hay in the box, the guinea pig will burrow comfortably and will not panic. It is not likely to gnaw its way out of the box if housed here only for a short time, but never leave it where cats or dogs could gain access to it.

GUINEA PIG HYGIENE
The hutch should be cleaned out thoroughly at least once a week, with the bedding making ideal compost.

◆ ABOVE
Once it realizes that it will not be hurt when picked up, a guinea pig will lie comfortably in this position. This is a male, known as a boar.

Always keep a close watch on your guinea pig's droppings because these give a vital insight into its state of health, and they can be particularly significant in the case of older boars. In later life, boars are especially susceptible to a condition known as rectal impaction, when the muscular contractions necessary to force the faeces out of the anus become weak, causing the droppings to accumulate. This results in a painful swelling at the end of the digestive tract.

The problem will be apparent if the guinea pig is examined from beneath. Although it is a highly unpleasant task for both parties, the only solution will be to pour olive oil carefully into the anus and then gently massage the obstruction out wearing disposable gloves (your vet will do this for you if you prefer). A general purpose dietary supplement may be needed to prevent further deterioration.

WINTER CARE OUTDOORS
During the colder winter months, it is a good idea to bring the hutch into a sheltered, well lit outbuilding. If you leave the guinea pig outside, be sure that it has enough bedding to stay warm and check it daily. Check also that there is an adequate supply of drinking water available. It is not

recommended to use an earthenware bowl for this purpose, because it will quickly become fouled with bedding. A better option is to use a bottle that can be attached to the outside of the cage. Take precautions with this system if the temperature is set to drop below freezing point: do not fill the bottle to the top or when the water expands, as it changes into ice, it may crack the bottle. Check also that the stainless steel spout is free from ice, as this will stop the flow of water. Squeezing the bottle when it is full is the best way of checking for a blockage.

◆ BELOW
Take care when carrying guinea pigs in this way that they do not become scared, wriggle free and fall to the ground.

BREEDING

◆ BELOW
It is relatively easy to identify the sex of guinea pigs. This is a female, known as a sow. There is a membrane which may be visible over the opening, apart from when she is ready to mate.

◆ BELOW
A male guinea pig or boar. Gentle extrusion of the penis, as shown here, identifies the male, even in the case of immature individuals where the testes are less visible.

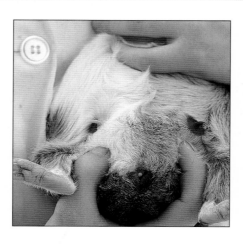

It is potentially dangerous to wait until a guinea pig sow is a year old before allowing her to have a litter. As the sow grows older, her pelvic bones will fuse together, and they will not expand easily to allow for the passage of young through the birth canal. This means that the risk of the young being trapped and having to be born by a Caesarean section is greatly increased. The ideal time for a sow to be mated for the first time is between five and six months of age. The stretching of the bones and muscles that takes place within the pelvis is then permanent, so that future litters born later in life are unlikely to result in a sow experiencing a difficult birth, which is known as dystocia.

◆ BELOW
It is preferable to restrict the breeding period to the warmer months of the year. The young of long-coated varieties, such as the sheltie, have shorter coats when newly born.

Males mature even earlier and are able to mate successfully at only one month old. It is necessary, therefore, to separate males from females at an early stage, although it is usual to wait until the age of four months or so before using males for stud purposes.

Sexing of guinea pigs is reasonably straightforward. With a boar, gentle pressure either side of the genital opening will bring the penis into view. In the case of sows, there is usually a membrane over this orifice. Breeding is straightforward, with the female being placed in the male's quarters. More than one sow can be housed successfully with a boar, provided that the hutch is sufficiently large. Sows come into season approximately every 16 days, so that leaving a pair together for about five weeks should give adequate time for mating to take place.

The sow should then be transferred back to separate quarters to give birth. You can usually tell if a female is pregnant about six weeks after mating occurred, as the movements of the foetuses will be clearly discernible from this stage onwards. Do not squeeze her body to detect the offspring though, as this could inflict serious damage on them. A dietary

◆ LEFT
Young Himalayan
guinea pigs are
predominantly white
in colour at birth.
The darker markings
on their bodies will
develop with age.

◆ BELOW
A female
tortoiseshell and
white Abyssinian
with her litter. Note
the variability in
their markings.

supplement of Vitamin C may be useful during pregnancy, when the sow will double her requirement for this important vitamin.

The young are born – very often during the night – after a gestation period of approximately 63 days. Around this period, you may not know with any certainty if the young have been born. Take particular care when opening the hutch door to the sleeping quarters for an inspection, to prevent any newborn babies tumbling down on to the floor.

CARING FOR THE YOUNG

Baby guinea pigs are miniature adults, fully developed at birth, with their eyes already open. They may be somewhat darker in colour, however, and, in the case of long-haired breeds, they will have much shorter fur. A typical litter is made up of three or four offspring, but if the litter is much larger, keep a close watch on the female for signs of a serious condition known as pregnancy toxaemia. Typical signs include loss of appetite and twitching, followed by convulsions. Obese sows are the most at risk. Rapid veterinary treatment will be needed if the sow is to recover.

Young guinea pigs are born in an advanced state of development, which means that they can eat solid food almost immediately, although they still benefit greatly from their mother's milk. If a litter is orphaned, supplementary feeding is not so critical to their survival. They can be handreared on evaporated milk, diluted with two parts of cooled boiled water, and mixed with a cereal baby food and a vitamin supplement.

GROOMING AND SHOWING

♦ BELOW
The grooming requirements of the different breeds of guinea pig differ significantly. Long-haired breeds, such as the coronet shown here, must be groomed every day.

The grooming requirements of guinea pigs vary greatly from minimal to fairly heavy, depending on whether your pet is long- or short-haired. To keep a pet guinea pig tidy and clean, you will need to make sure there is no food or bedding material lodged in its fur. If you have a long-haired guinea pig, you will also need to give the coat a regular brush to keep it free of tangles and mats.

SHOW PREPARATION
If you want to show your guinea pig, you will need to make some finishing touches before the show to make sure it looks its best.

With a Peruvian guinea pig, you will need to train its hair, using brown paper strips and small blocks of balsa wood, from the age of three months. This helps to encourage the sweep of the hair, which, for the purpose of the show, extends over all parts of the guinea pig's body, including the head. The wrappers, which are like hair curlers, are folded in a concertina

shape with the balsa block held inside and kept in place with rubber bands. Each wrapper measures 15 cm (6 in) in width, with the balsa block being 5 cm (2 in) wide and 2.5 cm (1 in) across. In the case of young Peruvian guinea pigs, wrappers are placed first on the sweep at the tail end and on each side of the body, with further wrappers being added as the guinea pig grows older and its coat develops.

Preparing an Abyssinian guinea pig for a show will involve brushing the animal with a toothbrush, using a brush with natural bristles, to avoid introducing static to the animal's coat. Brushing in this way will emphasize the rosettes and ridges that are so characteristic of the Abyssinian's coat.

AT THE SHOW
When it comes to judging, Peruvian guinea pigs are placed on a special judging stand – a hessian- (burlap-) covered platform measuring 45 cm (18 in) square and standing 15 cm (6 in) off the ground – to display their magnificent coats in all their finery. With any exhibition guinea pig, it will be necessary to train it to stand still while being judged. Guinea pig shows are held often, although they are rarely advertized outside the pages

♦ LEFT
A Peruvian guinea pig being prepared for a show. It is standing on the typical hessian-covered show stand.

◆ BELOW
Guinea pigs in their show pens. Advertisements
of such events can be found in the specialist
press, as well as club newsletters, usually giving
the address of the show secretary.

of specialist publications. Even if you are not exhibiting, it is interesting to visit a show and see the many varieties of gunea pig that now exist. This is also a good place to meet breeders, who will often have stock for sale.

If you are interested in exhibiting your guinea pig, attending shows provides an opportunity to see what the judges are looking for. This will give you a much clearer idea than trying to visualize what is required by reading show standards and pouring over pictures in books. At both local and national shows, there may not be only guinea pigs on view, but also other small mammals, such as rabbits, rats and other rodents.

If you are wanting to see the rarer colour varieties of guinea pig, you will need to visit the bigger national events. If you are interested in exhibiting your own pet, however, it will be better to start out at local level, by joining a club in your area, before progressing to larger events with stronger competition.

◆ RIGHT
A group of smooth-coated guinea pigs being judged. The temporary spots on their ears correspond to their pen numbers, enabling individuals to be identified easily.

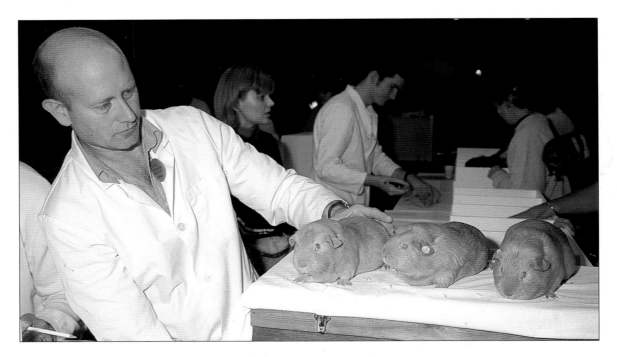

HAMSTERS

These small rodents are very popular throughout the world. They are bred in a range of colours and coat types, yet they still retain the rather nocturnal instincts of their ancestors, sleeping through most of the day. Bear in mind that hamsters are anti-social by nature, especially the Syrian or golden hamster, and they must be housed on their own. Hamsters make good children's pets, and they can be handled, although they may bite occasionally.

INTRODUCTION

Hamsters are a group of mainly small rodents with a wide distribution throughout the Old World. The common hamster (*Cricetus cricetus*) is the biggest member of the group, measuring 33 cm (13 in) in length and weighing approximately 475 g (17 oz). It is found in parts of Europe, where its numbers have declined significantly over recent years.

The appeal of hamsters as pets is relatively recent, and dates back to the capture of a female Syrian hamster (*Mesocricetus auratus*) and her young, in a field on a mountainside near Aleppo in Syria, in 1930. It was hoped that they could shed some light on a parasitic blood disease

◆ LEFT
Only when they are young can Syrian hamsters be housed together safely. They are otherwise likely to fight severely, even when introduced for mating, which needs to be closely supervised as a result.

◆ LEFT
The coat of the dwarf Russian, hamster becomes white in the winter.

but, before they could be taken to the University of Jerusalem, a number of the family had escaped and could not be recaptured.

The group that remained proved to be quite prolific, however, and before long these hamsters were sent to both the United States and the United Kingdom. Again, they bred well, and ultimately stock from London Zoo was passed to private breeders. This marked the start of the hamster's rise to popularity as a pet, and the first hamster club was formed in the United Kingdom in 1945. However, this was not

Dwarf Russian hamsters have become very popular over recent years, with an increasing range of colour forms being developed. They are smaller than Syrian hamsters.

the first time that Syrian hamsters had been kept in Britain. In the late 1880s, the former British Consul in Syria had returned to the United Kingdom with a breeding colony, but this ultimately died out during the 1920s.

When they were first introduced to the public, these hamsters were described as golden hamsters because of the golden colour of their coat. Today, this name has become less appropriate as a wide range of colour varieties has been developed. Now they are better known as Syrian hamsters, which also helps to distinguish them from the Russian and Chinese hamsters. The Russian forms in particular have grown greatly in popularity over recent years, partly as a result of their more sociable natures. They, too, are now being bred in different colours and coat types.

The dwarf Russian hamster (*Phodopus sungoris*) occurs in the eastern part of that country, and in two different forms. The most striking feature of the dwarf winter white (*P. s. sungoris*) is its coat, which changes colour, as its name suggests, before the onset of winter, losing its colour pigment and turning white. This form originates from Siberia and northern Kazakhstan, whereas the dwarf Campbell's Russian hamster (*P. s. campbelli*) ranges as far east as

northern China. This hamster, which was not discovered until 1905, is closely related to the winter white. Both forms are also known as Djungarian hamsters.

The third dwarf hamster from this part of the world is Roborovski's hamster (*P. roborovskii*), whose home is the desert area of Mongolia. It can be distinguished easily by the lack of a dark stripe down its back. All three forms of dwarf hamster have only been widely available to pet-seekers since the 1980s.

The Chinese hamster (*Cricetulus griseus*) is less commonly kept than the other breeds, and is therefore less widely available. This hamster is distinguishable from other breeds by the length of its tail, which measures about 2 cm (¾ in). These hamsters originate from northern China, and have a dark stripe down their back. The coat itself is shorter and sleeker than that of the Russian dwarf.

On average, a pet hamster can be expected to live for between two and three years.

In spite of their size, dwarf Russian hamsters are very active by nature, and will appreciate having a special hamster wheel in their quarters for exercise purposes.

SPECIES AND BREEDS

A wide range of colours have now been developed for the Syrian hamster, and an increasing number are emerging in the Russian species in particular. The wide choice of colours has helped to increase the hamsters' popularity with fanciers.

SYRIAN FORMS

The original golden form of the Syrian has a golden coat with black ticking on the individual hairs. The underparts are a contrasting shade of ivory white, and the ears are dark grey. There is also a darker golden form, with more extensive ticking and black ears, as well as a dilute form known as the light golden. The latter has no ticking on the coat and pure white underparts.

Among the other colours that have now been created is an attractive cream form, available in red-, ruby- and black-eyed variants. The yellow resembles the black-eyed cream, but can be distinguished by its darker coloration, which produces tipping on the guard hairs. The honey is very similar to the yellow, but can be easily distinguished by its paler ears and red eyes. The most colourful form of hamster is the cinnamon, which has orange-coloured fur.

The three different forms of white Syrian hamster are distinguished by the pigmentation of their eyes and ears. The albino is a pure red-eyed white with no colour pigment present, in contrast to the dark-eared form.

The third form is the black-eyed white, recognizable by its black eyes and pink ears. All three forms have a pure snow white coat. Several grey forms of the Syrian hamster are also now established, as well as the dove,

✦ LEFT
Smaller in size than their Syrian relative,
Russian hamsters, too, have become popular
in recent years. Colour and coat varieties of
these hamsters are now becoming established.

The most distinctive colour of the
dwarf campbell's is the argente,
which has a ginger-coloured coat and
a chocolate-coloured stripe down its
back. There is also a true albino form,
which is entirely white in colour,
with the characteristic pink eyes.
A satin-coated mutation has also been
developed in recent years, and, as the
name suggests, this variety boasts a
noticeably sleek coat.

which has a lilac tinge to its colour.
Among other darker shades are the
chocolate, which is brown in colour,
and a new pure black variety.

In addition, there are a range of
marked colour varieties. These include
the banded, which has a white area
encircling the body, in combination
with any solid colour. Less rigorously
defined in terms of markings is the
variegated, with white and coloured
areas in its coat. The spotted is similar,
but in this case the markings are
circular. There is also a tortoiseshell
form, with yellow or black and brown
markings, which can also be combined
with white.

The potential for different hamster
varieties is enhanced by the various
coat types, which have been developed
to supplement the standard short-
haired form. The satin mutation can
be combined with this to make the
coat more shiny than normal. There

✦ BELOW
Syrian hamsters are being bred with specific
markings. The tortoiseshell and white seen here
has variable colour markings.

are also long-haired Syrian hamsters,
often known as teddies, and rexes,
distinguished by their curly coats.

RUSSIAN COLOUR FORMS
Of the dwarf Russian white, one of
the first colours to be created was the
sapphire. This is bluish-grey with a
stripe along its back and blue markings.
The pearl, which is greyish in colour,
has become popular in recent years.

CHINESE HAMSTER
The best-known colour variant of
the Chinese hamster is the dominant
spot, which displays one or more
white spots on its body. A white
patch on the head is also favoured as
a requirement for exhibition stock.
Still rare is the white form of the
Chinese hamster, which is recognized
by the dark stripe running down the
length of its back.

✦ LEFT
The colour of dwarf
Russian hamsters may
change through the
year. Their dark fur
will be replaced by
white at the start of
the winter.

✦ RIGHT
In spite of their large
eyes, hamsters do not
have good vision. They
rely very heavily on
their sense of smell.

HOUSING AND FEEDING

◆ BELOW
Tubular housing systems have become very popular for hamsters over recent years. The sections can be fitted together in various ways and expanded easily.

Looking after your hamster correctly involves providing it with adequate food and shelter. These basics will ensure that it stays healthy and happy throughout its life.

HAMSTER CAGES

Although the traditional hamster cage is still a popular option, other more inventive housing systems are now available. If you opt for a cage, check that the base fits securely to the mesh roof area. Should there be any weakness here, the hamster is likely to find a gap and escape into the room. This applies especially in the case of young Russian hamsters, since cages on the market are generally intended for the larger Syrian species.

Another important aspect of cage design to consider is the strength of the door. It will be easier to take your hamster out of its quarters if the door is on the side of the cage, rather than in the roof. Door hinges have a tendency to become weaker over time, so it is a good idea to invest in a small combination padlock as an extra security precaution.

A cage should have a sleeping area. Make sure the bedding is safe hamster bedding, which will not cause a potentially fatal blockage in the rodent's intestinal tract if swallowed. You can buy bedding at a pet store. Tease it out by hand, so that the hamster can burrow into it easily.

Another option is sectional housing, which mimics the layout of a hamster's burrow in the wild, and has specially designed tunnel systems with enlarged nest areas. It is a good idea to begin with a basic starter kit, and then add inexpensive extra sections. You can create an entire housing system this way, with the water bottle fitting into the design. Such systems provide a more secure environment for a

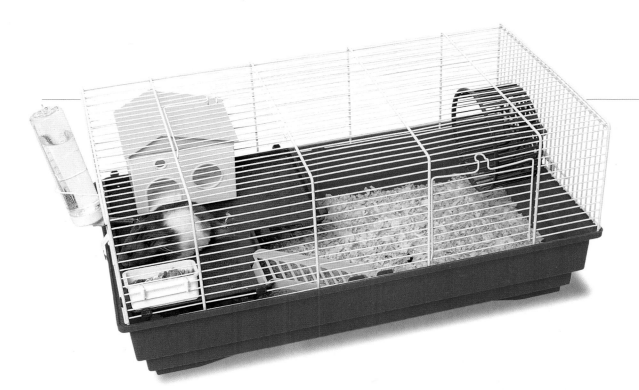

◆ LEFT
A typical hamster cage. Always check the door fastening is secure, because if a hamster escapes into the room, recapturing it is likely to prove very difficult.

hamster than a cage, but you should still check regularly to see that the rodent is not nibbling at the plastic at any one point, through which it might attempt to escape.

HAMSTER FOODS

Hamster mixes are readily available from pet stores. These will usually contain a variety of cereal seeds, as well as sunflower seeds and peanuts. These oil seeds should be offered in small quantities because of their high fat content, which can lead to obesity if they form the bulk of the hamster's diet. Commercial pelleted diets are

also available, although these tend to be the more expensive option. Use a small, heavyweight earthenware pot as a food bowl and provide fresh drinking water in a bottle, attached to the side of the hamster's quarters.

Do not forget to offer a little fresh food, such as a piece of sweet apple or greenstuff, on a daily basis as well. This can occasionally be sprinkled with a special small-animal vitamin and mineral supplement as an additional tonic. It is very important to match the amount of food offered to the hamster to the quantity being eaten because, otherwise, a hamster is likely

to waste food, carrying it back to its nest in its cheek pouches. Hamsters instinctively hoard food in this way, building up large supplies in their burrows when food is scarce above ground. Take particular care with fresh food, because this is likely to rot if left in the bedding material for a couple of days. It's a good idea to check the bedding regularly as this is likely to be harmful to your pet's health.

There are also a number of commercial treats now available to supplement your hamster's diet. These are useful for taming purposes, and can be offered directly by hand.

Feeding bowl

Mineral block

Hamster mix

GENERAL CARE AND BREEDING

It is important to provide a range of other items apart from food and water to ensure your hamster's well-being. Chews of various types will help to keep your hamster's incisor teeth in trim, although short branches cut from apple trees – which have not been sprayed with chemicals – can serve the same purpose. Crusts of bread roasted in the oven can be a valuable addition to the diet as well.

EXERCISE

It is vital to keep your hamster fit. In the wild, hamsters emerge from their burrows under cover of darkness, and may travel several miles in search of food or a mate. An exercise wheel will give your pet hamster a substitute for this night-time activity. Modern closed-wheel designs are the safest option, as a hamster could slip and injure itself in an open-weave wheel. Check regularly that the wheel is firmly in position and will not collapse on the hamster. Oil the wheel from time to time; it may be noisy when in use and, if the cage is in a child's bedroom, the wheel can disturb a sleeping child. Pregnant females seem to use a wheel most, and it may be that this helps to tone up their muscles in preparation for the birth of their pups.

◆ ABOVE
Syrian hamsters especially will benefit from having an exercise wheel. A closed wheel as shown is the safest option. Oil the wheel occasionally so that it moves freely.

◆ BELOW
A wide range of other toys are now available for hamsters. Being burrowing creatures by nature, they need adequate retreats of various types in their quarters.

Hamster play area

Sectional unit

Hamster nest

MATING AND PREGNANCY

Pairings of Syrian hamsters need to be carried out very cautiously to prevent injuries caused by fighting. Once mature, the female can be recognized by the rounded, rather than step-like, profile of her hindquarters when viewed from the side, and she will be larger in size than the male. Never be tempted to introduce him to her quarters, because she will almost inevitably attack her intended partner. Aggression is less likely if she is placed in alongside the male, because in the wild, it is the female who journeys in search of a mate. The other alternative is to introduce the pair on neutral ground in a container with a removable partition. If the female is receptive to her intended partner, then mating will normally occur within an hour, after which the pair should be separated again.

It is usually possible to tell when the female is ready to mate by stroking her back. If she stands still with her tail raised, this is a sign that she is ready. Female hamsters come into heat

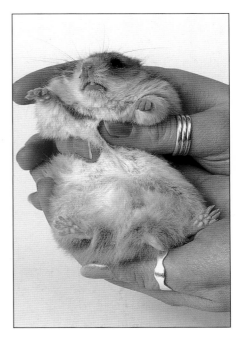

roughly every four days, so you will not have long to wait in any event. In pregnancy, the gestation period for hamsters is among the shortest of all mammals. A female Syrian hamster will produce her offspring just 16 days after mating, and the five to seven young pups will be totally helpless at birth. The normal gestation period for

Russian and Chinese hamsters will last about 19 days in both cases.

Avoid disturbing the nest as this can cause cannibalism. The young grow quickly and will start to emerge from their nest at about two weeks old. Within a further fortnight, they will be independent and should be moved to separate accommodation.

◆ RIGHT
A young Syrian hamster with its mother. Hamsters are not social by nature, and now that this youngster is feeding itself, it will need to be transferred to separate quarters to avoid fights breaking out between the pair.

GROOMING AND SHOWING

◆ BELOW
Grooming a smooth-coated hamster with a soft cloth. This can help to improve the gloss on its fur, and may also serve to remove loose hairs during the moult.

When it comes to grooming, or indeed showing, it is important that your hamster is tame and used to being handled. Hamsters have poor eyesight as, like many rodents, they spend much of their time underground in the dark. As a result, their sense of smell is significant. If you pick up a hamster too quickly, you are likely to be bitten. Instead, you need to accustom your pet to your scent. Place your hand on the floor of the cage and encourage the hamster to step on to it. You can then lift out the hamster by scooping it up, using your other hand like a cup. Avoid gripping your pet tightly, as it will then panic, struggle and bite. Occasionally, you may have to tempt your hamster into a container in order to take it out of its quarters without a struggle.

Ease of handling is another reason for starting out with a young hamster, as at this stage hamsters are far more responsive to being tamed. Taming will be virtually impossible with an older individual.

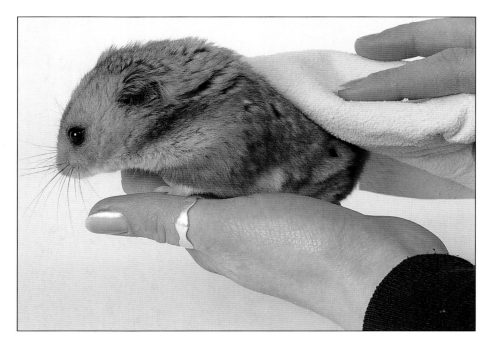

To restrain the hamster in an emergency – if it is out of its cage and is escaping under furniture, for example – hold the skin at the back of its neck. This will secure the hamster's head, so it will not be able to turn round and bite. You can then pick it up as normal to return it to its cage.

KEEPING CLEAN

Short-coated hamsters need very little grooming, although wiping them with a chamois leather, in the direction of the lie of the fur, is recommended before a show, to improve the appearance of the coat. Short-coated rexes have curly coats that do not lie flat. However, their coat care is quite straightforward as their hair is far less likely to mat. Hamsters are actually very fastidious about grooming and will usually keep themselves looking immaculate and sleek – if your pet does appear to be fluffed up with an unkempt look about it, it may indicate an illness.

Hamsters with long coats need combing once or twice a week, to prevent the hair from becoming matted and to remove bedding or pieces of food, which can get caught up here. Use a small comb with rotating teeth or a soft toothbrush. The former is a better option as it helps to break down any tangles that

◆ LEFT
When it comes to exhibiting hamsters, not all individuals will meet the show standard. You will need some luck when breeding colour varieties with markings.

are forming, rather than pulling at the coat. If there is a bad knot in the coat you may have to cut it out. If you have to do this, you won't be able to show your hamster until the hair regrows to its original length.

HAMSTER SHOWS

If you are interested in showing your hamster, it is a good idea to join one of the many specialist societies, which are generally a good source of information and equipment (such as show cages).

At the show, the judges will assess the hamsters' colouring and form, and it is vital that you are aware of the show standard for the type of hamster that you are exhibiting. As well as the overall appearance or "type" of the hamster, the judges will also consider individual requirements for the different colours and coat types. Do not despair if your initial attempts at

exhibiting do not result in any wins. This is partly because hamsters are only likely to win when they are in top condition. When being judged, the condition of each entry is significant, and a hamster may win at one show and fail to be placed at the next. Always make sure you turn out your entry in immaculate condition.

◆ ABOVE
The pairing of hamsters needs to be carried out with regard to their physical appearance or type, as well as coloration, if you hope to breed exhibition winners.

◆ BELOW LEFT
Grooming a long-haired hamster is a more involved task, which needs to be carried out a couple of times a week; otherwise, the coat will become matted.

◆ BELOW
Be careful which foods you offer your hamster before a show. Avoid carrot as the juice is likely to stain the fur on the face, and this will affect the coloration, albeit temporarily.

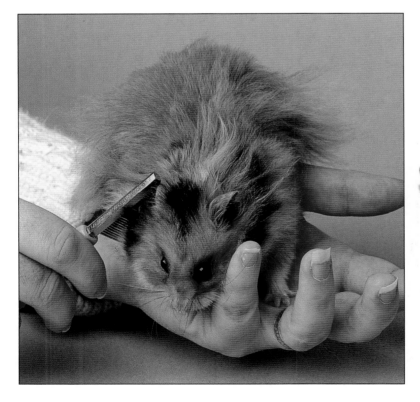

GERBILS AND JIRDS

This group of rodents is found in arid parts of the world. Like hamsters, they burrow to escape danger and the heat of the midday sun, but they are also far more agile. Their hind legs are especially well developed, and this enables them to jump long distances. In a home setting, you will need to handle them carefully to prevent them from escaping. The Mongolian gerbil has a social nature, and should be kept in pairs or trios rather than on its own.

INTRODUCTION

The Mongolian gerbil (*Meriones unguiculatus*) is the best-known member of this group – it is the most friendly of the pet gerbils – and has built up a strong following since first becoming available to pet-seekers during the 1960s. The first specimens were collected on an expedition to Mongolia by a Japanese scientist in 1954, and were bred in Japan before some stock was sent on to the United States, and then to Europe. These gerbils were actually discovered during the mid-1800s by the missionary Pere David, who travelled widely in this part of the Orient.

Mongolian gerbils are well adapted to living in desert areas, with the sandy colour of their coats and black tipping providing excellent camouflage when they are seen from above. Their underparts are white, to reflect the heat of the sand beneath them, while their long tail is also covered in fur. The tail serves as a stabilizer when the rodent is running, with its long hind legs helping to support its weight so

◆ LEFT
The natural colour of the Mongolian gerbil is called the agouti, and this helps to provide camouflage when the gerbil is viewed from above. The underparts are paler in colour.

that it can sit up and look around, jumping away if danger threatens, in a similar way to a kangaroo. Mongolian gerbils can leap 45 cm (1½ ft) to elude a would-be predator, and then quickly disappear down their burrow.

Internally, their bodies are well equipped to withstand the rigours of life in the desert. Their kidneys are incredibly efficient, allowing them

to produce a very concentrated urine. This in turn means that, unlike rats and mice, gerbils have no pungent odour associated with them.

Jirds are very similar to gerbils in their habits, and the descriptions of the two species are sometimes synonymous, as in the case of the Shaw's jird which is another member of the *Meriones* genus. Like gerbils, jirds are found in arid areas. Both gerbils and jirds are found in an area ranging from North Africa through the Middle East into Asia. Only in the case of the Mongolian gerbil, however, have colour variants become widely known at present, and you may well need to track down specialist gerbil breeders in order to obtain stock of other species.

◆ LEFT
An ever-increasing range of colour mutations and varieties has been created in the case of the Mongolian gerbil, and this has led to a growing interest in exhibiting them.

◆ BELOW
Gerbils use their long hind legs to stand up and explore their environment. You must ensure their housing is covered, to prevent any escapes.

◆ ABOVE
While balancing on its strong back legs, a gerbil may pick up and eat food using its shorter front legs, which serve rather like hands.

GERBILS AS PETS

The most important thing to bear in mind with gerbils is that they are highly social by nature, to the extent that they must be housed in groups, rather than singly. If you do not want them to breed, then you should keep them in single-sex groups. Their natural curiosity means that they are easily tamed and can be encouraged to feed quite easily from the hand.

As children's pets, gerbils have the advantage over hamsters in that they are not primarily nocturnal. Even so, they are not really pets that like to be handled or cuddled for any length of time, since they have very active natures and prefer to have the freedom to scamper about.

Although gerbils are not easy to recapture in a room because they are so agile, they are less likely to

disappear in these surroundings than a hamster, for example, which may well choose to slip down under a gap in the floorboards, or disappear out of sight. Gerbils often remain on the surface and, with care and patience, it is possible to net them, or persuade them into a large cardboard box placed on its side, if food has already been placed there as a bait.

Gerbils and jirds can be expected to live for up to three years.

◆ RIGHT
When it is standing up, the gerbil relies on its tail to help to support its body. In this position, it is not just looking around but also sniffing the air, to pick up scents.

SPECIES AND BREEDS

MONGOLIAN GERBIL

A number of different colour varieties of the Mongolian gerbil have been developed. The first originated in Canada and is known as the Canadian white spot. It has a white spot on the coloured area of the body, and often has white legs and white on the tail.

A pure albino form is identified by its reddish eyes and pink ears. Up until the age of about three months or so, when the dark fur develops along the tail, it is difficult to distinguish between the albino and the dark-tailed white. At the other extreme is the pure black gerbil, known for its glossy coat. Another popular variety is the lilac, which has a bluish-grey coat (with a rosy hue) and pink eyes. Although similar, the dove grey's coat is lighter and more silvery in colour. It also has pink eyes.

A very popular variety is the predominantly gold-coloured argente, which has a white abdomen and feet, and pinkish claw and ears. The dark-eyed honey is a more unusual colour; the young, in this case, undergo a colour change at about two months old. Up until this stage, they have a yellow coat with black fur on the extremities of the body, such as the

◆ LEFT
The lilac form of the Mongolian gerbil. This colour was originally developed from crossings between the black and argente varieties. Occasional white patches do sometimes crop up on their coats.

◆ RIGHT
The argente has been described under various names, including cinnamon, golden and, perhaps most accurately, as the white-bellied golden, with a very clear delineation between white and golden areas.

◆ LEFT
The black mutation was first recorded in laboratory stock housed at the USAF School of Aerospace Medicine in Texas. Ideally, these gerbils should be pure black, with no odd white patches at all.

legs, tail and nose, giving them an appearance rather reminiscent of a Siamese cat. When they moult for the first time, these dark areas disappear from the extremities, and then ticking appears on the yellow hair of the body. As the gerbil grows older, so its white

belly patch becomes more obvious. The eyes in this case are dark, as are the nails and ears.

In the silver agouti or chinchilla form, the beige and black of the normal agouti has been modified to silvery white and black, with the belly

◆ LEFT
The Mongolian gerbil has a natural agouti coloration, with dark and light banding running down each hair, making it hard to spot from above.

◆ RIGHT
Always check on
compatibility when
considering the
purchase of other
types of gerbil or
jird. Some, such as
the relatively large
Jerusalem jird shown
here, may need to be
housed on their own.

JERUSALEM JIRD

One breed that you may occasionally encounter among the other varieties of gerbils and jirds is the Jerusalem jird (*Meriones crassus*). This variety differs significantly from its smaller Mongolian cousin in its requirements, and is very solitary by nature – to the extent that it will need to be housed on its own. The coat of the Jerusalem jird has a more reddish hue, while in terms of temperament, it tends to be less friendly than the Mongolian.

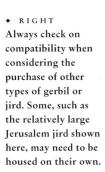

◆ RIGHT
A pallid gerbil.
Note the relatively
large eyes, indicating
that it becomes more
active as darkness
falls. Like other
gerbils, the pallid is
very active by nature,
and jumps well, with
its tail serving as
a counterbalance.

OTHER SPECIES

The attractive Egyptian gerbil (*Gerbillus gerbillus*) is sandy brown in colour. It lives on a colony basis and can become very tame. Shaw's jird (*Meriones shawi*) is found in parts of Egypt but, unfortunately, these rodents are not social by nature. Perhaps the most bizarre species of all is the fat-tailed or Duprasi's gerbil (*Pachyuromys duprasi*), which occurs in northern parts of the Sahara desert in Africa. These gerbils have a rounded body shape, and a broad, pink tail, which acts as a store for their body fat, keeping it aside to be metabolized when food rations are in short supply. The fat-tailed gerbil is nocturnal in its habits. Again, these rodents are not social by nature, and they should always be housed on their own to avoid fights.

being white. The eyes and claws are black. It has also proved possible to combine the chinchilla and dark-eyed honey mutations to create a variety known as the polar fox. This gerbil's silvery-white coloration replaces the honey coloration, although the characteristic change in markings, associated with the dark-eyed honey, is seen in this case as well. The unusual name of these gerbils stems from the similarity in appearance to the fox found in the Arctic region.

Gerbils are now being bred that display the Himalayan gene, which is responsible for the appearance of the Siamese and related cat breeds. The points of these gerbils – their legs and feet, ears, nose and tail – are dark in colour,

whereas the body is a lighter shade. Tonkinese and Burmese forms of gerbil, which show less contrast thanks to their darker overall body coloration, have also been bred; again, their names derive from breeds that exist in the cat fancy. Other new varieties of Mongolian gerbil are also being developed at present, including creams and sepia forms. These may not always be widely available.

◆ RIGHT
A number of other gerbils and jirds
are available from specialist breeders.
This is Shaw's jird, which, like its
Mongolian relative, displays a dark
tip on the upper surface of the tail.

HOUSING AND FEEDING

As gerbils are natural burrowers, it is best to house them in converted aquaria, as these allow more depth than wire-mesh cages.

GERBIL HOUSING

A lightweight acrylic tank is preferable to a glass tank because it is easier and safer to move. Equip the tank with a secure, ventilated hood to prevent the gerbils from using their jumping abilities to leap out, and to stop cats from reaching in. You should be able to acquire a special housing set-up for gerbils, which includes not only a hood but also a colour co-ordinated drinking bottle, which fits into the enclosure as part of the hood and can be removed easily from the outside.

One of the major advantages of keeping gerbils, compared with rats and mice in particular, is that they produce very little urine and so have virtually no odour associated with them. This makes caring for them more straightforward, as the lining

Gerbil mix

♦ BELOW RIGHT
Young gerbils born in a colony can be left with their parents, but you will need to check that their quarters do not become overcrowded.

♦ BELOW LEFT
Gerbils of different colours can be housed together without problems, but avoid adding newcomers to an existing colony, as this can result in fighting.

Clean out the gerbil's cage on a weekly basis, discarding the soiled shavings and replacing them with fresh ones. You will need to transfer the gerbils into a secure carrier while you clean out their quarters. A simple acrylic enclosure with a hood will suffice for this purpose, and can also serve as a suitable carrier should you need to take your gerbil to the vet. This type of carrier is much safer than a cardboard box, which gerbils will often gnaw their way out of.

in their quarters does not need to be changed as frequently. Coarse shavings, sold as small-animal bedding, should be used to line the cage. It is important not to use sawdust, as the gerbils' burrowing activities mean that their eyes can be irritated by flakes of sawdust. You can bury lengths of tubing in the substrate to allow the gerbils to explore these areas, as their own tunnels, built from shavings, could collapse. Do not forget to provide bedding material, which they can use to line nesting chambers.

SUITABLE FOODS

Feeding gerbils is straightforward, and the procedure is the same as for other small rodents. Gerbils feed mainly on a diet of seeds, greenstuff and vegetables, and they may also eat a few invertebrates, such as mealworms. However, do not feed them large quantities of oil-based seeds, such as sunflower, as these can cause obesity, which can prove fatal. A small amount of hay is important, not just as bedding but also to add fibre to their diet. An earthenware food pot, which they will be unable to tip over, makes an ideal feeding bowl.

CONVERTED AQUARIUM SET-UP

1 It is relatively easy to set up a home for a colony of Mongolian gerbils by converting an aquarium into what is sometimes described as a gerbilarium. Ensure the tank is clean and dry before tipping in coarse wood shavings.

2 Gerbils will want to have areas where they can retreat in their enclosure, and you can help by including cardboard tubing in the substrate. Food, water and a selection of toys should also be provided.

3 A secure covering over the enclosure is important, both to stop the gerbils jumping out and to protect them from cats or dogs. A secure covering can be made using wire mesh attached to a wooden framework. Make sure the covering can be securely fixed in place.

4 As a further precaution, weigh down the roof with blocks placed at each end, which will stop any cat from being able to dislodge the lid. Note how the water bottle is suspended from the roof, allowing the gerbils to drink without difficulty.

Although gerbils do not drink large volumes of water, it is important to provide them with a supply of fresh drinking water on a daily basis. The bottle should be fixed securely in place so that it will not leak – originating from an arid area, gerbils are very susceptible to damp surroundings, and can suffer from respiratory problems.

Before you obtain a gerbil, find out what it has been feeding on, and do not change this diet for the first two weeks after rehoming. Sudden changes made during this period can lead to a fatal digestive upset. Provide your gerbil with something to gnaw to stop its teeth from overgrowing, which would prevent it from eating properly.

GENERAL CARE AND BREEDING

♦ BELOW
Gerbils can be quite tame, but when moving your pet out of its quarters, restraining it by the base of the tail will prevent any escapes.

Gerbils are surprisingly agile creatures, able to escape encircling fingers by using their powerful hind legs to jump out of your grasp. They are not pets that enjoy being handled, although they will often feed from the hand.

HANDLING
When you need to restrain a gerbil, start by allowing it to sniff at your fingers, and then gently coax it on to your hand. Place your other hand on top, so that the gerbil can see out but will still feel reasonably secure. Since it is not being held tightly, it will also be unlikely to bite under these circumstances.

Handling a gerbil can sometimes be rather alarming because, acting on instinct, it will often faint in the same way that it would if caught by a predator. Some strains of gerbils are more prone to this behaviour than others. If a gerbil does react in this way, the best thing to do is to place it in a quiet spot and it will soon recover.

Although you can restrain a gerbil by gently holding the base of its tail close to the body, never grasp it by the tip of its tail. The skin here is very loose and sheds rapidly, resulting in

bleeding and even partial loss of the tail. Again, this is a defensive mechanism that helps the gerbil to escape from a predator. Careful handling should prevent this from being a problem.

MATING AND PREGNANCY
It is important to sex gerbils correctly at the outset as they will need to be kept in single-sex groups; if not, you will almost certainly end up with unexpected litters. Male gerbils can be identified easily by comparing the length of their ano-genital gap with that of the females, since this space is significantly longer. Once mature, male gerbils are also significantly larger than females and are nearly twice as heavy.

When breeding Mongolian gerbils, introduce the male and female carefully. Initially, place them both in neutral territory. Some acrylic containers have a divider, so, after a couple of days, the two gerbils can be allowed direct contact by removing the partition. Even so, watch for any signs of aggression, although normally there are no problems under these circumstances, and mating soon takes place. The pair should be left together for about a week, after which they can be separated.

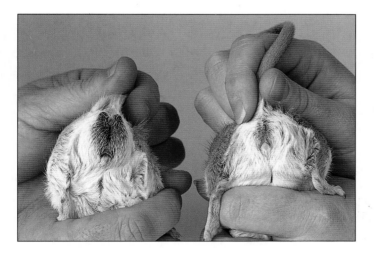

♦ LEFT
Sexing gerbils is straightforward, with the male shown on the left here. The swellings caused by the testicles will be less evident in younger males.

♦ RIGHT
When picking up a gerbil, do not hold it tightly in your hand but cup it gently, as shown here.

◆ BELOW
The long tail of the gerbil acts as a
counterbalance, helping to ensure that
when the gerbil jumps, using its powerful
limbs, it will usually land safely.

◆ BOTTOM
Young Mongolian gerbils can remain within an
established colony, provided that the group will
not be overcrowded.

It is not a good idea to leave the male with the female because she can mate again very soon after giving birth, and this will mean that the gerbils are likely to produce an unexpected second litter. About

24 days after mating, a female will typically give birth to five cubs, which are without fur and totally helpless at this early stage, usually measuring about 2.5 cm (1 in) in length. The young gerbils will grow

rapidly, and can be weaned once they are about five or six weeks of age. They are likely to be mature after a similar period of time, and will continue to breed well until the age of about 14 months old.

◆ LEFT
Young gerbils can
be weaned at five
or six weeks. They
will be mature about
6 weeks later, and
will breed well up
to 14 months.

GROOMING AND SHOWING

◆ BELOW
Gerbils being judged at a show. It is important
that exhibition gerbils are used to being
handled from an early age, so that they are not
frightened by this experience.

Gerbils need very little grooming
in order to look immaculate, partly
because no long-coated mutation has
yet been developed, and their coats
are not prone to becoming tangled.
In addition, gerbils frequently clean
themselves. However, for exhibition
purposes, a degree of tidying-up will
usually be necessary to ensure that
your gerbils are looking their best.

SHOW PREPARATION

The most common problem is that the
coat may have become stained by juice
from greenstuff, particularly the area
around the face. It is a good idea to
leave items such as carrot and cabbage
out of the gerbil's diet for a week
beforehand as it may be difficult to
remove these stains, especially as it is
not advisable to wash the coat. Aside

from the stress involved, there is a risk
that the gerbil could develop a chill.
Serious exhibitors often resort to
using corn flour to mask stained areas,
carefully moistening the area and
rubbing in the corn flour. Once it has
dried, the area needs to be brushed
very gently to remove all trace of the
powder. If you place the gerbil in a
hay-lined box, it will burrow in and

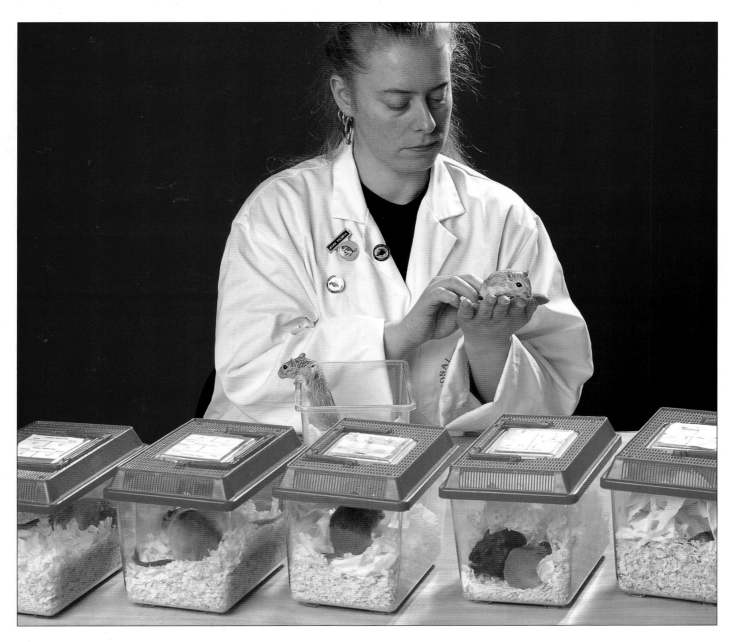

✦ BELOW
Condition is very important in exhibition gerbils. Beware of offering too much sunflower seed as this is fattening, and may even shorten the gerbil's lifespan.

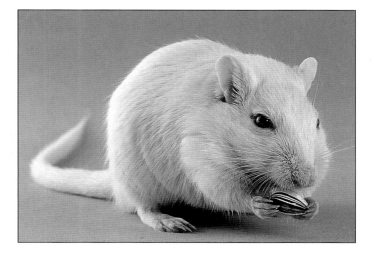

✦ RIGHT
Gerbils are shown individually, so you will have to wait until a female has given birth and her litter are independent before showing her again.

✦ BOTTOM
You will need to be familiar with the show standard for particular varieties, in terms of coloration and patterning.

✦ BELOW
Always ensure that your gerbil is in perfect condition prior to entering a show. Any loss of hair or damage to the tip of the tail will almost always count against it.

easily. It is also very important that the judge will be able to handle your gerbil without difficulty. If you hope to show your pet gerbil, you will need to train it when it is young to get it used to handling. In addition to the condition of the gerbil and

its tameness, the judges will also look at its surroundings. An otherwise excellent entry will be penalized if exhibited in a dirty or chipped show cage. It is important to maintain show cages or pens in top condition by washing them out after each show. After they have dried, keep them dust free by storing them in plastic bags until required again.

this will have the effect of grooming the coat. Finally, stroking the gerbil with a silk cloth helps to impart a good gloss to its fur.

GERBIL SHOWS
Standard show cages for gerbils are essential for serious exhibitors. For pet classes, however, the gerbils' regular home can be used, although you should cut down on the bedding for the show, so that the judge will be able to see your entry

One of the aspects of showing is its unpredictability. There is no guarantee that just because one gerbil won at its last show that it will do so again at the next event. The gerbil could be moulting, for example, so that its coat is not in top condition. As with other small livestock, the gerbils in a show class are not judged against each other, but rather against an ideal for the particular variety concerned. After the judging has taken place, most judges will be happy to offer advice concerning your gerbils.

RATS AND MICE

While these rodents may not top the list of everyone's favourite pet, they can turn out to be truly excellent companions, with rats in particular proving to be highly intelligent. Although rats and mice are very similar in appearance, rats are distinguished by their larger size. They must not be housed together, since rats will often instinctively attack mice. The choice of colours available in the case of rats is far less varied than it is with mice.

INTRODUCTION

Although rats and mice have a justified reputation for spreading various unpleasant diseases, the simple fact is that today's domesticated, or "fancy", rats and mice are far removed from their wild relatives, and are unlikely to present any significant health risks to people keeping them.

The process of domestication began well over a century ago, when rats were a major cause of disease in densely populated cities. The high death toll from rat-induced infections led to the employment of rat-catchers to keep a check on their numbers.

On occasion, the rat-catchers would catch rats that were different in colour to the normal type. These oddities were often kept on display at public houses, whereas their less fortunate relatives were killed by dogs in rat pits for customer entertainment.

✦ ABOVE
The brown rat is the original ancestor of all of today's fancy rats, although the black rat was also kept and bred for a period.

✦ LEFT
The wild form of the house mouse, with its typical brownish coloration – far removed from today's colourful domesticated mouse varieties.

By this stage in history, the brown rat (*Rattus norvegicus*) had become far more numerous than the black rat (*Rattus rattus*), and all of today's fancy rats are of brown rat descent, although different-coloured strains of black rat were kept during the 1920s.

The keeping of fancy rats lost favour for a period after this era until the 1970s. Since then, however, there has been much interest in keeping these intelligent rodents as pets and for exhibition purposes, and more colour varieties have been established.

◆ RIGHT
Rats are very adaptable creatures, able to swim well, although they will not thrive in damp surroundings.

◆ BELOW RIGHT
Mice are popular among fanciers for exhibition purposes, with judging standards being laid down for all the popular varieties.

RATS AND MICE AS PETS

When it comes to choosing between a mouse or a rat as a pet, it is worth bearing in mind that rats are significantly larger, averaging at least 25 cm (10 in) in length, and will consequently need more spacious accommodation. Mice typically measure around 15 cm (6 in) overall, including their tail. Rats have a significantly longer lifespan than mice, living on average for five years or more, while mice have a lifespan of around three years. Rats are also more likely to become tamer and are more amenable to handling. The strong odour of both rats and mice can be a

The domestication of the fancy mouse from its wild ancestor, the house mouse (*Mus musculus*), first began in the United Kingdom in the latter part of the 19th century. As in the case of rats, mice were widely used for medical experiments at this time, although their show potential was quickly recognized. The National Mouse Club in the United Kingdom was established in 1895 and is the oldest body of its kind in the world. Its creation led to the development of a vast colour range of fancy mice.

problem in the home environment, although females tend to produce a less pungent urine than males and may make a more suitable pet. While rats are typically kept on their own, mice can be housed comfortably in single-sex pairs or even trios.

It is important to buy pet mice and rats when they are young so that they accept being handled. They are then far less likely to inflict a painful bite when picked up.

Rats and mice are nocturnal by instinct, but they will usually be active during the day as well. Ensure that the fur looks sleek when you buy – if it is not, it could be a sign of ill-health, particularly if the rodent also appears to be hunched up.

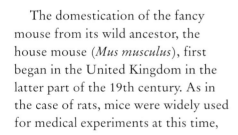

◆ BELOW
Rats can become very tame if handled regularly, and they will soon learn to identify their owners by their scent. They rarely bite, unless frightened or badly handled.

COLOUR VARIETIES

While there are now over 700 different varieties of mice, the number of fancy rat mutations is much lower, totalling less than 30. In most cases, the choice of colours available in most pet stores is small, so if you are seeking out some of the more unusual colours, you will usually need to contact a breeder. Look through the advertisement columns of specialist magazines or contact clubs. Details can usually be obtained through local libraries or via the Internet.

RATS
Breeds of rat that are furthest removed from the natural agouti form are the most popular. The most widely kept variety of rat is the albino form, sometimes called the white, which is distinguished by its pink eyes. Its lack of colour pigment also accounts for its pink ears and tail. Most of the new rat varieties have direct counterparts in

◆ ABOVE
The silvered mink is just one of a growing number of exotic colour varieties of the domestic rat. All are descended from the brown rather than the black rat.

◆ BELOW
A Himalayan rat, so-called because of the darker areas of fur present on the extremities of the body. These will be far less apparent in newly born pups.

the mouse fancy, with the exception of the mink. This rat is coffee coloured, with a bluish sheen to its coat.

Darker colours include the chocolate, which should be an even dark shade, as well as the black, which must also be pure in colour with no odd white hairs visible in its coat. In addition, there are other self (solid colour) varieties with pink eyes and a rosy hue – including the champagne, which is beige. The patterned colour variants include the hooded, which has a coloured area over its head and shoulders, extending down the back to the base of the tail. In the case of the capped form, there is no darker streak running back down the spine, and the remainder of the fur is white. There is no long-coated form, although there is a rex mutation, which has distinctive curled fur and whiskers.

◆ ABOVE
An agouti and white rat. The agouti colouring corresponds to that of the wild brown rat, which explains why these varieties are not the most popular choice as domestic pets.

◆ LEFT
A silvered black rat. At shows, it is not just the coloration of these rodents that is judged, but also their physical appearance, or "type".

◆ LEFT
A chocolate and tan mouse. This variety was first recorded in 1904 but has never gained great popularity. The chocolate coloration should be a dark shade.

The features of the long-coated and rex variants can be combined with any colour form or patterning. The scope here is truly enormous, and some fascinating specimens can be seen at the larger mice shows.

◆ BELOW
Even coloration is an important feature of the silver-grey variety. Sometimes, the body extremities may lack adequate silvering. This individual is a buck (male).

MICE

There are both self and patterned varieties of fancy mice. One of the most striking is the self red, which is a rich shade of chestnut. Its coloration is improved by the addition of a satin mutation, which gives a glossy sheen to the coat. The eyes are black, but some varieties, such as white and cream, exist in both pink-eyed and black-eyed forms. Evenness of colour through the coat is an essential attribute for self-coloured mice of all varieties.

Tan varieties are instantly recognizable by their appearance. Their underparts are tan coloured, while the remainder of the body is a contrasting shade. The feet should match the body colour on the outside and be tan coloured on the inside. Nor is it just dark shades such as black and tan that are regularly seen. Lighter variants, too, such as silver and tan, are quite commonly bred. Mice showing various other markings are also widely kept today. These include Himalayans, with dark points, and the Dutch, which has a similar pattern to that of the corresponding guinea pig or rabbit breeds.

◆ ABOVE
The chinchilla mouse is so-called because it resembles the wild chinchilla in colour. The individual hairs are tipped with black, and the undercoat is slate blue.

◆ BELOW
The black form of the mouse must be jet black, with a glossy coat. Mice of this colour were first recorded as far back as 1640. Any white markings are a serious flaw.

◆ ABOVE
A black and tan mouse. The tan underparts are most obvious when these mice sit up on their haunches. There must be clear delineation between the colours, as in this individual.

HOUSING AND FEEDING

Caring for rats and mice in the home does not present problems, providing the housing is roomy and secure and the diet is suitably nutritious.

ACCOMMODATION

The range of housing options for rats and mice has grown significantly over recent years. Special cages are now available that provide plenty of climbing space and are essentially escape proof – a highly important consideration when keeping these rodents in the home as, once free, they can be difficult to recapture. To be extra safe, it is worthwhile adding a small combination lock to the door.

If you prefer not to use a mesh cage – which can be a magnet to a cat – an acrylic container with a ventilated roof is a suitable alternative. This lightweight option is easy to move around but, as with any housing for pets in the home, be sure not to position the cage resting on furniture in front of a window. In hot weather, your pet may be affected by heat stress, with the glass magnifying the sun's rays. Rats and mice are also nocturnal creatures and bright daylight can upset their sleep patterns. Position cages in a draught-free place because, in spite of the hardiness of their wild relatives, domestic rats and mice are susceptible to chilling.

Most cages for rats are equipped with a detachable metal tray where the droppings collect. It is a good idea to line the tray with shavings but do not use this as a lining material in the rats' quarters, where they can burrow directly into it. A better option for this purpose is to use dust-free bedding also sold in pet stores.

Both mice and rats are shy creatures so it is essential to provide them with a thick layer of bedding in a corner of their quarters where they can retreat

◆ **ABOVE**
A cage for rats. Take care to ensure the rodents are not overcrowded. Otherwise, not only disease but fighting, too, can break out.

◆ **LEFT**
Toys of various types appeal to the inquisitive nature of rats and mice. If you provide a wheel, it must be of an enclosed design to prevent tail injuries.

◆ **RIGHT**
Paper bedding is one hygienic option and is readily obtainable from pet stores. It is less likely to trigger respiratory problems, being relatively free from dust.

Rat mix

Sunflower seeds

Peanuts

Dog biscuits

If you are not feeding your rodent a pre-formulated diet you may need to use a supplement to compensate for any nutritional deficiencies. Sprinkle the supplement over the rodent's favourite tidbits. When it comes to fresh food, it is best to offer it in small amounts on a regular basis. Although it will not contribute greatly to the protein intake, it will provide valuable vitamins and minerals. Large amounts of fresh food eaten at one time can trigger digestive upsets.

Avoid using mixes that contain significant proportions of oil seeds, such as sunflower or peanuts. These are not recommended for rats and mice on a long-term basis as they are likely to provoke skin irritations. There is no harm in offering other treats occasionally, such as small cubes of cheddar cheese and raisins.

The occasional sunflower seed or nut can be used when taming your rodent to feed from the hand. Otherwise, attempts to hand-feed could lead to bitten fingers.

A water bottle that attaches to the rodent's quarters and an earthenware food container are both essential.

and curl up to sleep. A wooden box surrounding this area will give them greater security. Special paper bedding is a better option than hay as both rats and mice are susceptible to respiratory diseases, and these can be triggered by the dust and fungal spores in hay.

SUITABLE FOODS
You can feed your rodent a seed-based diet, which contains cereals such as wheat and flaked maize (corn), or, preferably, a pelleted diet, which contains all the necessary ingredients to keep rats and mice in good health.

◆ ABOVE, BELOW LEFT AND BELOW RIGHT
Retreats are very important, allowing rats and mice to feel secure in their quarters; the natural instinct of small mammals is to stay hidden, out of sight of possible predators.

GENERAL CARE AND BREEDING

You can purchase accessories of various kinds for the enclosure, but bear in mind that mice and especially rats can inflict damage on plastic items, and these may need to be replaced in due course. It is actually much better to provide them with wooden blocks for chewing purposes or dried crusts of bread, on which they can wear down their incisor teeth. Avoid exercise wheels which have an open-weave design, as the rodent's long tail may become trapped.

Some household items can also be used to amuse your rodent, such as the lining tubes out of paper towelling, which make excellent tunnels. Rats are very playful by nature, and glass marbles that can be rolled along with their paws are another item that often appeals to them; glass marbles will also prove indestructible.

HANDLING
The handling of rodents requires particular care, as rats and mice have poor eyesight and rely more on their sense of smell for information about the world around them. If you attempt to pick one up too suddenly, you are likely to be bitten. Instead, allow the rodent to sniff at your fingers, and then gently scoop it up from beneath. Your new pet will quickly come to recognize your distinctive scent and will become much more amenable to regular handling. Even so, take care not to clench your pet tightly – this will make it panic and it could then bite – but allow it to rest in your hand. If necessary, mice can be restrained from scampering off by gently grasping the base of their tails.

◆ ABOVE
Handling a mouse. Do not try to grip your pet tightly in order to restrain it. Instead, encourage the rodent to step on to your hand and hold it gently by the base of the tail.

◆ LEFT
Rats are slightly more difficult to hold than mice because of their larger size, but they will rest in the hand for short periods, being cupped in this way, without attempting to bite or struggle.

◆ ABOVE
Rats will step readily from one hand to another, usually sniffing cautiously before they do so. Many will also perch on your shoulder.

NEWBORN RATS

Young rats are helpless and blind at birth. Do not disturb them at this stage because it could cause the doe to abandon them. Dark markings indicate black fur.

One of the features of rodents is the speed at which their young develop. This litter of rat pups is 12 days old and their coloration is already apparent. They sleep together for warmth.

A three weeks old, these young rats are moving and exploring their environment. It will be a further two weeks, however, before they are fully weaned and able to go to a new home.

◆ RIGHT
The rapid growth of young rodents can be seen by comparing the size of the younger four-week-old rat here with its larger companion, which is just a fortnight older.

MATING AND PREGNANCY

This is a relatively straightforward procedure. Male rats and mice, known as bucks, have the typical longer ano-genital gap and a visible scrotal sac. Females (does) in general are smaller in size. If you want to encourage mating, introduce the pair to neutral territory and leave them together for up to a fortnight, by which time mating will have taken place. The doe should then be housed on her own in preparation for the birth. Pregnancy lasts about 23 days in the case of rats, and a couple of days less in the case of mice. Rats may have slightly larger litters on average, comprising ten or more pups, which can be separated from their mother at five to six weeks old. Young mice pups should be weaned at three weeks old. Mice will often reach maturity at three months of age.

NEWBORN MICE

The breeding cycle of mice is faster than that of rats, but otherwise similar. No special foods are required for rearing purposes.

Young mice aged ten days old with their mother. The pup on the far right is smaller than its nest mates and is the runt of the litter.

Mice at 25 days, which have been weaned. The genetics surrounding the breeding of different colours have been intensively studied.

GROOMING AND SHOWING

Coat care for rodents is generally minimal, although long-coated mice do require grooming to prevent the hair becoming matted or soiled by bedding underneath. Exhibitors often have their own particular ways of conditioning their stock prior to a major show but, in many cases, it is possible simply to take rats or mice from their regular cages, transfer them to show cages and go on to win without any further preparation.

SHOW PREPARATION

To improve the sheen on your pet's coat, gently groom it with a piece of silk in the direction of the lie. As condition is very important in the judging process, do not expect your rodent to win if it is moulting. There is nothing that can be done here other than allowing the new fur to grow. It is worth noting, too, that a mouse or rat that is out of condition could be vulnerable to illness.

◆ ABOVE
Rats and mice need little grooming, and keeping the fur free of food or bedding is usually the most that will be required.

◆ BELOW
The condition of the mice is very important for show purposes, and those that are moulting are unlikely to excel. The Maxey show cage is typically used for exhibiting mice.

AT THE SHOW

It is well worth visiting shows, even if you are not entering any rats or mice yourself. This will give you the opportunity to study the entries and build up an image in your mind's eye of the ideal for your particular variety.

To gain even greater insight into the exhibition side of the hobby, you could volunteer to steward at show events. Stewarding itself entails taking the entries and facilitating the judging process by removing the hay, for example, from the Maxey show cages, allowing the judge to remove the mice more easily so that they can be examined individually. As a steward, you will be able to see how judges assess the entries at close quarters, and, after judging has occurred, you can ask the judge about the points that have influenced the placings.

Judging standards are laid down for the different varieties. These relate firstly to the overall appearance of the rats and mice in general terms, specifying what is considered to be desirable, such as the shape of the head

♦ BELOW
A wide variety of different retreats can be
purchased for mice, although plastic designs
are preferable to wood, because they will not
become stained by urine.

♦ BELOW
It is not a good idea to allow your pet mouse
to exercise in the garden, as these rodents are
very nimble and can quickly run off and
disappear from view.

and ears. They also highlight serious
flaws, such as kinked tails, which
would merit penalties – including
possible disqualification – although
it is unlikely that rodents with these
weaknesses would have been entered
in the first place.

Then there are the more specific
requirements – depending on the
variety concerned – that specify the
pattern of markings or the desired
depth of coloration. Condition is not
overlooked either, with obese entries
being penalized, while ease of handling
is another important factor that can
help to influence a judge's decision.
Those varieties that are not yet
standardized because there are too
few examples in existence, are usually
grouped together. Assuming that the
popularity of these varieties continues
to grow among fanciers, and no major
weaknesses crop up in the bloodlines,
then these are likely to be recognized
with specific official standards in due
course and will be transferred into
classes of their own.

♦ RIGHT
**Red-eyed white mice are popular pets. This
may be linked to the fact that they appear
very clean, thanks to the colour of their fur.**

CHINCHILLAS

The requirements of these rodents are rather different from other members of the group. Chinchillas are also more costly to purchase, although this is balanced to some extent by their relatively long lifespan. As quite new entrants on the show scene, chinchillas are not widely exhibited as yet. However, there are signs that this state of affairs is changing, particularly as new colour varieties are becoming more commonly available.

INTRODUCTION

Chinchillas belong to the caviomorph sub-group in the rodent family and, as such, are closely related to guinea pigs. Like guinea pigs, chinchillas originate from the Andean region of South America, on the western side of this continent, and are found at relatively high altitudes where the temperature can become very cold, particularly at night. They are well equipped to survive in this type of terrain, however, thanks to their very dense coat. In fact, the coat is so dense (there can be 70 or more hairs growing from a single hair follicle) that parasites cannot become established in it.

Unfortunately, this very dense, soft fur proved ideal for clothing and accessories, and this led to the Spanish explorers of South America taking

◆ LEFT
The mountain viscacha, which lives in the Andean region of South America, is closely related to the chinchilla. It has similarly dense fur but much larger ears.

◆ BELOW LEFT
A young viscacha in the wild. All members of the family Chinchillidae produce fewer offspring than other rodents and after a longer gestation period.

chinchillas back to Europe in the early 1500s. The growing European and North American demand during the 1800s led to the determined hunting of these rodents for the fur trade. By the early 1900s the chinchilla was becoming an endangered species.

The first efforts to farm chinchillas for their fur proved unsuccessful, and by the time a mining engineer called M. F. Chapman tried to obtain chinchillas for a further attempt during the 1920s, they were on the verge of extinction. It took 23 men three years to obtain just 11 live examples for him. Fortunately, this was sufficient to establish the first chinchilla fur farm, and also, ultimately, to safeguard the future of these unique rodents.

After careful acclimatization from the Andean mountains to sea level, the chinchillas were taken by ship to California, where they started

breeding rapidly. Stock initially changed hands at high prices, but by the 1960s the appeal of chinchillas started to grow. They started to be sold as pets for the first time, and the market for their fur began to decline.

CHINCHILLAS AS PETS

Chinchillas are now highly popular around the world as companion animals. They are still more expensive than other pet rodents but their exclusivity and clean image has helped them to become favourite pets. As chinchillas tend to be more active at dusk, they are a good choice of companion for people who are out at work all day, and they can become very tame, especially if handled regularly from an early age. Unlike the guinea pig, the chinchilla is very much a household pet and it will require special care and grooming. Chinchillas have sharp incisor teeth, which can inflict serious damage on plastic food containers and play equipment in their cages; these will need to be checked and replaced on a regular basis.

Unlike many rodents, chinchillas have an unusually long lifespan, and can live for over a decade. Some have been known to live for over 20 years.

◆ BELOW
The charcoal variant of the chinchilla, which is
of a darker shade than the standard. Although
more expensive than the usual form, their care
needs are identical.

COLOUR VARIETIES

The typical wild form of the chinchilla, known as the standard, is variable in colour, with light and dark bands encircling the individual hairs, creating a slightly mottled impression over the body. The depth of colouring differs between individuals, ranging from shades of grey through to black, with the hairs darkest at the tips. In contrast, the fur on the underside of the body is pure white. The eyes are always black and the ears, too, are dark in colour.

WHITE FORMS

The palest varieties now available are the white forms. The true white is pure white in colour, sometimes displaying odd darker patches. It is not a true albino, as it may have some black hairs on the body and has black ears and eyes. This is in contrast to the

◆ BELOW
The alert nature of the chinchilla is clearly displayed by this standard individual, with its large ears helping to pinpoint the direction of sounds with great accuracy.

pink white where the presence of any pigment is restricted to traces of beige colouring. The ears and paws are both pink, and the eyes may vary in colour from pink to red, emphasizing the lack of dark melanin pigment in the white chinchilla form.

BEIGE FORMS

There are two forms of beige chinchillas, and these differ in their genetic make-up and thus, their coloration. The pure homozygous beige is paler in colour than its heterozygous counterpart, and is a very pale shade of cream with a slight pink suffusion. The eyes in this case are also a pale shade of pink, with a whitish ring surrounding the pupil at the centre of each eye. Heterozygous beige chinchillas vary in colour from cream through to shades of dark beige, with significantly paler underparts, as in the standard variety. The eye coloration of the heterozygous is often more clearly defined, ranging from pink through to red.

BREEDING AND SHOWING

Although they mature between three and five months of age, it is not recommended to breed from chinchillas for the first time until they reach seven months old.

MATING AND PREGNANCY

Female chinchillas have a shorter gap between their anal and genital openings than males, and are smaller in size when adult. The female has a relatively long breeding cycle and only comes into heat once a month. Pairings need to be made carefully to avoid genetic incompatibility and to minimize any risk of fighting when the pair are introduced. Place them in adjoining cages and then, after a few days, if they are showing an interest in each other, transfer the male into the female's quarters. Assuming all goes well, he can be left in there with her until after the young are born and are independent.

One of the most reliable signs of pregnancy is the presence of a white plug of mucus, called a stopper, on the floor of the cage. This is produced by the female. She may also adopt an unusual sleeping posture, although the impending arrival of a litter is not the

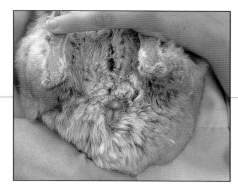

only cause of this. Pregnancy lasts for 16 weeks. Three young will be born in an advanced state of development, as miniature adults, with their eyes open. At this stage, they weigh up to 55 g (2 oz), less than a tenth of the weight of an adult. The young chinchillas, known as kits, will be suckled by their mother for six to eight weeks before they are fully independent.

EXHIBITIONS

Chinchillas are not commonly exhibited at present but as the number of colour varieties

◆ BELOW
An older fawn chinchilla. The coat by this stage is much more developed, and the brush of longer fur on the tail is clearly apparent, compared with the youngster.

◆ ABOVE LEFT AND ABOVE RIGHT
The sexing of chinchillas is done by examining their underparts. The female is seen here on the right. Note the swelling of the male's scrotal sac.

◆ LEFT
A fawn chinchilla baby at two days of age with its mother. The difference in size is very obvious, and it will be at least six weeks before the youngster is independent.

◆ BELOW LEFT
A young chinchilla. Note the relatively short tail, and the covering of short fur here. It has a long potential lifespan, often living for ten years or more.

continues to increase this situation is changing. Chinchillas may be seen at larger small-animal shows, as well as at events organized by chinchilla clubs. Standardization of the chinchilla's type is underway because of pressure on coat quality, following selective breeding for fur over the generations.

When travelling with chinchillas it is vital to remember that they are highly susceptible to heat stroke in temperatures above 25°C (77°F). This applies even in the home, where they may need to be transferred to a cooler location on particularly hot days.

OTHER SMALL MAMMALS

Several other different types of rodents and other small mammals are becoming popular with enthusiasts, although their requirements tend to be more specialist than in the case of the more regular pet rodents. These mammals make original and charming pets, but they can be expensive to buy and you will often need to spend more time tracking down appropriate food and equipment suppliers.

SPECIALITY PETS

Always aim to find out as much as you can about the needs of your pet before you take it home. The breeder from whom you buy the animal will be able to advise on most aspects of its care.

CHIPMUNK

One of the most widely kept members of this group is the Siberian chipmunk (*Eutamias sibiricus*). This is an attractive shade of brown with darker stripes running down its back and white underparts. These rodents measure about 10 cm (4 in) long, with a slightly shorter tail. They can be housed either indoors or out, in an aviary-like structure. Provide plenty of branches for climbing purposes.

The wooden supports of the cage should be built on the outside, out of reach of the chipmunk's strong teeth. The mesh for the frames should be 16 gauge in thickness, with a strand size no bigger than 2.5 x 1 cm (1 x ½ in). The base must be solid to prevent escapes and to ensure that other rodents cannot tunnel their way in.

◆ RIGHT
A Korean chipmunk housed in a large indoor bird cage. These rodents are very lively and agile by nature. Note the nest box provided as a retreat, and the wooden branch for climbing purposes – this may also be gnawed on occasion.

◆ BELOW LEFT
The spikey appearance of the fur is one of the characteristic features of spiny mice. These rodents need to be handled with particular care, since their tails are easily injured.

While chipmunks are naturally active you should not expect to handle them as you would a conventional pet rodent, although they can often be tamed enough to feed from the hand. A seed mixture makes a good basic diet, with added nuts, vegetables, apple chunks and mealworms.

Provide a nest box for roosting and breeding. Between four and eight young will be born after a gestation period of 31 days. The young leave the nest at seven weeks and will become independent shortly afterwards. If housed outdoors, the chipmunk will be less active in cold spells of weather.

SPINY MICE

Several different species of mouse are being bred by enthusiasts, of which the best known are probably spiny mice (*Acomys* species). Originating from parts of North Africa and the Middle East, these mice have unusual spiky fur, as their name suggests. Ideal housing for a spiny mouse would be a converted aquarium with a ventilated hood. Because of their small size, they may find a cage too spacious to make them feel secure. Care needs to be taken when handling these mice as their tails are easily injured. Damage to the tail can also result if the mice are housed in overcrowded accommodation, even if it is only for a relatively short time.

The breeding habits of spiny mice are unusual for small mammals. They have a long pregnancy, lasting around 38 days, and usually only give birth to two or three pups in one litter. The young are active almost from birth and are covered in grey fur at this stage. In addition to seeds and greenstuff, spiny mice will also eat mealworms.

SUGAR GLIDER

The small marsupial known as the sugar glider (*Petaurus breviceps*) originates from Australia and New Guinea. Its main diet should be a nectar solution mixed fresh each day. Fresh fruit and vegetables can also be provided, along with nuts and seeds, a few mealworms and other sources of protein, such as commercial dog or cat food.

Sugar gliders need indoor aviary-type housing, and it is a good idea to make sure this is easy to clean: the sticky nature of their droppings means that the gliders' quarters must be cleaned out on a daily basis.

A nest box for sleeping purposes should be included in their enclosure, and add tree branches, such as apple, to simulate their natural habitat and provide them with an opportunity for regular exercise.

As marsupials, the newborn young move after birth to their mother's pouch, where they will remain for the next ten weeks. Weaning occurs about five weeks later. Young sugar gliders mature at around ten months old and may go on to live for a decade or more.

◆ ABOVE
A pair of sugar gliders. They require an aviary-like structure, equipped with branches to allow them to climb freely. Their quarters need to be designed so that they can be cleaned easily.

◆ LEFT
Sugar gliders reproduce in a different way to the small mammals more usually kept as pets. They are marsupials, forming part of the group that includes kangaroos.

HEALTH CARE

Once established in their quarters, small animals usually prove to be very healthy. One of the more common causes of serious health problems in small mammals is a sudden change in their diet, which is likely to lead to digestive upsets. Treatment of these animals is not always straightforward because, in many cases, they will react adversely to certain antibiotics. Seeking veterinary advice early offers the best hope of recovery from illness.

SMALL MAMMAL HEALTH

◆ BELOW
Rabbits often need to have their claws trimmed back. If overgrown, walking will be difficult.

Once they are settled in their housing, small animals are usually healthy, and need very little in the way of routine health care. Sometimes though, you may need to clip back their claws if these become overgrown. If you prefer, you can ask your vet to do this for you. However, clipping claws is straightforward, provided that you have a suitable pair of clippers for the purpose.

Guillotine-type clippers with a sliding blade are to be recommended. This makes it easier to control the amount of the nail which you will be trimming off, as the claw is placed within the ring of the blade. It is helpful to have someone else to restrain your pet, so that you can concentrate on clipping the claw

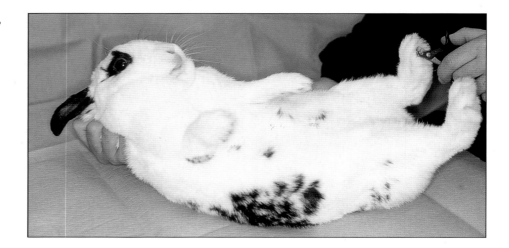

safely. If left, the claws can otherwise curl back into the pad, causing great discomfort to the animal. Guinea pigs are most susceptible to overgrown claws, but rabbits can also suffer from this problem.

Carry out claw clipping in a good light, so that you can detect the quick, visible as a pink streak running down the claw from the base. You then need to cut at a point where this disappears towards the tip of the nail, so as to avoid bleeding. In the case of individuals with black claws, however, it may be impossible to spot the end of the quick, and particular care needs to be taken in these cases. If you do nick a claw too short, or it is injured and starts bleeding, pressing on the tip for a few moments should help to stem the blood flow. A styptic pencil, as sold in chemists (drug stores) for shaving nicks, may also help.

◆ BELOW LEFT
If the incisor teeth do not meet correctly in jaws, it will soon be impossible for the rabbit to continue eating.

◆ BELOW RIGHT
Hair loss is a relatively common condition in many of the smaller mammal breeds.

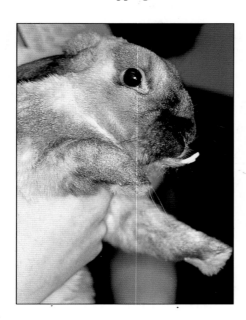

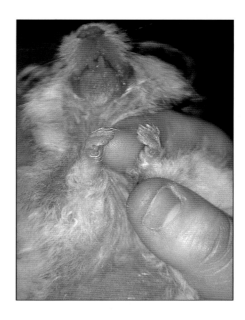

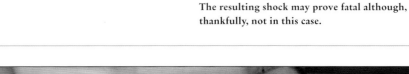

◆ BELOW
Vitamin C deficiency can arise quite easily in
guinea pigs. It results in scurvy, reflected here
by the dry, scaly skin. This is a dietary problem
which can be treated fairly routinely.

◆ BELOW
Rabbits are especially at risk from being
attacked by dogs and even cats on occasions.
The resulting shock may prove fatal although,
thankfully, not in this case.

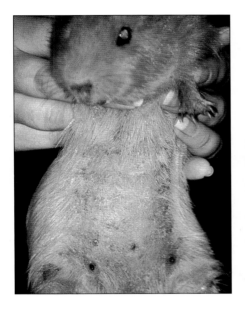

Overgrown teeth, caused by
malocclusion, when the top and
bottom incisors do not meet properly,
are a more serious proposition to deal
with, and these are best attended to
by your vet. The teeth are likely to
need trimming back every eight weeks
or so, to allow your pet to continue
eating without difficulty.

Nutritional problems are rare in
small animals, particularly now that
specially formulated diets are widely
available. Even so, cases of Vitamin C
deficiency do occur occasionally in
guinea pigs which, unlike other small
animals, cannot manufacture this
vital vitamin in their bodies. It must
therefore be present in their diet. If
you are housing a rabbit and guinea
pig together and offering them rabbit
pellets, then a deficiency, giving rise
to the condition known as scurvy, is
likely to occur before long. Dry, flaky
skin which can bleed readily is the
commonest sign. Vitamin C supplementation, and the regular use of a
guinea pig food which will contain this
vitamin should lead to a cure.

Hair thinning in hamsters is a sign
of old age rather than a nutritional
deficiency, and there is really nothing
that can be done about it. Equally,
another quite common condition
which is difficult to deal with in
elderly male guinea pigs is a distended
rectum, which leads to swelling as the
result of a build-up of faecal matter

here. This appears to be the result of
the loss of muscular tone. Increasing
the fibre content of the diet may help
but, ultimately, the rectum will need to
be emptied manually, gently massaging
the affected area with a little olive oil
first to loosen the obstruction. This
can be done at home but your vet can
perform it for you, if you prefer.

◆ LEFT
Hair loss in hamsters
can be difficult to
resolve, with the
coat often becoming
noticeably thinner
in old age. Distinct
bald patches may
indicate parasites.

BACTERIAL ILLNESSES

✦ BELOW
Rabbits are prone to upper respiratory infections – a condition known as snuffles. A nasal discharge, as seen here, is one of the most common signs.

✦ BOTTOM
A sick guinea pig. A mite infestation which results in fur loss can lead to a more generalized illness if left untreated. This is the case for most small mammals.

It is not difficult to recognize signs of illness in a small animal, as when sick an individual will usually be less active than normal and it may lose its appetite. It is likely to sit in a hunched-up fashion, with its fur held out from the body, creating a ruffled appearance. Even so, it can be very difficult to diagnose the cause of the illness accurately, because the symptoms of many infections are fairly similar.

As a result of their small size, pet rodents especially will lose heat rapidly from their bodies, which results in their condition deteriorating quickly. As a first step, therefore, it is important to provide some additional heat, while leaving a cooler area where your pet can retreat if it starts to feel too warm. A heat lamp will be useful for this purpose.

A small mammal that is sick needs urgent veterinary attention, but unfortunately, the choice of drugs which can be used to treat infections in this group of creatures is more restricted than in other pets because they react very badly to a number of antibiotics. Some antibiotics will have

a harmful effect on the beneficial bacteria in the digestive tract, and this can prove fatal. You should never be tempted to use remedies prescribed for other pets for treatment purposes.

Young, recently-weaned rodents are perhaps most prone to bacterial illnesses, particularly if their diet is changed suddenly, because this can allow harmful bacteria to colonize the digestive tract, and interferes with the digestion of food. The stress of rehoming can also be significant.

Tyzzer's disease for example can strike young mice, rats and gerbils in particular. It is caused by a bacterium

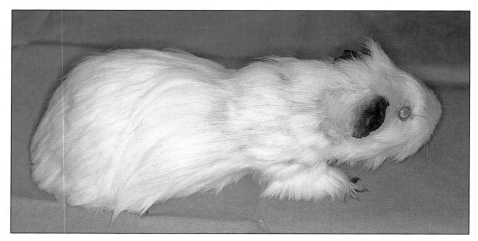

known as *Bacillus piliformis*, with symptoms typically including diarrhoea; sometimes in epidemics, a large number of young animals will die suddenly from this. Young hamsters can suffer from an infection known as wet tail, or proliferative ileitis, which again is often linked with a bacterial infection. Diarrhoea

✦ LEFT
Illnesses can be spread easily when guinea pigs are being housed together. This applies especially in the case of skin ailments, such as mites and ringworm.

✦ BELOW
Health problems can be caused by unsuitable
bedding. Eye and associated nasal irritations
in gerbils can be triggered by allowing them
to burrow into fine sawdust.

✦ BELOW
There is now much more that veterinarians
can do to prevent and treat illnesses in small
mammals, but much depends on owners seeking
professional advice at an early stage.

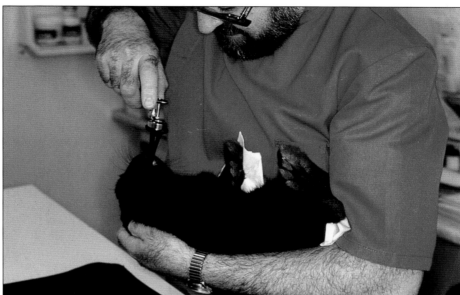

affecting the area under the tail
causes the fur here to appear wet,
while internally, the part of the small
intestine known as the ileum will be
badly inflamed. Again, treatment is
difficult, but it can be successful,
especially if carried out before the
hamster becomes badly dehydrated.

Other illnesses may be more
localized. Rats and mice are
particularly vulnerable to infections
of the upper respiratory tract, which
result in runny noses and noisy
breathing. Similar symptoms can be
triggered by dust from unsuitable
bedding, which will provoke an
allergic reaction. Rapid treatment
is vital before the infection spreads
further down into the respiratory
system, causing pneumonia. Rabbits
can suffer from a similar condition,
often referred to as snuffles.

Guinea pigs are especially prone
to pneumonia, which can be caused
by a range of different bacteria.
This is often linked to poor
ventilation in their quarters, or

damp surroundings, and there may be
few, if any, early-warning symptoms.
Only if the unfortunate guinea pig
is autopsied will the cause of death
become known. Laboured breathing

and loss of appetite are the most likely
indicators of this problem. Antibiotic
therapy may help a sick individual,
although pneumonia in any small
animal is a very serious condition.

✦ BELOW
You can prevent dental problems
in small mammals by providing
them with various chews, which
will help to keep their teeth in
good condition.

♦ BELOW
Myxomatosis is a killer viral disease which
relatively few rabbits will survive, and there
is no treatment available. All pet rabbits should
be protected by vaccination.

VIRAL AND FUNGAL ILLNESSES

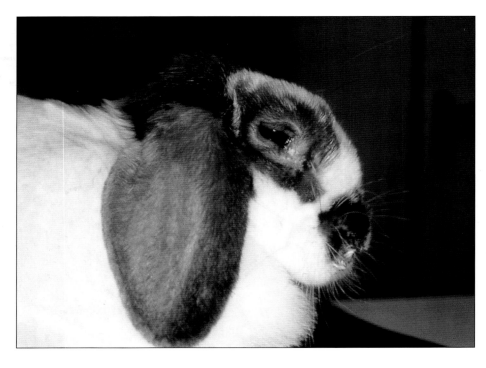

The most significant viral illnesses for owners of small animals occur in rabbits, and both have been developed with a view to controlling wild rabbit populations by biological means.

MYXOMATOSIS

This is a virus which can be spread to domestic rabbits by wild rabbits visiting their hutches; for this reason it is recommended to stand hutches at least 60 cm (2 ft) off the ground in areas where wild rabbits are prevalent, and to double-wire runs on both faces of the timber around the perimeter. Outbreaks of myxomatosis tend to occur in the summer in more temperate areas because biting insects, such as mosquitoes, are also capable of spreading the infection, and these are most numerous at this time of year.

The earliest signs of infection are inflammation of the eyes, quickly accompanied by a whitish discharge. By this stage, the rabbit will be seriously ill and will have lost its appetite. Sadly, there is no treatment for myxomatosis, and most affected

individuals will die within a couple of days. Those which survive beyond this stage develop scabs around their eyes, and their ears become badly swollen and start to droop. With virtually no hope of survival, therefore, it will be kindest to have a rabbit which has contracted myxomatosis painlessly

♦ BELOW LEFT
A guinea pig that is housed with a rabbit does not need to be vaccinated against myxomatosis or VHD, which only affect rabbits.

♦ BELOW
Ringworm on a rabbit's face. This fungal ailment is usually characterized by its circular pattern of spread, with accompanying hair loss.

✦ BELOW
A vaccine to protect against VHD being administered. The vaccine is essential, especially in exhibition stock, to guard against this relatively common killer rabbit disease.

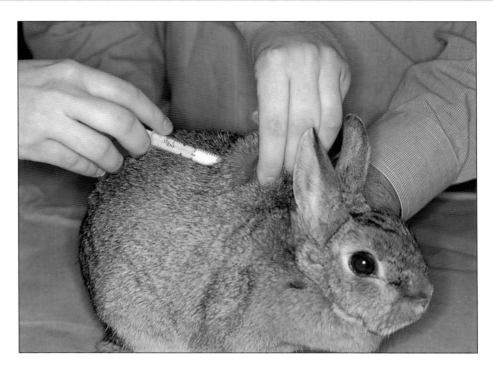

euthanased after diagnosis. In areas where this infection crops up regularly, it is vital to have pet rabbits protected by vaccination, since they are more vulnerable to the disease than wild rabbits, which may have some immunity to this illness. In areas where a vaccine is not available, then keeping domestic rabbits isolated from wild rabbits, and screening their quarters from insects, should offer some protection against myxomatosis.

VHD

Viral haemorrhagic disease (VHD) has only been recognized in rabbits since the 1980s, but has spread through the wild population and infected domestic stock as well. There are very few symptoms, and an affected rabbit will usually die suddenly. One tell-tale sign is a slight haemorrhaging of blood from the nose. There is no treatment, and vaccination against this disease is important, particularly for show stock because the virus survives well in the environment. It is spread by contaminated food and water bowls, housing pens and even clothing, as well as directly from one rabbit to another.

Because rabbits are prone to digestive upsets, viruses may have a role in some cases of digestive illness, although the role is not yet clearly understood. The hope of recovery stems from preventing dehydration, which accompanies severe diarrhoea, from becoming life-threatening. This should enable the body's own defence mechanisms to overcome the illness.

RINGWORM

Viruses are less important to small mammals such as hamsters, which are usually housed on their own in the

home, and are therefore at a much reduced risk of acquiring this type of infection. But very occasionally, small mammals may be afflicted by the fungal disease called ringworm. This causes a loss of the coat in circular patches. The risk is that this condition can be spread to human beings, where it will show up as red blotches, in the shape of circles, on the arm where the infected area of fur was in contact with the skin. Fortunately, it can be treated.

Ringworm is transmitted very easily by fungal spores on grooming equipment. If you suspect ringworm, avoid using this on any other animal in your collection. The spores will linger in hutches and elsewhere for years, so thorough disinfection is essential after an outbreak, using a hexetidine preparation to kill the fungus. Wear gloves when cleaning out the quarters and burn the bedding, which is likely to be contaminated with spores.

✦ RIGHT
Hamsters rarely suffer from viral illnesses. However, the hamster plague virus will cause fits, and an affected hamster will die within 24 hours.

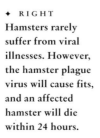

PARASITIC ILLNESSES

Rabbits and guinea pigs in particular are both prone to external parasites living on their bodies. Rabbits can often suffer from ear mites, which cause the condition sometimes described as canker. The mites cause irritation within the ear canal, resulting in the formation of brown scabs here, with the resulting discomfort causing the rabbit to scratch its ears more frequently than normal. If left, the mites are likely to spread into the inner part of the ear, permanently damaging the rabbit's sense of balance.

Do not attempt to pick off the scabs but, instead, dust the ears with flower of sulphur, a yellow powder available from pharmacies, which will kill off the mites effectively. Disinfect the hutch thoroughly once the rabbit has recovered fully, to eliminate any risk of reinfection as far as possible, although there is a risk that the mites could be reintroduced on dusty bedding material such as hay.

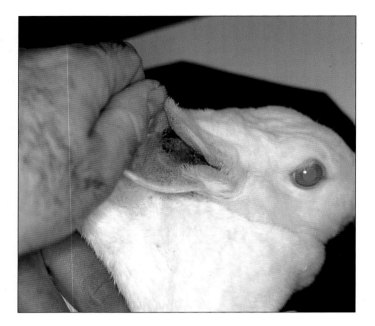

♦ LEFT
Ear mites attack the inside of the ear, creating brownish, crusty deposits here. These parasites can spread easily from rabbit to rabbit but can be treated easily.

Guinea pigs are vulnerable to skin mites, which again may lurk in contaminated bedding. You may miss the initial stages of infection, when the mites cause tiny white spots under the fur. Skin shedding, in the form of pronounced dandruff then follows, along with hair loss. At this stage, a

♦ BELOW
Rex breeds of rabbit may suffer fur loss because of their housing conditions, rather than as a result of illness.

mite infestation may sometimes appear like ringworm, and skin scrapings from an affected area will be necessary to identify the mites under a microscope.

Treatment by injection using the drug ivermectin at the appropriate dilution is now the simplest way to kill off these mites, although this treatment will be needed over a period of a month or so, with injections being given every fortnight. The cage must also be thoroughly disinfected, to kill off any surviving mites. Other guinea pigs sharing the hutch will probably need to be treated as well. The susceptibility of guinea pigs to skin problems means that a thorough examination will be necessary to determine the cause of the problem, which is not always infectious. Some sows, for example, lose patches of their fur when pregnant, but this should regrow in due course.

It is always very important, particularly if your rabbit or guinea pig has suffered recently from diarrhoea,

◆ BELOW
Diarrhoea in rats or mice can be caused by
parasites, but tests will need to be carried out
by your vet to obtain a definitive diagnosis.

◆ BELOW
A severe case of mange in a guinea pig.
Treatment by a series of injections will be
required, but always seek advice at an early
stage to minimize your pet's suffering.

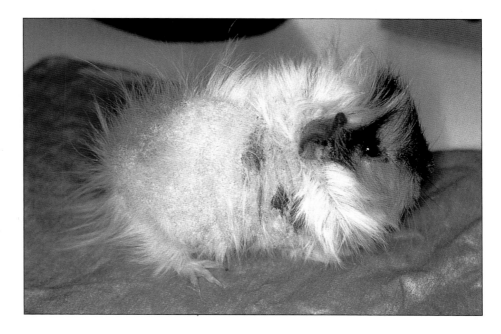

to check there is no soiling of the fur around the animal's rear end. Otherwise, your pet could become parasitized by the larvae of blowflies, responsible for the condition often described as fly strike. Bluebottles and similar flies will be attracted to the soiled fur, laying their eggs here which hatch rapidly into larvae. These literally bore into the flesh, releasing deadly toxins. This is why it is so important to remove the larvae without delay because, otherwise, they will kill the rabbit or guinea pig. Your vet will be able to remove them with special forceps; a wound powder may also be used to promote healing.

A wide range of microscopic, single-celled organisms, called protozoa, can be found in the intestinal tract of small mammals, often helping to digest the food here so that the nutrients can be absorbed into the body. Some of these protozoa are likely to be harmful however, giving rise to the disease known as coccidiosis. They can cause diarrhoea, which may be blood-stained,

and permanent damage to the lining of the intestinal tract, so that a young rabbit will not grow properly.

In order to protect against this infection, drugs called coccidiostats are sometimes incorporated in the rabbit's food. Another form of the infection attacks the liver, causing what is described as hepatic coccidiosis, which can also be fatal.

Actual treatment of coccidiosis will be possible using specially formulated sulphur-based compounds available from your vet. Cleanliness is equally vital, however, because the infection is transmitted via the rabbit's droppings.

◆ BELOW
If you have a number of guinea pigs, use
separate grooming tools for them. This will
help to prevent the spread of skin mites.

PET BIRDS

Birds have been popular as pets for over 5,000 years. The ancient Greeks used to marvel at the ability of parrots to learn different languages. This ancient link is commemorated today by the Alexandrine parakeet (*Psittacula eupatria*), which was first taken back to Greece by soldiers in the army of Alexander the Great.

Overseas voyages of discovery brought European sailors into contact with a large number of previously unknown birds. When Christopher Columbus returned from his successful sailing to the New World in 1493, he brought back a pair of Cuban Amazon parrots (*Amazona leucocephala*).

Soon afterwards, small finches with an attractive song were brought from the Canary Islands, off the west coast of Africa, and these became immensely popular. These rather dull-looking green birds were the ancestors of today's amazing range of canary breeds. The pure yellow coloration of the birds of today did not emerge until domestication was well underway, around the early 1700s.

When it comes to coloration, of course, it is the budgerigar that now reigns supreme. These popular parakeets originate from Australia, and first started to become well known in Europe during the 1840s.

◆ OPPOSITE

A pair of masked lovebirds. These small parrots make highly attractive aviary occupants. Males and females cannnot be distinguished visually from each other.

◆ LEFT

Budgerigars have been bred in a huge range of colour varieties and this has enhanced their popularity. These birds are talented mimics and will breed readily.

CANARIES AND OTHER FINCHES

These attractive and often colourful small birds are very popular occupants of garden aviaries, as they are neither destructive nor noisy by nature. Some members of the group, especially canaries, are also highly prized by pet-owners on account of their singing prowess, while others, such as zebra finches, will nest readily, even when housed in a cage indoors, although they are unlikely to become as tame as some members of the parrot family.

INTRODUCTION

All of these birds are easy to cater for in terms of food and housing needs. They feed primarily on seed, although other foodstuffs, such as greenstuff and small invertebrates, are also significant in the diets of many species, particularly during the breeding season. At this stage, finches, such as waxbills, become highly insectivorous and their young are unlikely to be reared satisfactorily without a supply of livefoods such as hatchling crickets, which are available commercially, and aphids, which are found in parks and gardens.

The housing of canaries and finches is also straightforward, thanks in part to their small size. Most finches average between 10 and 15 cm (4–6 in) in length and, unlike most parrots, finches will not destroy their quarters. If they are housed in an outdoor aviary in temperate areas, they are likely to need additional heat and lighting to see them through the cooler and darker days of winter. This can add significantly to the expense of keeping them, and you should calculate this expenditure at the outset. As an alternative, you can bring the birds indoors and house them in a flight over the winter period. They can then be released back into the aviary in the spring when the risk of frost has passed. Few finches, with the notable exception of the canary and its close relatives such as the singing finches,

are talented songsters but many, such as the Gouldian finch (*Chloebia gouldiae*), are beautifully coloured.

As finches are often social birds, it is not uncommon for pairs of several species to be housed together in the same aviary. You need to ensure that they will be compatible in these surroundings, however, and are not overcrowded as outbreaks of fighting

may otherwise occur, particularly during the breeding period when the birds' territorial instincts will be at their strongest.

Most finches have a life expectancy of around seven years, although, on occasion, individuals have been known to live much longer – for more than 20 years in the case of some green singing finches.

♦ LEFT
The Gouldian finch
is one of the most
colourful finches
in the world today.

♦ BELOW
Cock singing
finches will display
their talents as
songsters, especially
during the breeding
period, although
their fluency of song
does not match that
of the canary.

SEXING

It is often possible to sex finches
by differences in their plumage but,
where this is not possible, you can
start off with several individuals of the
same species, which should ensure
that you have at least one breeding
pair in the group. It can be virtually
impossible to distinguish between the
sexes when canaries are moulting, as
cock birds will not attempt to sing at
this stage. At other times, patience is
important so that you can watch the
birds carefully, picking out which is
likely to be a cock in the group.

BREEDING BEHAVIOUR

Certain finches, notably male weavers
and whydahs, undergo a dramatic
change in appearance during the
breeding period when they become
much more colourful. Their breeding
requirements differ quite markedly
from other finches as well, with male
weavers building ornate nests and
needing to be kept in harems
comprising a single cock and perhaps
three or four hens. Male whydahs
have an elaborate display dance, while
the hens will deposit their eggs in the
nests of waxbills, rather than
incubating them themselves.

The typical breeding behaviour of
weavers and whydahs may represent
a challenge, even for the experienced
bird-keeper. However, other species
of finch will breed readily, and will also
make popular exhibition subjects as
they have been developed in a wide
range of attractive colours and feather
types. The Bengalese finch, which is
better known in the United States as
the society finch, and the zebra finch
are among the most widely kept
finches for this reason.

SPECIES AND BREEDS

CANARIES

Since wild canaries (*Serinus canaria*) were first brought to Europe several centuries ago, a number of different breeds have been developed, and the process of evolution is still continuing today. Canaries are divided into three basic groups: singing breeds, type breeds and breeds developed for their coloration, known as new colours.

Of the singing breeds, the ancestral form, called the roller, is still the best known and most widely kept. Although all cock canaries have an attractive song, top rollers are unrivalled, both in terms of the quality of the song and their range, which can extend over almost three octaves.

The type breeds are characterized by their appearance, which must conform as closely as possible to the official standard laid down for judging purposes for the breed concerned. This is a large grouping, with some breeds, such as the attractive Gloster canary which occurs in both a crested and plainhead form, having established an international following, whereas others remain localized. The unusual frilled breeds are also included in this category, with the names of many such canary breeds traditionally reflecting their area of origin, as in the case of the Parisian frill.

The third category of canaries are the new colours, which have been bred primarily for their coloration. They include the stunning red factor birds, which were

✦ LEFT
The crest of the Gloster corona should be even, and must not obscure the eyes. The neck should be relatively thick. This is a variegated bird, with both dark and light areas in its plumage.

✦ BELOW
The green singing finch is a close relative of the canary, found over a wide area of mainland Africa, and has an attractive song. It needs similar care in aviary surroundings. The hens can be identified by the black spots across the throat. They have been known to live for 20 years or more.

✦ LEFT
The hens originally bred from pairings between canaries and black-hooded red siskins were infertile until the third generation. Today, the fertility of red canaries, such as this intensive clear red, is normal.

created in the 1920s as the result of an attempt to create pure red canaries by way of cross-breeding experiments involving a South American finch, the black-hooded red siskin (*Carduelis cucullata*).

GREEN SINGING FINCH

The green singing finch (*Serinus mozambicus*) is the closest wild relative of the canary that is widely

◆ LEFT
The markings of the cock bird, here on the left, can be clearly seen in this exhibition pair of chestnut-flanked white zebra finches.

◆ BELOW
In the fawn mutation of the zebra finch, it is easy to distinguish the sexes. The grey plumage has been replaced by a warmer shade of brown.

kept today. Smaller in size, averaging about 12.5 cm (5 in) in length, these finches can be sexed easily: cock birds display more yellow coloration on their heads and lack the black throat spots seen in hens. These finches need similar care to the domestic canary, and may breed successfully in a breeding cage, although success is more likely in a garden aviary. They build a cup-shaped nest and, as with canaries, two rounds of chicks may be reared in succession. Provide daily supplies of egg food for rearing.

WAXBILLS

These birds make ideal companions for singing finches in aviary surroundings, although they are often more difficult to breed. Sexing in most cases is straightforward. For example, the hens of the red-eared waxbill (*Estrilda troglodytes*) have paler plumage on their underparts. These finches may use a domed nesting basket or they may prefer to construct their own nest from vegetation found in the aviary – clumps of dried grass, sticks, moss and similar materials.

The blue waxbills can also be housed as part of a colony as they all require similar care but, since they can be aggressive towards others of their

own kind, only one pair should be kept in an aviary alongside other finches. The red-cheeked waxbill (*Uraeginthus bengalus*) is a good choice, not only because of its attractive appearance, but because pairs are easy to distinguish: only the cock bird displays the red cheek markings.

◆ BELOW
Waxbills such as this attractive pair of red-cheeked cordon bleus require careful management at first, but may then live for a decade or more.

ZEBRA FINCH

These birds (*Taeniopygia guttata*) rank among the most widely kept of all finches. Their name comes from the black and white striping usually seen on the chest of cock birds, although this feature may not be apparent in some of the colour forms that have since been developed. Hens can be identified by the more orangish rather than red coloration of their bills. Zebra finches are lively little birds, and they are highly social by nature, living well in groups or as single pairs. They can be housed with waxbills and other non-aggressive finches as part of a collection. Pairs are equally adaptable in breeding terms, using open-fronted finch nest boxes or nesting baskets for this purpose.

Among the popular colours are chestnut-flanked whites, which replace the grey coloration of the normal variety on the head, back and wings with white. Pieds with variable white and coloured areas are also popular, although it is not possible to predict the markings of chicks from those of their parents. Fawn, silver and cream varieties are equally well established, while among the newer variants is the black-breasted, with the barring on the chest of the cock replaced by solid black coloration. There is also a crested form.

BENGALESE FINCH

The origin of the Bengalese (*Lonchura domestica*) is mysterious – this finch does not occur in the wild, and is thought to be the result of cross-breeding with the striated mannikin (*L. striata*). Bengalese finches are thought to have been developed at least 500 years ago, probably in China. Their coloration is shades of brown. The fawn of the species is pale compared to the darker chestnut, while the chocolate colour is regarded as the original form. These colours also exist in combination with white, and the crested Bengalese, as they are known, are very popular. Visual sexing is impossible with these finches, and it is only the cock's song that distinguishes them.

✦ ABOVE
Red-eared waxbills are hard to sex outside the breeding season. Two birds preening each other does not signify they are a pair because they are social birds by nature.

GOULDIAN FINCH

The stunning Gouldian finch (*Chloebia gouldiae*) is unusual in that it occurs in the wild in three different head colours – red, black and yellow

✦ RIGHT
The Gouldian finch is often called Lady Gould's finch in the United States. It was named by the Victorian explorer John Gould after his wife, Elizabeth. This is the black-headed form.

✦ ABOVE
The self chocolate variety of the Bengalese or society finch, as seen here, is closest to the ancestral form of this domesticated finch.

The amazing
appearance of the
male Fischer's
whydah, with its
elongated tail
plumes, has led to
these birds also being
known as straw-
tailed whydahs.

(which is in reality a more orangish
shade). With domestication there
have been other changes in colour,
including the introduction of white-
breasted variants among others.

Gouldians are delicate birds and
must be given heated accommodation,
certainly through the winter. They
can be bred either on a colony basis
or, more commonly, in breeding cages.
The bills of cock birds take on a
cherry-coloured tip as they come
into breeding condition.

ORANGE WEAVER

The orange weaver (*Euplectes orix*)
is also highly coloured, as least in the
case of cock birds during the breeding
season, when you may see them
advertized as "I. F. C." (in full colour).
These birds can be rather bombastic,
however, and they should not be
housed with small companions such
as waxbills. Once they have become
properly established, both they and
whydahs, such as the pin-tailed (*Vidua
macroura*), will be quite hardy, and

they can be
comfortably
housed through
the cold months
without artificial
heat, provided that
they have well lit, snug
roosting quarters. It is
not suitable to keep them
in cages as the long tails
of the cock whydahs
in their breeding finery
will soon be damaged.

The cock bird of this pair
of orange weavers is in
his breeding plumage.
Colour feeding at the
time of the moult can
help to maintain the
intensity of the orange
feathering, although this
is not always necessary.

HOUSING

◆ BELOW
Cages with vertical bars are most suitable
for finches and canaries, which do not climb
around their quarters. The perches need to
be placed near the raised food pots.

A wide range of cages is available for pet canaries and other finches, but as a general rule it is best to choose as large a design as possible. You can also buy attractive flight cages, mounted on castors, or indoor aviaries that are sold in self-assembly form. To assemble, they simply require screwing together. For breeding purposes, however, your birds may appreciate a greater sense of security. This can be provided by a breeding cage, in the form of a box-type design with a finch- or canary-type front. These cages are used in birdrooms as well, where they are arranged in tiers supported off the ground. They are equipped with a sliding tray that can be lined with a sandsheet or sheets of old newspaper weighed down with bird sand as an absorbent floor covering.

Building an aviary for finches is quite straightforward, as there are a growing number of manufacturers

◆ BELOW
Additional lighting can be very valuable in a birdroom, particularly in temperate areas, allowing the birds' feeding period to be extended on dull days. Fluorescent strip lights give off a natural light but they cannot be operated with a conventional dimmer switch.

advertising in bird-keeping magazines who offer designs in sectional form to be delivered to your door. The panels should be covered with 19-gauge mesh, with strand dimensions that are ideally 1 cm (½ in) square and not exceeding 2.5 x 1 cm (1 x ½ in). These units simply need to be fixed together on secure footings.

In the case of finches, it may be better to choose a chalet-type design, which has mesh confined to the front of the flight only. This will give the birds better protection from wind and rain than an open flight. The siting of the aviary is also important. It should be located in a sheltered part of the garden, preferably not in the path of the prevailing wind. A location near the house, where the birds can be seen easily, is ideal because, if you intend to house them here throughout the year, running an electrical supply for heating and lighting purposes will be easier and less costly. The work of

◆ BELOW
Finches can be housed with other species of
birds, but take care with more aggressive species
such as pheasants. A planted aviary will provide
cover and will minimize the risk of aggression.

wiring the electrical cables to the
aviary will need to be undertaken
by a qualified electrician.

There are aviary designs available
that incorporate the shelter into a
larger birdroom area, and so provide
more flexibility. This additional space
can be useful for breeding cages and
the storage of seed and other items.
There may also be space for an indoor
flight as well. Supply heating in the
form of tubular convector heaters,
which can be operated under
thermostatic control. Fan heaters

are much more costly to operate,
and can become clogged with dust.
Lighting can be operated on the basis
of a time-switch. Birds should be given
no more than 12 hours of artificial
light every day, so as not to interfere
with the moulting cycle.

Within the flight, a variety of plants
can be grown for decoration and to
provide interest and perches for the
birds. The vegetation within the flight
can be watered from the outside with
a hose to avoid disturbing the birds
when they are breeding. The other

option is to set the plants in containers,
on a concrete or paving slab base; this
base will be easier to clean thoroughly
than an earth floor.

Plants that provide dense cover,
such as conifers and bamboos, are
often favoured for nest-building by
the birds. Climbing plants can help to
disguise artificial nesting sites, making
them more appealing to the birds. You
will need to provide supports for the
climbers, as the weight of the growing
branches may damage the mesh, and
seasonal pruning will be necessary.

FEEDING

◆ BELOW
Millet sprays. These seedheads are
very popular with finches and smaller
members of the parrot family, including
budgerigars and cockatiels.

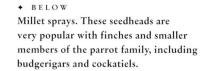

The dietary needs of finches fall into
two groups. There are the true finches,
such as canaries and green singing
finches, which require a diet consisting
of a mixture of cereal and oil seeds,
and all other finches, such as waxbills
and zebra finches, which need to be
fed primarily on cereal seeds. Suitable
seed mixes are available from pet
stores, or they can be ordered from
specialist seed suppliers listed at the
back of bird-keeping publications.

It is better to purchase seed either
in packets or sacks, rather than loose
seed in bins, which is more likely to
have been contaminated by dust and
dirt, and could be a cause of disease.

A canary seed mixture is made up
mainly of plain canary seed, which is
brown and oval in appearance, and
red rape, a dark reddish, circular seed.
Other ingredients may include hemp,
which is a dark shade of brown and is
significantly larger than the other
seeds, as well as niger, which is long,
thin and black. A typical finch mix
comprises plain canary seed and a
variety of millets, which may range in
colour from shades of pale yellowish-
white through to red. Millet sprays or
seedheads are given separately. They
are considered a valuable rearing food.
Other seeds offered to canaries at the
rearing stage include teasel, fed as
soaked seed, and blue maw, which is
valued for weaning purposes and is
sprinkled directly on top of egg food.

SOAKED SEED

Soaking seed in water, prior to feeding
it to the birds, triggers a variety of
changes, including stimulating the
germination process of the seed and
improving its nutritional value.

Canary seed

Millet

Niger

Egg food

Red rape

To prepare soaked seed, start by rinsing the required amount of seed in a sieve under running water and then immerse it in a container of hot water. Leave the seed to stand overnight, then rinse thoroughly, and offer to the finches in a separate food tub. Soaked seed will quickly turn mouldy, and any left uneaten should be removed at the end of the day and discarded.

FOOD SUPPLEMENTS

Bird seed is deficient in a number of key ingredients, and you will need to supplement the birds' diet to make up for these shortcomings. Some seed mixes contain vitamin and mineral supplements coated on to dehulled seeds, so that they will not be wasted as there is no husk for the bird to remove. Other mixes contain added pellets of nutrients, although birds will often avoid eating these nuggets, choosing to eat only their regular seeds, and it will be less easy for you then to monitor their diet.

As an alternative, try a vitamin and mineral powder, which will stick well to damp greenstuff, or a similar product added to the drinking water. Feeding fresh natural foods, such as chickweed, dandelion and seeding grasses, can also help to compensate for any deficiency.

Calcium is an essential mineral and is particularly important for the hen during the breeding season as it is the main constituent of eggshells. Cuttlefish bone is a valuable source of calcium, and this will also help to keep the birds' bills in trim as they peck at the powdery surface. Scrape a little off the surface at first to make it easier for them to start nibbling.

Grit will supplement mineral requirements and will assist in the birds' digestive process. Oystershell grit dissolves more readily than mineralized grit in the acid of the bird's gizzard, where seed is broken down. Cuttlefish can be held in place in the aviary with a clip, while grit can be offered in a small container, which will need to be topped up regularly.

Tubular drinker

◆ LEFT
A selection of food and water containers used for small birds.

Food container

Small seed hopper

Small container suitable for grit

GENERAL CARE AND BREEDING

Finches need to be given fresh drinking water each day and fed as necessary. Since canaries in particular can be very wasteful in their feeding habits, it is better to feed them on a daily basis, providing just the required amount for that day rather than leaving several days' supply at one time, which is likely to end up scattered around the flight or cage.

Always put food containers for aviary birds in the shelter rather than the aviary to ensure the seed stays dry and to reduce the possibility of attracting rodents. Use heavyweight pots as food bowls, and brush off discarded seed husks with your hand before the pot is topped up. Perishable foods should be provided in separate pots, and any spillages cleaned up thoroughly before they can turn mouldy or attract wasps and insects.

HANDLING

Finches are very agile little birds and, although it can be relatively easy to catch them within the confines of a cage, it will be much harder doing so in aviary surroundings. Taking down the perches initially and then shutting the birds in the aviary shelter will simplify this task. You may want to use a special bird net to catch them, but do ensure this is well padded around its rim, to minimize the risk of injury to the birds, and only try to catch one bird at a time.

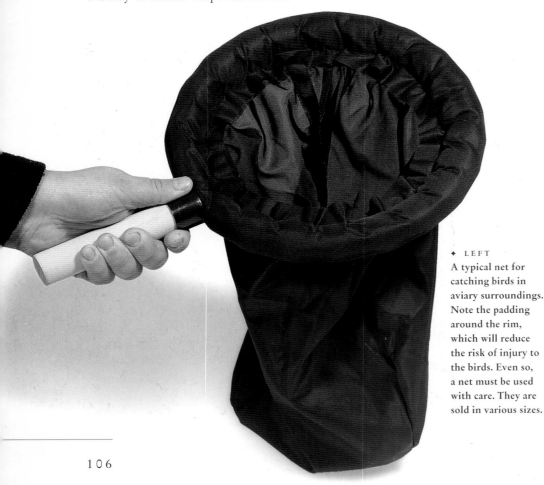

◆ LEFT
A typical net for catching birds in aviary surroundings. Note the padding around the rim, which will reduce the risk of injury to the birds. Even so, a net must be used with care. They are sold in various sizes.

The other option is to catch the birds with your hands. This is what you will need to do in cage surroundings, and it can be easier and safer in the aviary as well. Gently place your hand over the bird and scoop it up with your hands, with the aim being just to restrain it. This is easily done once its wings are confined in the palm of your hand. The majority of finches will not try to nip with their bills, and so there is no need to worry about being bitten.

BREEDING

In the spring, as the breeding season approaches, position a choice of nesting sites around the aviary, in the form of nest boxes, baskets and canary nest pans. These can be screwed to the aviary framework or, in the case of baskets, held in place with netting. Take care to ensure they are positioned under cover, in a secluded part of the flight. Nesting materials such as moss, dried grass and coconut fibre should all be provided.

Two designs of finch nest box, made out of plywood. These should be suspended in a secluded part of the aviary, at a relatively high point under cover.

A wide range of nesting material may be used by finches. Canary nest pans are lined with circular felts, with softer material added on top. Longer lengths of coconut fibres are also used.

A woven nest site for finches and a canary nest pan. While canaries and singing finches build a cup-shaped nest, other finches build much more elaborate nests.

One egg a day is laid. In the case of canaries it is usual to take away the first three eggs on the morning they are laid, replacing them with dummy eggs and storing them in a cool place until the morning when the fourth egg is due. When the final egg has been laid, return the stored eggs to the nest. This will delay the incubation process so that the eggs hatch together and the chicks will be a similar age; this will increase their chances of survival.

Egg food should be fed to parent birds throughout the rearing period, to provide the vital protein necessary for the growth of their young. Waxbills will require tiny livefoods, such as micro-crickets, which can be sprinkled with a nutritional balancer. It helps if the live crickets are cooled beforehand, as they will then be easier for the birds to catch. Most pairs will nest twice during the breeding season. When the young have fledged, the cock bird will take over feeding duties.

The wide gape of the chicks ensures that they swallow their food. Food passes to the crop at the base of the neck, and the chicks cease begging when this is full.

BUDGERIGARS AND OTHER PARROTS

Members of this group of birds have been popular pets for centuries, and in recent years, even those species which had a reputation for being difficult to breed are now nesting quite regularly in aviary surroundings. Some are much better mimics than others, however, and if you are seeking a parrot as a pet, be sure to choose a young bird which has preferably been handreared, so that it will already be tame, with no instinctive fear of people.

INTRODUCTION

There are more than 330 different species of parrot found in tropical areas throughout the world, but only relatively few are popular as household companions. The talking abilities of the different species vary quite widely, but the budgerigar and the African grey parrot are considered to be the champion chatterboxes. Both can amass a vocabulary of more than 500 words, although individuals vary in their talking abilities and much depends on the skills of their teachers.

In contrast, other larger parrots, such as cockatoos, are limited in terms of their talking abilities and are rarely likely to master as many as 30 words; the harsh natural calls of these birds are more likely to lead to complaints from neighbours. Cockatoos can also be destructive, and accommodating them either in the home or outdoors in aviary surroundings can be costly. Handling, too, can be difficult.

BUDGIES AS PETS

Few birds are as versatile as the budgerigar, which makes an excellent pet and aviary occupant. It is also a popular bird for showing, and if you are interested in this, you should contact a breeder of exhibition budgerigars for sales stock.

◆ ABOVE
Light green and sky blue budgerigars. Both these birds are cocks, as shown by the blue ceres above the bill. Light green is the budgie's natural colour.

◆ LEFT
The broad crest feathers that help to distinguish the umbrella cockatoo, along with its white plumage, can be clearly seen here.

The cere itself is important in determining the budgerigar's gender, although sexing is more difficult in recently fledged chicks than in older individuals. The cere of a young cock is a deeper purple shade than that of a hen, whose cere turns brown as she reaches maturity.

There are many thousands of colour combinations of the budgerigar. Among the most popular are red-eyed lutinos, which have deep yellow plumage; snow white albinos; and rich violets, which can be bred with either white or yellow faces. Colourful pieds, with their variegated appearance, and rarer

crested varieties are just some of the other options available from breeders. Budgerigars may live for ten years.

PARROTS AS PETS

In the case of parrots, a handreared chick is the best option if you are seeking a pet bird to house indoors. The chicks should be independent by approximately 16 weeks of age. Young grey parrots, for example, are distinguished from adults by their dark rather than straw yellow irises. Visual sexing is impossible so, if you want to know the sex of your pet, you will need to take a feather sample to a laboratory for DNA testing. Grey parrots, like many of the larger parrot species, have a life expectancy roughly equivalent to our own, and this adds to their appeal.

✦ ABOVE
The collar of the adult Indian ring-neck will identify the male, but it may take up to two years for this feature to become apparent in young birds.

If you are looking for a pet budgerigar, you need to choose one between six and nine weeks old as young birds will settle more easily in a new home. Solid-coloured eyes that have no white ring around them are the most reliable means of recognizing a budgerigar of this age. Other features that may be apparent, depending on the colour variety, include a dark tip to the upper bill, with the barred markings on the head extending down to the cere at the top of the beak. The throat spots are also likely to be smaller at this stage.

✦ RIGHT
A young grey parrot, as shown by its dark eye – adults have straw-yellow irises. Grey parrots are the best mimics of the parrot family, and are capable of building a vocabulary of hundreds of words.

SPECIES AND BREEDS

The choice of parrots suitable for housing outdoors in an aviary in urban areas needs to be made carefully to avoid complaints about the noise from neighbours. As a general guide, the smaller species are quieter by nature, and also less destructive.

COCKATIELS

Aside from the budgerigar, one of the most popular and widely bred birds for aviaries is the cockatiel (*Nymphicus hollandicus*). You can house these gentle birds in a collection with finches. Cocks of the normal grey form have bright yellow facial feathering, with orange ear coverts. The faces of hens are a greyer shade with yellow markings on the underside of the tail feathers. Young birds, which can make superb companions, are similar to hens, but have shorter tail feathers and pinkish ceres.

   The striking lemon-yellow lutino retains the orange cheek patches seen in the grey. Other popular colours include the cinnamon,

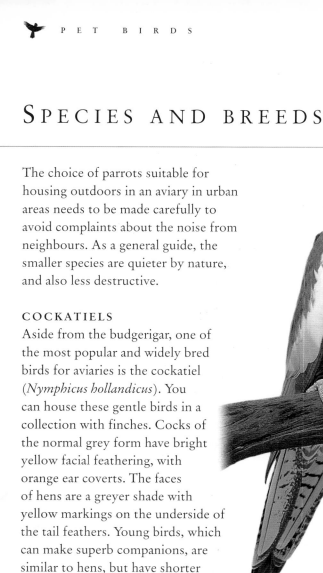

✦ ABOVE
Grey is the usual colour of cockatiels, as shown by this pair. Cockatiels breed well in outdoor aviaries, while the young birds can develop into excellent companions.

✦ BELOW
Peach-faced lovebirds are now being bred in a wide range of colours in addition to the normal green form, such as the popular cremino variety seen here on the right, and various yellow forms.

which has a brownish hue to its plumage, and the white faced; these are entirely white in colour in the case of the cock birds, while the faces of the hens are greyish. Pied variants are also common.

Although cockatiels can be bred in colonies the results are often better if they are housed in individual pairs. You should feed them on budgerigar seed and sunflower seed, along with a suitable nutritional supplement, which can be sprinkled over greenstuff, sweet apple or carrot.

GRASS PARAKEETS
The needs of grass parakeets, such as the splendid (*Neophema splendida*), are very similar to those of cockatiels. Also known as scarlet-chested parakeets, the cock can be recognized by his red breast feathering. A greenish-blue variety, in which the breast colour has been modified to salmon-pink, has also been bred.

PEACH–FACED LOVEBIRDS
Although rather underestimated as pets, peach-faced lovebirds (*Agapornis roseicollis*) are full of character. You can recognize young fledglings by the dark markings on their upper bill. Pairs will breed readily in aviaries, but sexing can be difficult. Only when they are in breeding condition does the gap between the pelvic bones above the vent enlarge in the case of hens, to the extent that they can be distinguished from cocks; at other times DNA sexing can be used. When breeding, these lovebirds are unusual among parrots in requiring nesting material,

◆ ABOVE
The celestial is the most widely kept parrotlet. These birds can be very aggressive, however, in spite of their small size. Like most parrots, they need to be housed individually or in pairs.

which they will carry in their bills. A wide range of colours are now established, of which the most colourful is possibly the lutino, with its bright yellow, rather than green, plumage offset against the peach-coloured feathering on the face.

PARROTLETS
These rank among the smallest members of the parrot family, but they can be quite savage and should be housed on their own in pairs. Always cover both sides of an intervening partition between flights with mesh, to prevent neighbouring birds from biting each other's toes. Chicks must also be removed as soon as they are independent as the breeding pair are likely to want to nest again, and the cock in particular may then attack his older offspring. The celestial (*Forpus coelestis*) is one of the most widely kept species, with hens lacking the blue plumage seen on the cock birds.

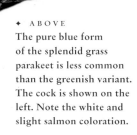

◆ ABOVE
The pure blue form of the splendid grass parakeet is less common than the greenish variant. The cock is shown on the left. Note the white and slight salmon coloration.

111

CONURES

Originating from parts of Central and South America, conures are a group of parakeets whose common name derives from their older generic name, *Conurus*. They can be broadly divided into two groups. Members of the Pyrrhura group are significantly quieter and less destructive by nature than their Aratinga cousins. Pyrrhuras are also called scaly-breasted conures because of the characteristic scaly markings on their breast feathering. The rest of their plumage is predominantly green, with red markings on the wings and sometimes on the underparts. These birds are quiet by nature and can become very tame, even in aviary surroundings. Feeding is straightforward as their inquisitive natures mean they will eat a variety of foods.

A number of species are commonly bred, including the black-tailed (*Pyrrhura melanura*), red-bellied (*P. frontalis*) and green-cheeked (*P. molinae*). It is not

✦ ABOVE
When they fledge, sun conures have greenish backs and a greenish tone to their underparts. Their distinctive coloration takes two years to develop over successive moults.

possible to sex these conures by sight, and DNA sexing will be necessary. Breeding pairs are quite prolific. They are relatively hardy but will require a nest box, for roosting purposes, throughout the year.

HAHN'S MACAW

The Hahn's macaw (*Ara nobilis*) is rather like a conure in terms of its size and coloration, but the bare facial patches of skin on the face confirm that it is in fact a macaw. Although social by nature, even this smallest member of the macaw clan is relatively noisy. Young handreared birds do make good pets, however, although they are not talented talkers.

✦ ABOVE
The plum-headed parakeet is an ideal choice for a garden aviary. Quiet, colourful and graceful in flight, these birds are justifiably popular.

+ LEFT
The white-fronted Amazon is instantly recognizable by the white area above the cere and the adjoining area of red plumage, which forms a narrow band around the eye. These parrots are sometimes called spectacled Amazons.

Pairs are likely to breed in the early summer and require a stout nest box for this purpose, which they will use for roosting for the rest of the year. It is best to feed them a complete diet although, if a parrot mix is used, then at least half of the food intake must consist of fruit and vegetables, ranging from pomegranates and peas to grapes and peeled carrots, sprinkled with a vitamin and mineral supplement.

PLUM-HEADED PARAKEET

In contrast, the plum-headed parakeet (*Psittacula cyanocephala*) is another species that is ideal for a typical suburban aviary as its calls are unlikely to cause offence. Hens and cocks are easily distinguished because only the cock bird has the distinctive plum-coloured feathering on the head. The immature cock birds resemble adult hens, however, so it is always better to obtain a proven pair rather than buying odd birds in the hope of obtaining a pair. The nest box must be located in a sheltered part of the aviary because these parakeets do not brood their chicks closely, and there is a real risk that they could become fatally chilled in cold weather. This is especially disastrous because plum heads usually only lay one clutch of eggs in a year.

AMAZON PARROTS

There are over 30 species of Amazon parrot, most of which are predominantly green in colour. The white-fronted (*Amazona albifrons*) is the smallest species, but its calls are almost as strident as those of its larger relatives. These parrots are very destructive by nature but can be housed in an aviary clad with 16-gauge mesh. Sexing, in the case of the white-fronted Amazon, is straightforward, with red feathering running down the edges of the cock bird's wing.

+ ABOVE
Even smaller members of the parrot family, such as this Hahn's macaw, are likely to be destructive. They are relatively hardy once acclimatized, especially if provided with a nest box for roosting purposes.

HOUSING

Because of their generally destructive natures, parrots will require much stronger housing than finches. Even budgerigars can whittle away easily at wood, and it is especially important that aviaries for all these birds have mesh on their inner faces, when they are assembled, to cover and protect the timber frame. The wire gauge also needs to be correspondingly thicker to resist the bills of parrots.

OUTDOOR ACCOMMODATION

If you are buying an aviary flight, check the mesh is firmly attached to the timber framework by proper netting staples rather than ordinary staples, even if this means having to reinforce them yourself before assembling the aviary. The mesh should be anchored to a blockwork base by means of frame fixers, with the base itself extending at least 30 cm (12 in) below ground level to provide support and exclude rodents. The panels themselves, as before, can be held together with bolts, which should be well oiled and fitted with washers so that the flight can be moved easily – if you move home, for example.

Entry should be via a safety porch, located at the rear of the aviary, leading into the shelter. This will ensure that the birds do not escape when you enter the aviary. It is important that the safety porch door opens outwards, however, to give you easy access to the interior of the aviary; both the aviary door itself and the connecting door leading into the flight should open inwards.

Where parrots are housed in individual pairs, as is usual, then a deep layer of gravel can be used as a floor covering, and paving slabs can be placed under the perches where the

◆ LEFT
A small parrot cage, suitable for a Senegal parrot, for example. The bird should be let out of the cage each day for a period of exercise.

◆ LEFT
A block of raised aviaries intended for parrots. The birds are fed at the back of the structure, and the raised floor area will usually have a mesh base.

nearest the shelter, as well as guttering to carry away rain water. This will also be needed on the shelter itself.

INDOOR QUARTERS

Space is extremely important when selecting a cage for indoor birds; it should be as large as possible as cramped quarters can trigger feather plucking. Always replace the plastic or dowel perches supplied with most parrot cages with fresh cut branches, as these will help to prevent any sore patches developing on the bird's feet, which can easily become infected.

It is normal for a pet parrot to gnaw the perches away, and these should be replaced as necessary. Only use branches from trees that have not been sprayed recently with chemicals as perches. Most fruit trees, such as apple, elder and sycamore, are suitable but avoid poisonous trees, such as yew, lilac and laburnum.

majority of droppings will accumulate. The perches themselves should be positioned across the flight, to provide plenty of flying space, but not so close to the end that the birds will damage their tails when they turn around here.

The floor covering in an aviary of budgerigars should be concrete, which can be hosed down regularly and disinfected at intervals. The floor needs to be sloped away from the shelter so that cleaning and rain water can drain away through a hole bored into the floor at the opposite end.

Although parrots are hardy once acclimatized in their quarters, they still need protection from the elements. You can provide this by fixing corrugated plastic sheeting on to the roof and sides of the flight

◆ ABOVE
Cleanliness is important in a colony aviary, such as this, where a number of birds are housed. Establish a regular cleaning routine and keep to it.

◆ RIGHT
A view from inside an aviary showing a safety porch in use. The purpose of the porch is to stop birds escaping when you enter the aviary by means of a double-doored entry system.

FEEDING

◆ LEFT
A hopper used for budgerigars. Seed is tipped into the top section, with the husks collecting in the drawer located below the level of the perch.

Most larger parrots are traditionally fed a seed mixture mainly comprising sunflower seed and peanuts, and lesser amounts of foods such as flaked maize, and pumpkin and safflower seeds. In comparison, cockatiels and parakeets are offered a higher percentage of cereal seeds in their diet, such as canary seed and millets, including millet sprays, as well as groats, which are a particular favourite of Pyrrhura conures. Seed mixes for budgerigars consist exclusively of small seeds, notably millet and canary seed, which can be provided more easily in a seed hopper than in an open food container.

As with seed mixes for finches, however, even the best of these diets will not meet all the nutritional needs of the birds. They are generally deficient in key dietary ingredients such as Vitamin A and calcium, which is why a comprehensive vitamin and mineral supplement will be required, along with daily portions of fresh, diced fruit and greenstuff.

In recent years, manufacturers have developed a range of complete diets suitable for small parrotlets up to large macaws. It is not always so easy to persuade birds to sample them, in spite of the fact that they have a superior nutritional value to seed. Young parrots that have been hand-reared on complete diets in a liquid form will usually continue eating them, once they are weaned, but older individuals that have lived on

Large pine nuts

Small pine nuts

Groundnuts

Groats

Safflower seeds

White and striped sunflower seeds

♦ LEFT
Taming a budgerigar sufficiently to have it eat
from your hand will often be possible, especially
if you have had the bird since it was young.

♦ BELOW
Tame birds such as this blue and gold macaw
will often be keener to sample new foods,
compared with aviary birds. Seed alone does
not provide a balanced diet.

sunflower seed for years can be very reluctant to sample something new. Certain types of parrot are worse in this respect than others, with cockatoos being especially reluctant to try unfamilar foods, including fresh fruit and greenstuff.

Complete diets are more expensive than seed on a weight-for-weight basis but there is very little wastage with them (providing the bird will co-operate) whereas, with seed, the husks will be discarded. There is an additional saving with complete diets in that there will be no expenditure on vitamin and mineral supplements because these components are already present at the required levels within the formulated food. Complete foods need to be kept dry, as with seed, and must be used before their stated expiry date in order for the birds to gain maximum benefit from them.

Never try to switch the birds' diet just prior to or during the breeding season. If you want to change your birds' diet, the simplest way is to mix some of the new food into the old, gradually increasing the quantity as the birds start to take the unfamiliar food, until it has entirely replaced the familiar diet. The other option is simply to remove the familiar food and present the birds with the new food, effectively forcing them to eat it. However, this may give rise to digestive problems and can result in loss of condition as well.

Special drinking bottles are normally supplied to larger parrots, although tubular drinkers can be given to budgerigars. In both cases, these will keep the water clean. In an outdoor aviary, check on cold mornings that ice has not formed in the spout, blocking off the flow of water. Birds must always have free access to clean drinking water, particularly when they are eating a dry diet.

♦ LEFT
Clean drinking water is essential for all birds. This bottle-style drinker can be suspended in an aviary or left standing on the floor. Keep it in a shaded spot, out of direct sunlight.

GENERAL CARE AND BREEDING

✦ BELOW
Greenstuff can be used to encourage a pet bird, such as this cockatiel, to feed from your hand. Always wash greenstuff and fruit thoroughly before offering it to birds.

Parrots are more difficult to handle than finches, thanks to their powerful bills, although they can usually be caught in a similar way. It is worthwhile wearing a pair of thin leather gloves when handling parrots as these will protect you against being bitten; take extra care when wearing gloves not to injure the bird by holding it too tightly. You can restrain the bird's head easily, between the first and second fingers of your left hand (assuming that you are right-handed), so that it will not be able to bite.

Gloves can also be useful when you are training a young parrot, whose claws are likely to be especially sharp: they will wear down once the bird is perching regularly. Most handreared birds will perch readily on the hand so it is always better to encourage them to do this rather than physically restraining them, partly because they may then grow fearful of the gloves.

Only allow your parrot out of its cage into the room when you are present, particularly because there are likely to be a number of dangers

lurking here. While some hazards, like dangerous plants such as cacti with their sharp spines, and potentially poisonous plants, such as winter cherry with its orange berries, and poinsettia, can be kept elsewhere in the home, window glass is an ever-present hazard. Net curtains or blinds indicate the presence of a barrier.

Always check that the windows are closed before letting your parrot out of its quarters. Any fires in the room should be adequately guarded to keep your pet away from the flames.

When first allowed out within the confines of a room, a young parrot is likely to fly around wildly, and may crash-land, knocking over ornaments.

TAMING A YOUNG PARROT

1 Start by encouraging the bird to take food from you by offering a tidbit, such as a piece of fruit, with one hand. In this way, persuade the bird first out of its quarters, then on to your hand.

2 As the parrot approaches, extend your other hand to encourage the parrot to step on to it. This will also make it easier for the bird to reach the fruit. Be patient.

3 In due course, your young pet parrot will step readily on to your outstretched hand, especially when food is being offered. If its claws are quite sharp, you may prefer to wear gloves.

In the case of aviary birds that will not talk, then either ringing or microchipping will be necessary. The microchip unit, about the size of a rice grain, is inserted by a vet into the bird's breast muscle. The chip is read by a special reader to identify the bird. It can prove vital in cases where birds have been stolen and then recovered.

BREEDING

Parrots housed outdoors should only be encouraged to breed during the warmer months of the year. In the case of budgerigars breeding on the colony system, their nest boxes must all be positioned at roughly the same height to prevent fighting. All nest boxes should be located under cover, preferably in the aviary shelter.

Birds will like to rest from time to time, and it helps if you provide perches in the form of stands around the room, which your pet will be able to use. Toys are also a good idea, and even a parrot play area that includes a play-gym, if you have the space.

◆ ABOVE
In many cases, cock birds are more colourful than hens, but there are exceptions, as with Ruppell's parrot, which is an African species.

TRAINING

If you place your finger alongside the perch your parrot should soon step on to it. When it comes to teaching a bird to talk, pick a word or short phrase and repeat this regularly. Training sessions should be kept short to maintain your pet's concentration, although you can reinforce these lessons with the use of a recorded audio cassette tape. One of the first things that a bird needs to learn is its address or telephone number, so that if it does escape and is found, there is at least some chance that you will be traced and reunited with your bird.

◆ RIGHT
Some birds prefer a deep, natural nesting site. This Levaillant's barbet has bored into an old log to create its nesting chamber.

HEALTH CARE

The care of sick birds has advanced considerably in recent years, but much still depends on the owner spotting that an individual bird is off-colour at an early stage. This will greatly increase the likelihood of a successful recovery.

Allow time each day to check your birds for signs of illness, especially when they are housed in aviary surroundings. It is critical that a sick bird is dealt with quickly, otherwise its condition will deteriorate rapidly.

BIRD HEALTH

Birds are very adept at concealing signs of illness. By the time the symptoms are clearly apparent, the bird is likely to be seriously ill, with its chances of recovery much reduced.

DETECTING ILLNESS
It is difficult even for an experienced avian vet to diagnose the cause of illness in some cases without tests, because the symptoms of many serious bird diseases are very similar. Sick birds will be less active than usual, with their feathers fluffed up

◆ LEFT
A commercially available hospital cage for smaller birds. The heat controller on the side of the unit makes it possible to reacclimatize the bird.

◆ LEFT AND INSET
An alternative system of providing warmth for a sick bird is to suspend a dull infra-red lamp over the cage, to supply heat rather than light. Position food and water containers away from the perches to avoid the contents being contaminated by the bird's droppings.

and not preened. They lose interest in food and in their surroundings, will remain huddled up, and may become too weak to perch. Their droppings are likely to turn greenish in colour as a reflection of the fact that they have not eaten properly for some time.

CARE FOR SICK BIRDS
Sick birds must be kept warm because they lose body heat rapidly and, since they are unlikely to be eating properly, are vulnerable to hypothermia. A sick bird therefore needs special care – to be kept warm and helped to feed. For this, it is possible to buy hospital cages for smaller birds, or a better option may be to invest in an infrared lamp with a reflector hood. This can be suspended over the cage,

✦ LEFT
Examining the bird closely gives a valuable insight into its body condition, particularly the breastbone in the centre of the body. This should be well-covered with muscle.

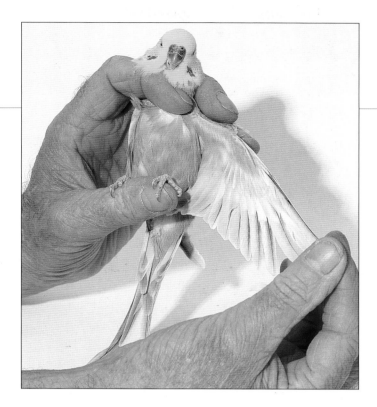

✦ BELOW LEFT
It may be necessary to give medication by means of a tube that has been passed down into the crop. Never attempt to do this without the advice of an avian vet.

✦ BELOW RIGHT
Accidents involving birds may result in fractures, as seen in this radiograph. It is often possible for a vet to repair such injuries successfully.

until the bird has recovered fully and is eating normally again. In the case of birds that fall ill outdoors over the winter months, it may be better to keep them in a birdroom or indoor aviary until the following spring.

ACCIDENTS

It is not just illness that may require emergency care. Birds can sometimes fracture their limbs and when this happens they will need veterinary attention immediately. A fracture of the skull may occur if a bird tries to fly through a window pane that has no curtains to clearly indicate a barrier. There is often little that can be done in these cases, however, particularly if internal haemorrhaging occurs.

Injuries to the feet or claws are fairly common and these may cause bleeding to varying degrees. If this happens, pressing on the affected area with a clean paper tissue for two minutes should stop the bleeding. If you have any worries about your bird's health, consult an avian vet.

ensuring also that there is a cooler area where the bird can go if it feels too warm. Reduce the heat output as the bird starts to show signs of recovery.

It is equally important to ensure that the bird can reach its food and water easily. If it is too weak to perch, place these containers on the floor of its quarters. You can often rekindle the appetite of a sick bird by providing soaked rather than hard seed; this is

especially true in the case of finches, which can usually be persuaded to eat soaked millet sprays. Seek veterinary advice if you experience problems getting a larger parrot to feed.

As the bird recovers, so it will need to be gradually reacclimatized first to room temperature, and then to an outdoor existence. Never try to rush the bird back to its former way of life, and do not even start rehabilitation

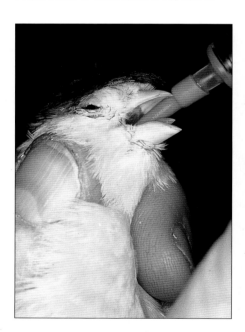

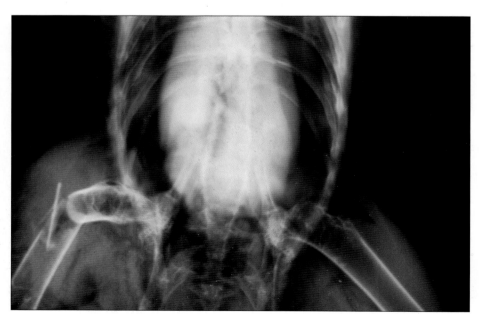

INFECTIOUS ILLNESSES

Infections are most likely to spread in aviary surroundings where a number of birds are housed together, rather than affecting a pet bird in the home. However, if dirty seed is used, then any bird is vulnerable. This is why it is important to ensure that only top quality foodstuffs are fed to the birds, and a good standard of hygiene is maintained in the preparation area.

ANTIBIOTICS

These can be very helpful in combating many of the common bacterial illnesses to which birds are susceptible. Always use antibiotics with care, particularly in countries where they can be bought over the counter without veterinary guidance. Never be tempted to stop treatment until the course has been completed. Stopping treatment too soon means that not only may the infection recur, but that the bacteria concerned may become resistant to the antibiotic. The only way to determine this is to carry out a series of tests, which will involve culturing the bacteria and testing for the most appropriate antibiotic for treatment purposes.

+ ABOVE
Birds living in groups, such as canaries, are the most vulnerable to infections.

+ BELOW
An antibiotic sensitivity test. The disks contain different antibiotics, while the cloudy areas show bacterial growth. The most effective drugs, on the left, have the largest clear areas around them, showing inhibition of bacterial growth.

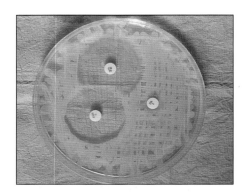

+ BELOW
A cockatiel with a badly inflamed eye. This could be the result of an injury, or it might indicate an underlying infection, especially if both eyes are affected.

Antibiotic treatment often comes in the form of medicated seed or a powder that has to be added to the bird's drinking water. It can be difficult to ensure that a sick bird consumes sufficient amounts of the medication to reach a therapeutic level in its body, which is why your vet may start by giving an injection, to help the bird over the critical phase of its illness.

PRECAUTIONARY HYGIENE

Always remember to take sensible precautions yourself when handling a sick bird, because there is a slight possibility that the infection could in turn spread to you.

Clean out the sick bird's quarters thoroughly, particularly if it is being housed with a group of birds, to stop the infection spreading. Wash and disinfect food and water containers as a priority, as well as changing the floor covering in the shelter and scrubbing off the perches. If there is a bad outbreak of disease try to find the source. New birds should always be isolated for the first two weeks to ensure that they are healthy as, otherwise, they could introduce an infection into the aviary. Attend to the needs of sick birds after those of healthy stock, and do not wash their food containers in the same water.

+ LEFT
Small birds such as finches are especially at risk from hypothermia when they fall ill.

◆ ABOVE
Enteric injections are relatively common in budgerigars but they can often be treated successfully with antibiotics. Green droppings are a typical sign of enteritis.

Some ailments can be treated topically, as in the case of minor eye infections. If you are using an ointment, hold the bird for a few minutes afterwards to allow the medication to start dissolving into the eye, because otherwise the bird may simply wipe the treatment straight off on to the perch. Drops may be easier to apply, but if the bird blinks, they may not reach their target. Recovery from eye ailments is usually very quick, but you must maintain the treatment to the end of the course to prevent the symptoms recurring. Eye treatments need to be given often, as the tear fluid will wash the medication out of the eyes.

FRENCH MOULT AND PBFD
Not all infectious diseases can be treated successfully, notably those of viral origins. These include French Moult, which affects young fledging budgerigars, causing them to drop their flight and tail feathers, and Psittacine Beak and Feather Disease (PBFD), a chronic and invariably fatal disease, which affects cockatoos and other parrots. This causes feather loss and distortion of the bill and claws, which soften and become flaky. The emphasis in combating viral diseases is essentially on prompt diagnosis and vaccination to protect individuals that are at risk.

You also need to be vigilant to the possibility of rodents entering the aviary and soiling the food. Rodents can introduce unpleasant bacteria, such as *Salmonella* and *Yersinia*, both of which are hard to treat successfully, and will cause widespread mortality.

◆ ABOVE
Some groups of birds are more vulnerable to certain types of infections. Australian parakeets may develop infections of the upper respiratory tract, for example.

◆ LEFT
Sick birds have a dull, depressed demeanour and ruffled plumage. They lose interest in their surroundings and will be reluctant to fly.

PARASITIC ILLNESSES

Although parasitic illnesses are most likely to affect collections of aviary birds, they may sometimes occur in pet birds housed on their own, particularly budgerigars.

EXTERNAL PARASITES

Budgerigars are prone to the disease known as scaly face, and in most cases they will have been infected with the parasites that cause the illness while still in the nest. This is a relatively easy condition to identify. Symptoms include tiny white spots, which start

◆ LEFT
Scaly face mites result in crusty swellings on the bill and cere. Early treatment is important because if left, not only does the bird represent a hazard to others, but it can also suffer permanent damage to the bill.

◆ LEFT AND INSET BELOW
Lice can be seen with the naked eye (*left*), lying close to feather vanes. Lice have strong mouthparts, as revealed under the microscope (*below*). Spraying the bird with an aerosol recommended for red mite will kill lice. The treatment will need to be repeated after about 14 days.

out on the bird's upper bill and spread to the sides of the face, causing coral-like encrustations here. Treatment is with a proprietary cream spread over the affected area.

You will need to continue treating the bird for a period after the obvious signs have disappeared, to be sure of eliminating any mites that may still exist in the skin. Otherwise, the infection can recur. It is important to replace the perches at this stage, because the bird may have transferred mites, which could reinfect it in the future. Scaly mite can also affect the legs in some cases, resulting in the appearance of white scaly swellings on this part of the body.

Red mite is another common avian parasite and this is often spread during the breeding season. The mites lurk within breeding cages and nest boxes, and they emerge to suck the blood of the chicks, which gives them their characteristic coloration. Covering the cage with a white cloth overnight is likely to reveal the presence of red mites in the morning, with their coloration standing out against the cloth. A specific avian aerosol can be

A roundworm expelled with the droppings after treatment was given. Australian parakeets and lovebirds (*right*) are especially at risk from these internal parasites.

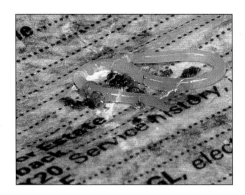

used to kill these parasites, and the birds' quarters should also be washed thoroughly. The best of the products now available commercially have a residual action and will offer some protection against reinfection. Aside from resulting in anaemia, especially in chicks, red mite can also cause the condition known as feather plucking.

Mirrors can help to keep a pet bird occupied, but on occasion, cock budgerigars may end up feeding their reflections repeatedly. This phase will usually pass as the bird's desire to breed subsides, but there may be another, more sinister cause of the behaviour. A crop parasite called *Trichomonas*, often passed from adult birds to their chicks in the nest, can

flare up, causing the budgerigar to regurgitate its seed. On closer examination, the crop, at the base of the neck, will also be swollen with air. It is usually possible to treat trichomoniasis successfully, but be aware that the condition may recur again, should any of the parasites have survived.

INTERNAL PARASITES
The most common internal parasites in birds are roundworms. These are a particular problem with Australian parakeets because of their habit of foraging on the ground, which makes them far more likely to come into contact with the microscopic worm eggs. It is possible to determine whether a parakeet is infected by examining a sample of its droppings. Direct treatment via a crop tube is the most effective way of eliminating the problem, and this should only be carried out by an avian vet. Treatment administered via the drinking water can also be used.

In order to minimize the likelihood of reinfection, disinfect the aviary thoroughly, as the roundworm eggs can survive for well over a year outside the bird's body. This must be done at the same time as treatment is given. Breeders often routinely de-worm their birds twice a year, just prior to and after the breeding season, to prevent a build-up of the parasites. Roundworms may cause relatively few symptoms in adult birds but can often be fatal in young, recently fledged chicks, which acquired them in the nest from their parents.

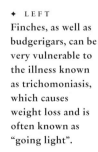

✦ LEFT
Finches, as well as budgerigars, can be very vulnerable to the illness known as trichomoniasis, which causes weight loss and is often known as "going light".

✦ RIGHT
Tapeworms, such as this one trailing out of a parrot's vent, have a more complex life-cycle than roundworms. They cannot usually be spread directly from bird to bird.

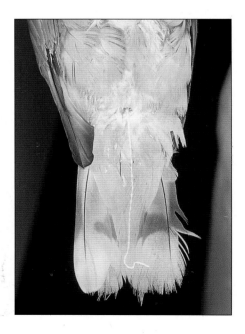

HERPTILES AND INVERTEBRATES

Interest in this group of creatures as pets has grown greatly over recent years, partly because of the ease with which they can be maintained in domestic surroundings. Yet, although most species are relatively easy to take care of, you need to bear in mind that some will grow quite large and can rapidly outgrow their accommodation. This is an important consideration when making your choice of pet. Another significant factor is that although a number of these creatures, such as the bearded dragon lizard (*Pogona vitticeps*), can become tame and will respond well to handling, many others, including the invertebrates, are very much to be admired from a distance rather than handled regularly.

Individual feeding needs may also affect your choice. Snakes, for example, are carnivores, whereas some lizards and a number of invertebrates are herbivores. Lifespan may be another consideration. Although tortoises are famed for their longevity there are some surprises as well, in that female tarantulas can potentially live for over half a century. Toads and some other amphibians can also have a lifespan measured in decades, whereas for snakes and lizards ten to 15 years is the average.

◆ OPPOSITE

Amphibians such as the stunning red-eyed treefrog are popular vivarium subjects. They require a rainforest-type set-up in order to thrive in these surroundings.

◆ LEFT

Tortoises are reptiles with very widespread appeal. Some species, typically those of Eurasian origin, can be housed outdoors in temperate areas for part of the year.

SNAKES

No group of reptiles is more misunderstood than snakes, but as people have been keeping and breeding them on an ever-increasing scale over recent years, this has helped to dispel many of the misconceptions. Snakes are interesting vivarium occupants, and there is a wide choice of species now being bred, including some attractive colour variants. The snakes featured here are chosen for their suitability as pets: are all non-poisonous and handling is relatively easy.

INTRODUCTION

◆ BELOW
Many of the most widely-kept snakes, such as ribbon or garter snakes, originate from North America.

Snakes evolved from lizard-like ancestors around 120 million years ago, and one of their most obvious features is an absence of limbs, although traces of limbs can be seen in certain snakes, such as boas. This loss of legs originally came about to help snakes burrow and today they are not noticeably handicapped by their absence. In fact, snakes can move very effectively; they are very able escape artists and can usually slip out through the smallest of gaps.

Snakes have adapted to live in a wide range of habitats, and a careful study of their body shapes can help to reveal the environment that they prefer. Those with raised nostrils, for example, tend to be aquatic by nature, while those with shiny scales and blunt-ended tails are burrowers.

◆ BELOW
A young Amazon tree boa. This tropical species undergoes a change in colour on maturity, becoming emerald green with white markings.

Colour can also be significant. Green coloration invariably indicates those snakes that spend most of their time off the ground, such as the green tree python (*Chondropython viridis*), in contrast with snakes that are predominantly brown and terrestrial in their habits. However, this is not an infallible guide: the boa constrictor is brownish with dark, irregular markings, which help to break up the outline of these large arboreal snakes.

Snakes have a wide distribution, and although the majority of species are found in tropical and sub-tropical areas, some, including the most commonly kept species, range into temperate areas. The type of vivarium and general management that these

♦ RIGHT
A snake shedding its skin. This process is often described as "sloughing". The skin should come off easily in one piece, as here, if the snake is in good health.

snakes require differs quite widely from that of their tropical cousins.

All snakes are predatory by nature. In the wild they will hunt prey but it is quite possible to persuade captive snakes to eat artificial substitutes, in a number of cases. This means that it will not always be necessary to keep a stock of dead rodents or chicks, which many people find unpleasant. It helps,

more problematic, especially in the case of young snakes. There are techniques available to identify true pairs: your vet should be able to advise you on this. In most cases, it is not a good idea to allow a pair of snakes to live together; snakes are often solitary hunters, and they can turn cannibalistic when living in close confinement with each other.

in this respect, if you obtain a young snake that has been reared only on artificial substitutes.

As they grow, snakes will shed their skin. This is often an anxious time for new owners who are not expecting this to occur. The snake's eyes will become a milky white colour and its appetite will decline. Rather than a sign of illness, this is normal; a healthy snake will shed its entire skin, including the eye covers. Incomplete, patchy moulting is a sign that the snake is not in good health and, if the so-called "spectacles" covering the eyes remain after the moult, they will need to be removed by a vet. Not surprisingly, young growing snakes moult most frequently but the process will continue throughout their lives.

Breeding snakes in vivarium surroundings is not especially difficult, but sexing in the first instance can be

♦ ABOVE
The frequency of shedding depends on the age of the snake. Young snakes which are growing fast will slough more frequently than adults.

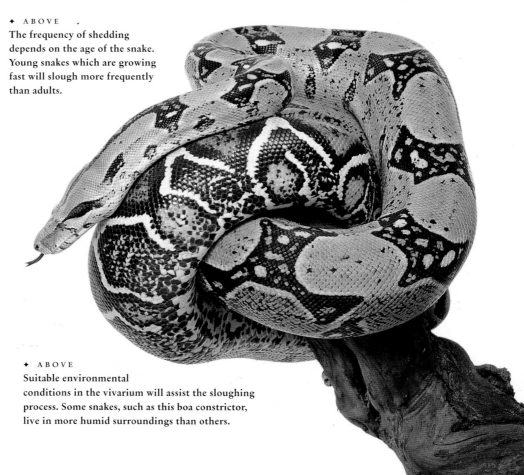

♦ ABOVE
Suitable environmental conditions in the vivarium will assist the sloughing process. Some snakes, such as this boa constrictor, live in more humid surroundings than others.

◆ LEFT
Ribbon snakes are recommended as a good choice for beginners. They require similar care to garter snakes, and will grow to a similar size.

SPECIES

It is no coincidence that some of the smaller and more colourful snakes are among the most popular, and for this reason the most widely bred.

COMMON GARTER SNAKE
The snake known as the common garter snake (*Thamnophis sirtalis*) has the widest distribution of any snake in North America, and takes its name from its narrow girth. Its needs are quite specific. It has to be housed at a temperature of about 25°C (77°F) in the summer, which can be allowed to fall back to a maximum of 15°C (59°F) in the winter, mimicking the changes that occur naturally in the snake's habitat. The vivarium temperature can then be raised gradually.

Although they are often found in areas of water, it is important that the substrate in the garter snake's vivarium stays dry. Provide a large water bowl in which the reptile can immerse itself – without flooding its surroundings, as dampness can trigger skin infections. It is also very important to feed the

◆ RIGHT
There are many localized forms of the milk snake, which differ in terms of their patterning. They feed primarily on mice, and will grow up to about 130 cm (52 in) long.

◆ ABOVE
A chequered garter snake. These snakes give birth to between six and 12 live young. Garter snakes will grow to 70–100 cm (28–40 in) long.

◆ BELOW
The Sinaloan form of the milk snake. It used to be thought that these snakes fed on cows' milk, because they are often found in open areas; however, they do not.

correct diet to these snakes if they are to remain in good health. There are now specially prepared foods, available from reptile stockists, which contain a range of the important nutrients.

MILK SNAKE
Bright colours in nature usually signify danger, and this fact has been exploited by the milk snake (*Lampropeltis triangulum*), whose appearance closely resembles that of the deadly coral snakes (*Micrurus* species). The natural forms of the milk snake are variable in appearance; for example, the Central American subspecies are far more brightly coloured than those of North American origin. They also produce

◆ BELOW
Corn snakes can grow up to 150 cm (5 ft) in length. Colour variants of the corn snake have helped to increase the popularity of these snakes as pets.

larger hatchlings, and this makes the young easier to rear successfully on whole pinkies (dead day-old mice). The Central American milk snakes do need to be kept at a slightly higher temperature as they originate from nearer to the Equator.

CORN SNAKE

A large number of colour varieties of the corn snake (*Elaphe guttata*) have now been developed, including the "snow corns", which are white to reflect their native habitat. Usually, however, corn snakes have a red, orange or grey background colour and red or orange markings. Corn snakes are adaptable by nature, and will make a good introduction to snake-keeping as they reach maturity at around two years of age.

RAT SNAKE

Although the most commonly available rat snakes are from North America, Asiatic species are also occasionally available. There are often distinct colour differences between young and adult rat snakes. Colour mutants have also cropped up, as in the case of the black

rat snake (*Elaphe o. obsoleta*). Young individuals, which display greyish markings, can be tamed quite readily and grow fast, but adults unused to handling are likely to remain wild. They are somewhat arboreal by nature, and will appreciate some opportunity to climb. Another popular subspecies is the yellow rat snake (*E. o. quadri-vittata*). It has dark stripes on a yellowish background when adult, and is closely related to the Everglades rat snake (*E. o. rossalleni*), which has an orange background colour.

◆ ABOVE LEFT
The attractive snow form of the corn snake. Females lay clutches of between ten and 20 eggs in the springtime.

◆ ABOVE RIGHT
An amelanistic corn snake. The lack of dark melanin pigment is responsible for their attractive bright coloration.

◆ ABOVE
Corn snakes hunt small rodents such as mice. These snakes can climb but they rarely do so.

◆ BELOW LEFT
The colourful Everglades rat snake is also sometimes called the orange rat snake because of its coloration. It grows to 180 cm (72 in).

◆ BELOW RIGHT
As their name suggests, rat snakes will prey on rodents such as rats. Their quarters should allow them the opportunity to climb.

◆ ABOVE
While some forms of the common
king snake are banded, as here,
others have longitudinal stripes.
Speckled and spotted individuals
are also known.

COMMON KING SNAKE

There are many different forms of
the common king snake (*Lampropeltis
getulus*) but they all require similar
conditions. These snakes are boldly
marked in many cases and are a good
choice if you are looking for a species
that can be expected to breed well.
An albino form of the Californian race
(*L. g. californiae*) is also widely kept.
King snakes are not keen climbers and
their vivarium does not need to be tall,
but it must have suitable retreats, such
as cork bark, allowing the snakes to
hide, as they are rather shy by nature.
They can reach 180 cm (72 in).

INDIGO SNAKE

Another popular species is the indigo
snake (*Drymarchon corais*), which
again displays considerable variation
in its coloration and markings. Young
snakes in this case are banded, whereas
adults tend to be dark in colour.
They will make a sound with their
tails, rather like rattlesnakes, when
threatened. Pairs need to be supervised
when mating because male indigo
snakes can become very aggressive.

◆ ABOVE, CLOCKWISE FROM TOP
A colour variant of the Queretouro king snake;
a Sonoran Mountain king snake, one of the
tri-coloured species originating from Arizona;
the "Blair's form" of the grey-banded king
snake, found in Texas.

SMOOTH GREEN SNAKE

A less widely available species is the
brightly coloured smooth green snake
(*Opheodrys vernalis*), along with the

◆ BELOW RIGHT
A rough green snake. Daily feeding is usually
recommended for these insect-eating snakes.
They are arboreal by nature, and will grow to
about 50 cm (20 in) in length.

related rough form (*O. aestivus*),
which has a reputation of being easier
to keep. Green snakes require a
vivarium with plenty of branches for
climbing purposes, usually inhabiting
the lower levels of bushes in the wild.
In contrast to most snakes, they feed
on insects. Crickets are a useful basis
for their diet but supplementation is
essential, since they are vulnerable
to nutritional deficiencies. They also
need to be fed more frequently than
other snakes. Breeders have sought
to maintain the distinctive regional
differences that exist in many
North and Central American snakes
by careful pairings.

◆ RIGHT
The glossy black
coloration of the
indigo snake is
impressive. These
are quite large
snakes, growing to
a length of about
200 cm (80 in).

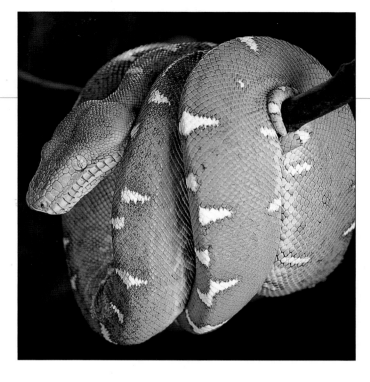

EMERALD TREE BOA

Reaching about 150 cm (60 in) long and needing thicker branches in its quarters is the beautiful emerald tree boa (*Corallus caninus*). These snakes originate from tropical parts of the world, where the climate is both hot and humid, and regular spraying is required, combined with good ventilation in the vivarium to prevent the development of moulds. These snakes may even drink the water that falls in their coils but do not spray them directly for this purpose – you should always provide a separate container of fresh water to supplement their fluid intake. Tree boas will hunt in the trees, spending most of their time there, and their food and water should be provided high up in the vivarium on a purpose-built shelf.

BOA CONSTRICTOR

The boa constrictor or common boa (*Boa constrictor*) is one of the most widely kept and bred of the large snakes. Occurring over such a vast range, their coloration varies. For example, those found in southern parts, such as Argentina, are darker in colour, with the dark pigmentation helping them to absorb more heat in the cooler areas of their natural habitat. A red-tailed boa originates from northern South America.

Young boas, which measure about 50 cm (20 in) at birth, are quite easy to care for and can be reared without difficulty. However, they will need much more spacious housing as they grow, and correspondingly larger quantities of food. Adult boas are quite capable of consuming dead rabbits and chickens, and will become more active at night, which is when they would hunt in the wild. Young boas will reach maturity when they are about three years old. A slight cooling in their quarters during the winter months, for up to eight weeks, will trigger breeding behaviour.

◆ LEFT
The coloration of the emerald tree boa helps it to blend in among vegetation. It is an arboreal predator, hunting birds and other creatures in the trees.

◆ BOTTOM
Boa constrictors range over Central and South America. They grow up to 3 m (10 ft), and can be difficult to handle at full size.

HOUSING

One of the most important basic features of vivarium design for snakes and other reptiles is the thermal gradient across the enclosure. In practical terms, this means that one end will be kept hotter than the other, allowing the snake to adjust its position in response to its body temperature. As the snake cools down it will move back to the warmer area. Since reptiles cannot regulate their body temperature independently of their surroundings – they are often described as cold-blooded – this is how they control their body temperature effectively.

Snakes are not especially active reptiles by nature and they do not need very large quarters, but their housing must reflect their needs. As a guide, allow between 30–45 sq cm (1–1.5 sq ft) per 30 cm (1 ft) length of the snake. Although there can be cases where snakes are housed together, this is not recommended, particularly as some species – such as king snakes – can be cannibalistic if housed with smaller companions. The height of the enclosure will be influenced by the size and habits of the species you are keeping. Generally, a height of 38–45 cm (15–18 in) is adequate in most cases, although taller designs are recommended for arboreal species.

Vivaria, in a range of suitable sizes, can be easily obtained from pet stores specializing in herptiles. Ease of cleanliness is a vital consideration, especially as snakes can be vulnerable to parasitic mites, which will establish themselves easily in the reptile's quarters. If you do not choose a seamless design of vivarium, and prefer a melamine design, seal the

joints inside with a special silicone sealant as used for fish tanks. Avoid sealants recommended for household use as they often contain harmful chemicals such as fungicides.

It is possible, especially with smaller snakes, to house them in a modified aquarium, but you will also need to invest in a special vivarium hood. These are manufactured in a

range of sizes and will fit snugly over the outside of the aquarium. Even so, it is important to secure the lid with a heavy weight because snakes can manage to force up the roof and slip out, escaping into the room where they can be very difficult to find.

There is usually a hole for an incandescent light bulb in vivarium lids; this is not necessarily the most

+ ABOVE
Lengths of wood may be useful in a vivarium to provide climbing opportunities for arboreal snakes.

+ LEFT
Plastic plants can serve to create a impression of a natural environment in the vivarium, as well as providing cover.

+ LEFT
Special fluorescent tubes will illuminate your snake, although the vivarium should never be brightly lit.

+ BELOW LEFT
An infrared heat lamp and surrounding reflector holder.

+ BELOW
Screening of the heat source is vital to prevent burns.

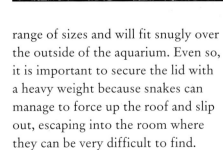

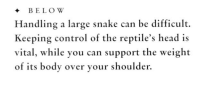

Snakes must not be gripped tightly when
being handled. Instead, they should be
encouraged to wrap around the hands.
A Durango king snake is shown here.

Check the heating
system in the vivarium
using two thermometers,
positioned one at either end, to
show the temperature differential.
The regulation of heat output is easy
to control by adjusting the thermostat.
Always keep a spare heating bulb,
as there is a chance that these will
stop working at a time when it is
impossible to obtain a replacement.

If you there is a power cut
(outage), switch off all the equipment
at the mains, and cover the vivarium
with a thick blanket, leaving a slight
space for ventilation, as this will help
to conserve the heat within. Once the
power is restored, remove the cover
and reconnect the power supply. Most
reptiles will survive these situations
without problems and will become
more active as they warm up again.

Handling a large snake can be difficult.
Keeping control of the reptile's head is
vital, while you can support the weight
of its body over your shoulder.

EVERYDAY CARE

Most snakes need feeding two or
three times a week when fully grown,
although young hatchlings are likely
to require feeding more frequently.
The water in their quarters must also
be changed on a daily basis, and the
substrate in the vivarium should be
cleaned as required, with soiled areas
being removed when necessary. A cat
litter cleaning scoop can be useful
for this type of spot cleaning.

Decor in the snake's quarters
should also be washed as necessary,
using one of the special vivarium
disinfectants now available. It is
not recommended to place
living plants in a vivarium
because they rarely thrive
in these surroundings. If you
choose to incorporate some of the
realistic plastic substitutes now
available, such as ivies and vines,
then these also should be washed
off at regular intervals. Perhaps
most important, however, is the
water container as this can very
easily become a focus for infection,
particularly if the snake is bathing
here as well. Wash out the container
on a weekly basis.

BREEDING

Snakes fall into two categories on the basis of their reproductive habits: many lay eggs; others, such as boas and garter snakes, give birth to live offspring, although they are not nourished in the body like mammals. Instead, the young snakes develop in eggs and these, in effect, hatch just at the moment of birth.

Unfortunately, one of the major difficulties when it comes to breeding snakes is that the sexes are usually very similar in appearance. On close examination, however, the tails of adult male snakes are often significantly longer, with a slight swelling in the vicinity of the external opening, called the cloaca. This is caused by the paired copulatory organs, known as the hemipenes. However, an internal examination performed by a vet is always required to confirm the gender of a snake.

MATING

There are a number of factors that are involved in encouraging snakes to breed successfully in vivarium surroundings. Firstly, they must be

✦ ABOVE
Snake eggs in an incubator box. Note the ventilation holes around the sides of the container. Snake eggs have leathery shells and will readily desiccate if kept too dry.

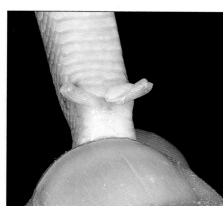

✦ ABOVE
The everted hemipenes of this Trans-Pecos rat snake can be clearly seen here. These reproductive organs are normally kept retracted within the body.

in good health and they must be mature. There are also significant external factors. In the case of the temperate species, the most important is the cooler "wintering period", which should last for two to three months. After this time the vivarium temperature should be raised again, and the level of light exposure should be increased to mimic the start of spring. After a further short interval, the snakes can be put together. Signs of courtship should soon be noted, with the male following the female around the vivarium and entwining himself around her.

SEXING A SNAKE WITH A PROBE

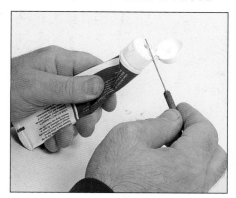

1 Probing a snake needs to be undertaken very carefully, to ensure that no injury results. In the first place, choose a probe of appropriate size and lubricate it well.

2 If you are uncertain about the procedure, seek expert advice. Never try to force the end of the probe into the snake's body, as this is likely to cause a fatal injury.

3 The inverted (withdrawn) hemipenes are located towards the tip of the tail, and so the probe will extend much further back in this direction in a male than a female.

◆ BELOW
A female python brooding her clutch of
eggs. These snakes remain in this position
throughout the incubation period, which
can last over 60 days, without feeding.

◆ BELOW
Most snakes, such as this Pueblan milk snake,
simply lay their eggs in a concealed locality, and
then leave them to hatch on their own. These
eggs need to be incubated.

◆ BELOW
Milk snake eggs hatching. An incubator set-up
for snakes does not need to be sophisticated but
the eggs themselves will need to be kept on a
moist substrate.

REARING YOUNG SNAKES

Those species that give birth to
live young require relatively little
additional care, although the pregnant
females are likely to spend longer
basking under the heat source in their
quarters. Egg-laying snakes, however,
will be keen to find a suitable area in
the vivarium where they can produce
their eggs. An area of damp sphagnum
moss is suitable for this purpose. The
eggs of snakes are all semi-permeable;
the shell is leathery in texture rather
than hard. They need to be transferred
to a reasonably sterile surface, such
as damp (not sodden) vermiculite.
This medium is kept within a plastic
container, which serves as a simple
incubator. The vermiculite must not
be allowed to dry out, and the eggs
must remain in direct contact with
it so that they can absorb water.

Keeping the container covered
slows the rate of
evaporation, and
this will lessen
the likelihood
of eggs drying
out during the
incubation period.
If this occurs it is
likely to be fatal.

Hatching will normally take
place within a period of two to three
months, if the eggs are kept at a
temperature of approximately 28°C
(82°F), but there is no closely defined
incubation period and you should not
be in too much of a hurry to discard
a clutch that has not started to hatch.

The young snakes can be kept
together for a time once they emerge
from their eggs, as they will not feed
until after they have shed their skins
for the first time. After this they will
need to be separated because of the
risk of cannibalism. Ventilated plastic
lunchboxes would make suitable
accommodation for the young snakes.
Pinkies (dead day-old mice) can be
used as a rearing food, although for
smaller, newborn hatchlings these
may have to be macerated before being
fed to the young snakes.

◆ ABOVE
Equipment needed to rear a young hatchling
snake: ventilated plastic accommodation,
substrate, a retreat and a container for water.

◆ RIGHT
Rearing a young hatchling snake. Keep a
watch on the appetite of a hatchling. Young
snakes should soon start feeding once they
have sloughed their skin for the first time.

LIZARDS

Lizards are a very diverse group of reptiles, both in terms of their appearance and requirements. Always consider the needs of a species with particular care, therefore, to ensure that you will be able to fulfil them. Most lizards are insectivorous in their feeding habits, with a few being carnivorous, while some require a vegetarian diet. Smaller lizards are likely to live for perhaps six or seven years, with larger species having a lifespan of up to 15 years.

INTRODUCTION

◆ BELOW LEFT AND RIGHT
Some lizards have sharp claws (*left*), while others have have expanded toe pads (*right*).

Lizards are found in many different habitats, ranging from desert areas to the edge of the Arctic circle, in spite of their cold-blooded (poikilothermic) reptilian natures. A highly adaptable group, their appearance is very variable, ranging from the seemingly leg-less slowworm (*Anguis fragilis*) to the quick-footed gecko and the dramatically colour-changing chameleon.

As pets, some lizards, such as geckos, can be easily accommodated thanks to their relatively small size, whereas others, such as green iguanas and water dragons, which can reach 1 m (1 yd) or more in length, require more spacious accommodation. A few lizards, particularly bearded dragons, are pets with real personality and are now being bred on a large scale to reflect their growing popularity. Green iguanas, too, are popular on this basis, but mature males in particular can become rather aggressive and may be difficult to manage; neutering can help with this problem.

Handling lizards can present particular problems. Geckos, for example, can be especially difficult to catch if they escape from their quarters. Worse still, if roughly handled, they may shed their tails, which is a natural defence mechanism designed to draw potential predators away from the head end of the lizard. This is why the tails of many small

◆ LEFT
The bearded dragon has become very popular as a pet, thanks to its friendly nature, although be sure to start out with a young hatchling, which can be tamed relatively easily.

It may look like
a snake but, in fact,
the slowworm is
actually a leg-less
lizard. The legs
here have virtually
disappeared.

✦ BELOW
One of the features distinguishing the slowworm as a lizard is its eyelids, which snakes
do not possess. The body of these lizards is also
relatively smooth.

lizards are colourful, compared with
their bodies. The tail, when separated,
twitches for a time, but the lizard itself
appears to suffer no pain or blood loss.
The tail will regrow to some extent,
although it rarely reaches the same
length as the original. Such individuals
are then described as "stub-tails".

CHOOSING A LIZARD

If you intend to purchase a lizard as
a household pet, especially one that
is to be allowed out of its quarters on
a regular basis, then it is vital to start
with a young hatchling, which you
can tame yourself. This will allow the
reptile to grow up with you so that it
feels secure in the home. Research
has shown that it is quite possible for
these lizards to recognize individuals,
and they do form quite strong bonds
with their owners.

If you are seeking breeding pairs,
starting out with young lizards has
the advantage that you can be sure
of their age, although distinguishing
the gender of young stock is often
more difficult. When it comes to
assessing whether a lizard is in good
health, animals should be relatively
plump, particularly over the
hindquarters, and alert and lively
by nature in the case of the smaller
species. Any obvious difficulties in
moving around may be indicative of
skeletal weakness; a vet will be able
to confirm this for you.

✦ ABOVE
Slowworms need to be handled with care.
Like many lizards, the ends of their tails
are very fragile and will break off readily,
although they will then regrow slowly.

Coloration is also significant, with
a brightly coloured individual likely
to be in good state of health. Darker
coloration is not necessarily a sign
of illness, however, but could simply
indicate an individual that is being
bullied by a dominant male – lizards
are territorial by nature. The skin
will also darken prior to a moult.

Before you buy, think about the
type of pet you want and whether you
can meet its particular requirements.
The bizarre appearance of many
lizards, such as chameleons, for
example, has helped to ensure their
popularity, and a better understanding
of their needs means that they are
easier to keep now than in the past.
However, chameleons have specialist
requirements. A large green iguana is
an imposing lizard, and trying to win
its confidence once it is adult will be
virtually impossible. You could end up
being badly scratched by its claws,
while its tail can inflict a painful blow. .

✦ ABOVE
It may look rather fierce, but this spiny-tailed
dab lizard feeds almost entirely on plant matter.

SPECIES

All the lizards on these first two pages are small and can be housed in a relatively small vivarium.

LEOPARD GECKO

The leopard gecko (*Eublepharis macularius*) is one of the most popular of all display lizards, thanks to its attractive patterning and compact size. These geckos can be kept in pairs or preferably trios, comprising a male and two females for breeding purposes, and they rank among the easiest lizards to breed in a vivarium. They grow to 25 cm (10 in) in length.

There is a distinct difference in appearance between young and adult geckos, however, with hatchlings being strikingly banded, displaying chocolate- and sandy-coloured stripes. As they mature these bands break up, giving rise to the speckled appearance of the adults. Colour variants are now being bred as well, although these are relatively scarce at present. Leopard geckos do not require a tall vivarium as, unlike most geckos, they do not climb. A sandy substrate, with rocks and retreats such as cork bark, suits them well. One corner should be kept damp to encourage egg-laying. The temperature under

the spotlight can be up to 40°C (104°F), with a temperature gradient across the vivarium, while at night the temperature can be allowed to fall back to 20°C (68°F).

DAY GECKO

The day gecko (*Phelsuma* species) is one of the most colourful of all lizards, and its brilliant emerald green coloration is patterned with striking markings of red, blue and gold, depending on the species concerned. The largest is the Madagascan (*P. madagascariensis*), attaining a length of about 25 cm (10 in) when adult. All require similar care: a tall vivarium, heated to about 28°C (82°F), falling back only very slightly at night. As for all lizards, lighting is

absolutely essential, both to maintain their appetites and to ensure bone condition and a healthy skeleton.

These geckos also feed on small invertebrates, such as crickets, which should be dusted with a suitable vitamin and mineral powder beforehand. In addition, they will enjoy a little honey water or bird nectar, which must be changed daily to ensure its freshness. Sexing is straightforward, and egg-laying will occur in bamboo or similar tubes of a suitable diameter. Gecko pairs must be housed on their own as males, especially, can be very aggressive.

GREEN LIZARD

The green lizard (*Lacerta* species) originates from temperate climes and is sometimes housed in outdoor

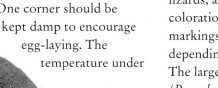

♦ LEFT
Day geckos are an attractive group of lizards. They can be prolific when breeding. Females only lay two eggs per clutch but they will produce these at regular intervals.

◆ LEFT
A common wall
lizard basking on a
rock. These are very
active lizards by
nature, scampering
around their
quarters. Retreats
and basking facilities
are vital for them.
Adults may measure
20 cm (8 in) long.

◆ BELOW
In spite of their name, green lizards are
quite variable in terms of coloration. This
is a mature male in breeding condition, as
shown by the blue area on the chin. Green
lizards can reach 40 cm (16 in) in length.

◆ LEFT
There are a number
of different wall
lizards, all of which
require similar care.
This is Danford's
wall lizard. They
are agile reptiles
by nature, and
are primarily
insectivorous,
feeding on crickets
of suitable size.

◆ BELOW
Various factors can affect the coloration of
lizards, with young green lizards being less
striking than adults. Cooler temperatures
will cause them to darken in colour.

vivaria in the summer months, which
need to be secure and yet adequately
ventilated to prevent overheating on
hot days. The green lizard takes its
name from its coloration: green
predominates although other colours,
such as blue spots on the flanks, are
also common. The colour patterning
differs between individuals, and can
be a reflection of regional variation –
it does not provide a means of
distinguishing the species.

Once mature, green lizard males
can be recognized by their larger, more
colourful appearance. The young, in
comparison, are a duller greyish-green.
It will take three years for them to
mature, although they will need to be
separated before this stage as males
are aggressive towards each other.

WALL LIZARD

The wall lizard (*Podarcis muralis*)
is also a member of the
lacertid group, and
will thrive in a similar
set-up, receiving full-
spectrum lighting.
They require an arid
environment, with
plenty of retreats for
hiding purposes, as well as basking
spots. The typical temperature in the
warmest part of the vivarium should
be up to about 31°C (88°F) during the
day, and reduced to about 17°C (63°F)
at night. Females often lay two
clutches of eggs in the summer
period. The diet for wall lizards should
consist mainly of invertebrates, with
the occasional offerings of sweet fruit.

BEARDED DRAGON

The bearded dragon (*Pogona vitticeps*) is now one of the most popular lizards in the world, thanks to its friendly personality and rather primordial appearance. Hatchlings are widely available, and they can become sufficiently tame to feed readily from the hand. They will grow to about 51 cm (22 in) in length. Their beard of spines under the chin, which form part of an inflatable throat pouch, may look fearsome, but in reality these projections are soft and harmless.

A number of localized colour variants have been recorded in the wild, and as domestication has taken place, breeders have also concentrated

◆ ABOVE AND TOP
The bearded dragon is so-called because of the spines on its throat and under the chin. They are quite prolific, with females laying clutches of up to 30 eggs.

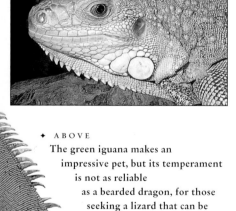

◆ ABOVE
The green iguana makes an impressive pet, but its temperament is not as reliable as a bearded dragon, for those seeking a lizard that can be handled regularly.

◆ ABOVE
Male iguanas develop a prominent crest running down their backs and a pronounced dewlap under the lower jaw as they start to mature, normally around three years of age.

on developing these shades. Red and golden strains are probably most widely kept at present. These lizards live well in groups, but, especially with hatchlings, it is important to check that they all have enough to eat, as weaker individuals will have to wait in order to feed.

There are now prepared foods for bearded dragons, or alternatively, they can be fed a wide range of plant matter, including dandelions, nasturtiums, and similar leafy plants. Carrots and even a little fruit can be supplied, augmented with a vitamin and mineral mix. Small invertebrates should also form part of the diet, especially for juveniles, which grow very rapidly. They are likely to be mature by a year old. A hot vivarium, plus full-spectrum lighting are essential for these lizards, which naturally bask for long periods.

GREEN IGUANA

Although hatchlings look cute, it is important to bear in mind that adult green iguanas (*Iguana iguana*) can become difficult to handle, especially as they become mature. They also require plenty of space, and it is better to prepare for this at the outset by starting out with the correct sized accommodation for this species. They can easily grow to a total length of 1.8 m (6 ft), with their powerful tail making up roughly half of this figure.

Green iguanas are quite arboreal by nature, and they require branches fixed securely in their quarters; this also allows them to bask under a heat source, protected with a grill, without burning themselves. Full-spectrum lighting for 12 hours a day is also necessary, helping to guard juveniles

The Asian water dragon is another
large lizard that will need spacious
accommodation. The banded patterning
on the tail often disappears after maturity.

◆ RIGHT
A panther chameleon. The ability
to change their coloration to blend
in with their surroundings is well
known in chameleons.

◆ BELOW
A veiled chameleon. The casque on the head
indicates that this is a male. Some chameleons
reproduce by eggs, whereas others give birth
to live young. Most average 30 cm (12 in) long.

◆ BELOW RIGHT
A Yemeni
chameleon. Note
how the tail is
carried curled up.
It can be used for
grasping branches.

in particular
from the
effects of
metabolic bone
disease. Their diet,
too, is important for
this purpose. It is very
difficult to sex young
green iguanas by sight,
but males develop a
distinctive crest extending
down their backs as they
grow older.

ASIAN WATER DRAGON

The Asian water dragon (*Physignathus
cocincinus*) is similar to the green
iguana – it will grow to about 91 cm
(36 in) overall – although it is a
member of the agamid family. But,
whereas green iguanas are essentially
vegetarian in their feeding habits,
these lizards require a diet based on
invertebrates and some fruit. As their
name suggests, they are found close
to water and their vivarium should
incorporate a pool area for bathing.
These lizards originate from the
tropics, so the temperature in their
quarters must not be allowed to dip
below 24°C (75°F) at night. Water
dragons like to climb, and will also
need full-spectrum lighting.

CHAMELEON

Chameleons rank among the most
fascinating of all lizards, thanks to
their colour changes, amazing eyes and
hunting agility, which allows them to

catch flies with a strike of the tongue.
Their requirements are specialized,
however, and, most importantly, they
are solitary by nature and can suffer
severe stress – losing their appetites if
closely confined together. The Yemeni
chameleon (*Chamaeleo calaptratus*)
is one of the most commonly bred
species at present, and it is
relatively easy to look after.
A vivarium for these arboreal
lizards must have branches
for climbing purposes.
The vegetation should
be sprayed with water,
as chameleons are often
reluctant to drink from
a water bowl. Offer a
choice of invertebrates
for their food.

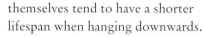

HOUSING

Lizards tend to be housed in an enclosed vivarium, often with a melamine interior, the surface of which can be wiped over easily. Ventilation grilles should be incorporated into the design, along with a door giving easy access to the interior. If required, you can make a vivarium of this type, with sliding glass or perspex doors at the front. Supply heating by means of a spotlight, located in the roof of the vivarium, where it should be set in a wire cage to exclude climbing lizards coming into direct contact with it.

Ceramic infrared heaters, with a reflector around them, are a popular choice, emitting no light. The heat output can be controlled quite easily by means of an adjustable thermostat, enabling you to lessen the heat output overnight, for example. Using ordinary light bulbs to provide heating is possible but the constant resulting light output can be harmful to the lizard's well-being, while the bulbs

✦ RIGHT
Lighting equipment for a lizard vivarium, including a control unit. Spotlights for basking purposes are very important, but ensure arboreal species cannot burn themselves.

✦ ABOVE
Special fluorescent tubes are available that emit the vital ultraviolet rays necessary for the lizard's calcium metabolism and growth.

✦ BELOW
The decor in the vivarium should match the natural habitat of the lizard. This set-up is suitable for a tropical forest species, but not for one of desert origins.

themselves tend to have a shorter lifespan when hanging downwards.

Ultra-thin heat mats, in various sizes and wattages, can also be used for heating. Although these mats are traditionally placed under the vivarium, they can be attached to the sides, though they do detract from the appearance of the vivarium here.

Another option that provides localized heating for small terrestrial lizards is to use what are normally described as "hot rocks". In the past, these have had a bad press because they would overheat, causing burns, but today's models should be safer – check the temperature control method prior to purchase, however.

LIGHTING
Correct lighting is absolutely vital in a vivarium for lizards. It is not a matter of using an ordinary light bulb or fluorescent tube, however, because these do not emit light of the same wavelength as sunlight, specifically light from the ultraviolet (UV) part of the spectrum. There are two components that are of significance to the well-being of reptiles – UVA, which acts as an appetite stimulant and generally encourages activity, including the onset of breeding behaviour, and UVB which is vital for the synthesis of Vitamin D3. This is vital in regulating the body's calcium

+ LEFT
Height is an important consideration of vivarium design when housing arboreal lizards. Be sure to provide them with adequate climbing opportunities here.

stores, and helping to ensure this mineral remains in the correct ratio with phosphorus.

Special full-spectrum fluorescent tubes can be fitted into the vivarium for this purpose. Their ultraviolet light output will decline over a period of time – most tubes need to be replaced after nine months of usage, even though they may appear to be still working. Black lights are also sometimes used in vivaria for lizards, but these do not have an adequate UVB output.

VIVARIUM LAYOUT

Provide hiding areas for your lizards, and make sure that the substrate used matches their needs. A wide range of bedding options are available. Lizards

+ ABOVE RIGHT, TOP
Substrates for a vivarium housing lizards. Fine gravel is not recommended for vegetarian species as it may be ingested with their food.

+ ABOVE RIGHT, BELOW
Retain the moisture in a tropical vivarium by including tree fern and peat slabs, which can be sprayed with water.

+ RIGHT
A piece of cork bark makes a good retreat for smaller lizards.

that are desert dwellers can be kept on calcium sand, which will be safe even if ingested with food. Chipped bark, in various grades, is suitable for lizards from forested areas as it is dark in colour. Other items, such as branches and living plants, can be included in the vivarium, if required, and these will respond well to the lighting. Never include any which could be hazardous though, such as cacti, and bear in mind that vegetarian lizards are likely to eat any live plants placed in their quarters.

◆ BELOW
Crickets are one of the most widely used livefoods today. Being available in a range of sizes, they are valuable for small and large lizards alike.

◆ BOTTOM
Invertebrates form a major part of the diet of many species of herptile. They are usually swallowed headfirst, as shown by this bearded dragon eating a locust.

FEEDING

There are various prepared diets available for the most popular types of lizards, such as green iguanas and bearded dragons. These diets are often in pelleted form and, although the foods can be fed in a dry state, they often prove to be more palatable to the lizards if they are moistened with water beforehand. Even so, it is still a good idea to offer a range of fresh foods on a regular basis, as these will add bulk and fibre to the lizard's diet. A good selection of fresh foods, ranging from sprouting pulses, such as mung beans, to alfalfa, can be grown quite easily even if you do not have access to a garden.

Other vegetables that can be fed to reptiles include carrots and cabbage in small quantities. Green lettuce contains little in the way of nutrients,

however, compared with red-leaved variants. Some lizards will eat fruit, including grapes, apple and melon, but avoid rhubarb, which could be toxic because of its oxalic acid content.

While larger lizards can munch whole leaves, food should be cut up into pieces, which can be swallowed

without difficulty, particularly in the case of carrot. Provide the food in a bowl that cannot be tipped over easily. It is also a good idea to sprinkle over a vitamin and mineral supplement to maintain the nutritional value. Read the labelling: overdosing is harmful, especially over a period of time.

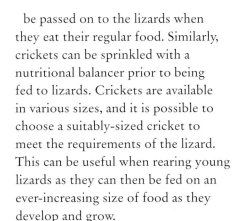

Some lizards, such as this skink, will feed mainly on fruit and greenstuff. Wash fresh foods thoroughly; it may be advisable to peel them if they could have been sprayed by chemicals.

INSECTIVOROUS LIZARDS

Catering for insectivorous lizards requires the use of a supplement as these foods are known to be deficient in terms of their calcium: phosphorus ratio, and this can be a cause of metabolic bone disease. There are now various ways of improving the nutritional values of the main types of livefoods to compensate for the nutritional deficit. One effective way of doing this is known as gut loading. This involves feeding smaller livefoods to the lizards' standard invertebrate livefood diet. The benefits should then be passed on to the lizards when they eat their regular food. Similarly, crickets can be sprinkled with a nutritional balancer prior to being fed to lizards. Crickets are available in various sizes, and it is possible to choose a suitably-sized cricket to meet the requirements of the lizard. This can be useful when rearing young lizards as they can then be fed on an ever-increasing size of food as they develop and grow.

Mealworms also range in size from the mini-mealworms through to giant mealworms, which are actually a different species. The giant type is only suitable for the biggest lizards, such as fully grown water dragons, but the smaller sizes will be eaten by a variety of lizards. Their tough outer-body casing means they may not be easily digested in some cases, especially by small lizards.

Waxmoth larvae are also very popular as a diet for lizards, and these are particularly valuable for rekindling the appetite of a sick individual and helping it to regain condition. The waxmoth larvae need to be kept cool to delay their pupation. If the larvae are allowed to develop, they will emerge as moths and can be fed to various lizards, such as chameleons, which will enjoy being able to catch their dinner themselves if the moths are emptied into the vivarium.

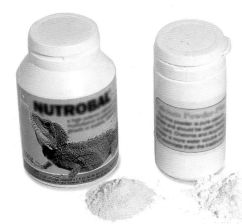

Water dragons will eat a diet based on invertebrates and some fruit. The substantial size of these lizards means that they will feed happily on giant mealworms.

Special nutritional balancers are available to compensate for shortcomings in invertebrate livefoods. These may be sprinkled over the invertebrates or added to their foods.

Crickets, like other livefoods, are low in calcium.

GENERAL CARE

The diversity in the size and shape of lizards means that there is no standard way of handling them. The tails of small species are fragile, whereas those of iguanas, for example, are strong and can cause a painful blow. Some lizards have sharp claws and can inflict deep and painful scratches. For these species it is always best to wear a pair of leather gloves and to avoid handling them with bare arms. Some lizards may even bite if they feel seriously threatened.

CATCHING LIZARDS

In the case of smaller species, such as geckos, the simplest means of catching them is to use a plastic container, such as the type used for transporting lizards, and gently steer the reptile into it. Place the lid over the top once the lizard is inside. Never try to catch several lizards at the same time as this will be near impossible; always concentrate on catching each of your pets individually.

A net, as used for catching tropical fish, can be helpful, especially in the case of any escapes into the room.

◆ RIGHT
Small lizards really should not be handled any more than necessary as they are very agile and can escape easily. It is often easier to catch them in a small container when they need to be moved.

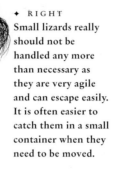

◆ LEFT
Large lizards, such as this green iguana, need to be handled carefully because they can scratch, bite and inflict a painful blow with their tails.

◆ RIGHT
Restraining small lizards, such as this day gecko, carelessly could easily result in tail loss.

You must shut the door as a priority, before attempting to recapture the lizard, as it could quickly dart out and disappear elsewhere in the home. If you do need to hold a small lizard directly, then try to cup it in your hand, and do not restrain it tightly.

When it comes to catching larger lizards, both hands will be needed. First, restrain the head, using your left hand (if you are right-handed)

◆ RIGHT
Male green iguanas develop a prominent dewlap as they mature. They can become more aggressive at this stage, and neutering may be advisable in some cases.

and then hold the tail and hind quarters with your free hand. This should help to stop the lizard struggling badly. If an iguana proves reluctant to return to its vivarium when allowed to roam around the room, the immediate solution will be to restrain it with a blanket or similar material. Avoid constantly chasing lizards if they prove hard to catch as this can be stressful for them and might even prove to be fatal.

MOULTING

There will be times when the lizard starts to moult, with the skin starting to lift from the body. In most cases, this doesn't cause a problem but, on occasion, difficulties may arise, especially with geckos. The old skin may stick around their flattened toes, and start to constrict here, and if it is not removed then the affected digit will be lost. Raising the relative humidity level in their quarters may help to overcome this problem.

PRACTICAL MATTERS

A vivarium is kept clean by removing soiled areas of substrate on a regular basis. It needs to be completely stripped down and washed out every two or three months on average; much will depend on the occupants.

If you go on holiday (vacation), you will need to find someone to look after your lizards. If transporting the vivarium to the helper's home – provided this is done quickly – there is no need to remove the lizards from their quarters; just take out water and food bowls and any heavy decor. Provide a spare heating element, in case this fails in your absence, as well as a supply of food.

◆ ABOVE
Pay close attention to a moulting lizard, in case it has problems shedding its old skin.

◆ BELOW
Keep the vivarium decor clean by washing it thoroughly in a special disinfectant solution.

◆ ABOVE
A tail that has been shed will usually regrow, but it may not reach its previous length.

◆ BELOW
Spot-cleaning the substrate means the removal of soiled areas. Wear disposable gloves.

BREEDING

◆ BELOW
Various herptiles give birth to live young, rather than laying eggs. In addition to lizards, certain snakes also reproduce in this way, as may some salamanders.

The smaller species of lizard generally represent the best prospects for breeding in vivarium surroundings, simply because they do not require such spacious enclosures, unlike green iguanas, for example. Although there are a number of specific features that allow the sexes to be distinguished in particular cases, there are also general guidelines that can be useful for sexing lizards.

Males are frequently brighter in colour, often with crests or head embellishments not seen in females. Geckos in general can be sexed by examining them from beneath in a clear-bottomed container. This allows the femoral pores, which extend down their hind legs, to be distinguished easily. These pores are indicative of a male lizard.

In many cases, male lizards are highly territorial, which is why they must be kept apart from each other. Even if there is no direct conflict, the weaker individual may be bullied to the extent that its condition may

deteriorate. Its growth rate, for example, is often significantly slower as it will be kept out of favoured basking sites and is unlikely to have the pick of the food on offer.

As with snakes, cooling during the winter followed by an increase in temperature in the spring will serve as a breeding trigger for lizards from

more temperate areas, whereas other factors, such as increasing humidity in the case of rain forest species, and even keeping pairs apart for periods, will be significant in some instances.

Most lizards engage in a mating display, which involves head-bobbing and similar movements. Mating itself can be quite aggressive in some cases

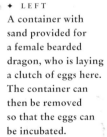

◆ LEFT
A container with sand provided for a female bearded dragon, who is laying a clutch of eggs here. The container can then be removed so that the eggs can be incubated.

◆ RIGHT
A tokay gecko hatching from its egg. When it comes to purchasing herptiles, younger, smaller individuals are invariably cheaper than adult breeding stock.

◆ BELOW
Young lizards, such as this ten week old Yemeni
chameleon, can be housed and fed in a similar
way to adults, although smaller livefoods
should be offered to them.

last five weeks to ten weeks or
more. The incubation temperature is
known to be significant in a number
of species as it can influence the
gender of the hatchlings. Some
experimentation will be necessary,
with the incubation temperature
generally being set around at the
30°C (86°F) mark.

Remove the young as they hatch
to rearing quarters. At first, they
will digest the remains of their yolk
sacs and so will not need feeding. A
separate vivarium is also recommended
for the young of live-bearing lizards,
which could otherwise be tempted
to prey on their offspring. Correct
lighting and a balanced diet are vital
for their subsequent healthy
development in all cases.

as the male anchors himself by biting
the skin of the female's neck. This
may result in some loss of scales, but
should not cause significant injury.

A few lizards, notably some
chameleons, give birth to live young
but the majority lay eggs. These may
have either a parchment shell or a
calcerous hard shell, which influences
the way in which they should be
incubated. The female will start to
swell with the eggs as these develop
in her body. Some lizards seek to bury
their eggs whereas others, such as
geckos, stick their eggs around their
quarters. It will be obvious when the
female has laid by the change in her
appearance, as she will become much
slimmer at this stage.

The eggs should be transferred
carefully to an incubator where they
can be hatched, hopefully under
optimal conditions. Damp vermiculite,
available from garden centres, is
commonly used as the hatching
medium and care must be taken to
ensure it does not dry out. This will

enable parchment eggs to absorb
water during the incubation period,
but hard-shelled gecko eggs can be
hatched without vermiculite.

Again, there is no set incubation
period, even for a clutch of eggs, so do
not discard them in a hurry. This can

◆ BELOW
In many cases, it is not a good idea to keep
young and adult herptiles together. In the case
of chameleons, such as the Parson's seen here,
bullying will occur.

TORTOISES, TERRAPINS AND TURTLES

With their distinctive shells and relatively slow, ambling gait, members of this group of reptiles are instantly recognizable. They are very popular as pets, often appealing to people who may not like other reptiles, such as snakes. The ease of their care depends to a degree on where you live, and whether you are intending to keep a tortoise, a terrapin or an aquatic turtle. Most can be tamed quite easily, to the extent of feeding from the hand.

INTRODUCTION

The names given to this popular group of reptiles can be confusing. Collectively, they are known as chelonians, since they belong to the order Chelonia. While the description of "tortoise" is usually reserved for those that live on land, the use of the term "turtle" is more varied – in the United States and Canada it is used for all aquatic chelonians, whereas elsewhere it is used to describe marine species, and these are not kept as pets.

This group of reptiles are some-times housed outside for part of the year, even in temperate areas, but care needs to be taken to ensure they do not become chilled. Tortoises, in

✦ ABOVE
The hingebacks are African tortoises characterized by the hinge which allows them to draw the hind part of their shell forward, protecting themselves against attacks from behind.

✦ LEFT
In sunny climates, this group of reptiles can be allowed to remain outdoors in safe accommodation for much of the year. Indoor housing is more usual in the temperate areas of the world.

◆ LEFT
A young Southern painted turtle, identifiable
by the orange stripe running down the centre
of its back. The quarters of these turtles must
include space for basking.

While terrapins in general are predatory in their feeding habits, tortoises are mainly vegetarian, and will require relatively large volumes of food as a result. Tortoises rely heavily on beneficial bacteria and other microbes in their digestive tract to help them to break down their food, and this can make them more vulnerable to digestive disturbances if their diet is suddenly changed – you should bear this in mind at the outset.

Eurasian tortoises such as Horsfield's tortoise (*Testudo horsfieldi*) spend part of the year hibernating underground. It is, therefore, important to ensure that tortoises are in a reasonable state of health before hibernating, and that their hibernation conditions are suitable. Otherwise, they can become seriously weakened and may even die during this vulnerable period.

particular, are vulnerable to respiratory diseases when kept at sub-optimal temperatures, and these can frequently progress to a fatal pneumonia. Advances in our understanding of the reproductive behaviour of these reptiles means that captive breeding of tortoises is now becoming commonplace with a number of species, but these young chelonians require rather different care from mature adults, needing to be housed in vivaria for most of the time.

The shells of chelonians are probably their most distinctive feature, offering them good protection from predators, with their skeletal system being encased beneath the shell. It is usually possible to distinguish between tortoises and aquatic chelonians on the basis of their shell shape; in most cases, turtles have relatively flat shells, whereas those of tortoises are more domed in appearance. In many cases, the shell is attractively patterned with highly individual markings. It is not true that the numbers of rings on the tortoise's shell give an exact indication of its age, however, as these do not correlate with all years of its life. There will be more in the young tortoises, and then in older individuals the shell becomes much smoother, with the rings

having been worn down. Tortoises, in particular, may have a lifespan that is equivalent to or even in excess of human beings.

TORTOISE OR TERRAPIN?
The choice between keeping tortoises and terrapins may depend on where you live, since if you do not have access to a garden, your tortoise will have to spend its time in a vivarium, rather than being able to roam freely outdoors on a lawn. If you have no garden, it may be better to choose a terrapin, but bear in mind that these can grow quite large, and may require a small indoor pond rather than a tank.

◆ BELOW
The attractive mottled patterning of leopard
tortoises is variable, allowing individuals to be
distinguished easily by their markings. They
can grow quite large.

TORTOISE SPECIES

Tortoises have a wide distribution through the warmer parts of the world, but for many years the Eurasian species have tended to be most commonly kept as pets.

◆ LEFT
A recently hatched tortoise set against a tomato. They hatch as miniature adults and grow slowly, with a life expectancy of over a century.

MEDITERRANEAN SPUR-THIGHED TORTOISE

Originating from the countries bordering the Mediterranean Sea, the Mediterranean spur-thighed tortoise (*Testudo graeca*), as its name suggests, is found on the opposite shores in both North Africa and Europe. Individuals are easily identified by raised areas, called tubercles or spurs on each side of the body between the hind legs and the tail. Their shell length can be 30 cm (12 in).

◆ ABOVE
The Mediterranean spur-thighed tortoise. The patterning of tortoises is as distinctive as fingerprints, with some displaying more darker blotches than others.

◆ LEFT
A Hermann's tortoise. These and Horsfield's tend to be slightly smaller than the spur-thighed.

HORSFIELD'S TORTOISE

Horsfield's tortoise (*Testudo horsfieldi*) has the most northerly distribution of any tortoise, ranging into parts of the former Soviet Union, as well as other Asiatic countries including Pakistan and Iran, and extending eastwards to China. It has not been widely available in the past, but is now quite extensively kept and bred with increasing frequency. As in

HERMANN'S TORTOISE

Hermann's tortoise (*Testudo hermanni*), whose distribution in Europe and Asia is constant through Spain, Turkey, Bulgaria and Greece, looks similar to the Mediterranean spur-thighed when viewed from above, but it lacks the spurs and is slightly smaller in size. The tail is much more elongated, particularly in the case of males, and terminates in horny tips.

◆ LEFT
Horsfield's tortoise has especially powerful front legs with strong claws for digging purposes.

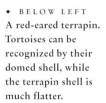

✦ BELOW RIGHT
A juvenile red-footed tortoise. These are tropical rainforest tortoises originating from South America and can grow to 50 cm (20 in). Fruit should predominate in their diet.

✦ BELOW LEFT
A red-eared terrapin. Tortoises can be recognized by their domed shell, while the terrapin shell is much flatter.

(*K. belliana*). The carapace in this case is domed at the back, forming a protective flap, and the shell coloration is highly variable, from plain brown to variegated with cream blotches. Other hingebacks are Home's (*K. homeana*), with its strange

other species, males have longer tails and a relatively concave base to the shell, known as the plastron. The feet of these tortoises are very strong and the upper surface of the shell, called the carapace, is relatively flat, allowing these tortoises to burrow, in order to escape from the blistering sun and freezing winters that prevail in the areas from where they originate.

LEOPARD TORTOISE

With increasing concerns about the wild populations of many tortoises, those available today are generally bred in captivity. Under suitable conditions, pairs can prove to be quite prolific, and as a result, Leopard tortoises (*Geochelone pardalis*), which occur over a wide area of Africa, are also often available. As their natural habitat is further south than the Eurasian species, they are only suitable for housing outdoors in the warmest weather in temperate parts of the

world, as they are especially prone to chilling. Their plastron is very attractively marked with a combination of striking dark and light blotches. As Leopard tortoises grow quite large – their shell can grow to a length of 40 cm (16 in) or more – accommodating them indoors as they grow can often be difficult.

HINGEBACK TORTOISE

The other group of tortoises from Africa which are seen occasionally are the hingebacks (*Kinixys* species), particularly Bell's hingeback

indented shell, and the eroded (*K. erosa*), which has a shell of a reddish shade. These are tropical forest tortoises with highly specific requirements. They need a more omnivorous diet than other tortoises, and must have an accessible container of water where they can immerse themselves. A relatively high level of humidity is necessary in the vivarium.

✦ BELOW
Hingebacks have a protective flange that can be lowered to protect their hindquarters. The hinge of softer tissue is present above the hind legs. The shell itself is 20–25 cm (8–10 in) long.

TURTLE SPECIES

SOFT-SHELLED TURTLES

Turtles vary quite widely in their requirements. Some, notably soft-shelled turtles (*Trionyx* species), are highly aquatic by nature, spending virtually their whole lives in water. This behaviour needs to be reflected in the design of their enclosure. They are also very territorial and aggressive, and even if you acquire two hatchlings at the same time then, almost inevitably as time passes, one will start to grow at a faster rate, and will start to bully its companion. Fights can often prove to be fatal because these leathery-shelled turtles are very susceptible to fungal infections if they sustain damage to their bodies. They are more aggressive than other turtles, and are carnivorous in their feeding habits. Adults will frequently reach more than 30 cm (12 in) long.

SIAMESE TEMPLE TURTLE

Much more placid by nature is the Siamese temple turtle (*Siebenrockiella crassicollis*), which is an attractive, gentle Asiatic species. It is black in

◆ LEFT
The American snapping turtle has a bad reputation. Its shell can measure 48 cm (19 in) in length.

◆ BELOW LEFT
The jagged shell turtle is an Asiatic semi-aquatic turtle, which may attain a shell length of nearly 20 cm (8 in).

colour, with large, pale yellow spots on each side of its head. The shell, in particular, is of an appealing ebony shade, with the skin being a greyish colour. These turtles are also aquatic by nature, especially as hatchlings. They are relatively small in size, even when adult, attaining a shell length of

approximately 20 cm (8 in). Their accommodation should incorporate a basking area where they can come out on to land, even though they are largely aquatic. Feeding is quite straightforward. As Siamese temple turtles grow larger, it is possible to distinguish the sexes. Males have larger, chunkier heads than females, with the space from the base of the tail to the ano-genital opening being longer than in the female.

AMBOINA BOX TURTLE

Originating from South-east Asia, the Amboina box turtle (*Cuora amboinensis*) has yellow stripes extending on the sides of its face. The shell is blackish and paler on the underside, with two flaps here that enable these reptiles to seal themselves into the shell entirely if danger threatens. Once they are used to being picked up, however, they will stop behaving in this way. These turtles

will spend considerable periods of time on land as well as in water, and this should be reflected in their accommodation set-up.

NORTH AMERICAN TURTLES

The North American box turtle (*Terrapene* species) can be recognized by its brown coloration. It spends much of its time on land, although there are a number of more aquatic turtles in parts of North America, where they are bred on turtle farms.

Among those that are quite regularly available as hatchlings are the painted turtles. There are four distinctive forms. The southern (*Chrysemys picta dorsalis*) is the most distinctive, with a bright orange stripe running down across the centre of the top of its shell. The western (*C. p. belli*) can be recognized by its yellowish markings here, and the mottled coloration on the underside of the shell. The colour of the plastron also serves to separate the other two types of painted turtle. The midland (*C. p. marginata*) has a dark stripe running down the centre of the shell. This same area is coloured clear yellow in the case of the eastern (*C. p. picta*). These turtles will all require a housing set-up which provides swimming water and an adequate land area, where they can bask and move around. *Chrysemys* turtles may grow up to 25 cm (10 in).

Map turtles are so-called because, in the case of hatchlings especially, the lines on their shells look like the contours on a map, although the lines may fade with age. Some types of map turtle also have knobbly tops to their shells, so they are often referred to as sawback turtles. Map turtles need similar housing to painted turtles – a reasonable amount of land and water. Mature females can grow to 23 cm (9 in) – twice the size of their mates.

◆ ABOVE LEFT
A red-bellied turtle sunning itself. It may be possible to house some of these *Chrysemys* turtles outdoors in escape-proof ponds during the summer months when the weather has become warmer.

◆ RIGHT
A red-eared turtle, identifiable by the red flashes behind the eyes. This is a male, as shown by the long front claws, used for display purposes.

◆ BELOW
When it is fine and warm, Mediterranean
tortoises can be allowed outdoors to browse
on a lawn; make sure that the lawn has not
been recently treated with garden chemicals.

HOUSING

The type of accommodation for this
particular group of reptiles will depend
very much on where your live, as well
as on the species concerned.

TORTOISE HOUSING

In the case of tortoises, it is especially
important to ensure they do not
become chilled, as this can often lead
on to a fatal pneumonia, particularly if
the conditions are damp as well. Young
tortoises are therefore normally kept
in a vivarium in temperate parts of the
world for much of the year, only being
allowed out into a sheltered outdoor
run when the weather is set to stay
warm and sunny during the day, before
being brought inside again at night.

The vivarium must be sited to give
the tortoises access to shade from
the sun, allowing them to adjust
their location according to their body
temperature. It is possible to let a
tortoise roam freely around a garden,
but under these circumstances, it is
likely to escape unless the boundaries
have been made secure. Some tortoises

◆ BELOW
A typical set-up for young terrapins. Note the
basking lamp suspended over the rock, which
provides easy access to and from the water;
keep the water level low.

are also very adept at climbing and
may slip away over a low wall in this
fashion. Even if your tortoise has not
actually escaped, you may still have
difficulty in locating it on occasions
if it is roaming freely outdoors,
particularly should the weather turn
unexpectedly cold during the day.
This will cause the tortoise to dig itself
in and, with its shell providing very
effective camouflage, the tortoise can
be very hard to spot.

INDOOR HOUSING

When housed indoors, smaller
tortoises can be accomodated in a
typical vivarium, equipped with a heat
pad beneath part of the enclosure,
and a spotlight. A natural-spectrum
fluorescent tube will be necessary to
ensure the healthy development of the
tortoise's shell and its appetite. A hide
to give the young tortoise somewhere

to retreat to should also be included. There should be a temperature gradient across the vivarium, and good ventilation is also important.

Old newspapers, which will be absorbent and are easy to change when soiled, make an adequate floor covering. However, if the newspaper becomes wet and the tortoise is being fed damp greens directly on the floor of its quarters – a practice not to be recommended – it may also consume the newspaper. Of the alternatives, wooden bark can be difficult to clean, while special sand can sometimes irritate the tortoise's sensitive eyes if it attempts to burrow into the substrate. Larger tortoises will require a tiled area as a base, with stout walls to their enclosure, plus a heat lamp suspended at one end of their quarters.

TERRAPIN HOUSING

Terrapins are usually accommodated in an aquarium, with a heat pad positioned under the tank, set under thermostatic control. The water temperature needs to be 25°C (77°F). A standard heaterstat for aquaria can be used, but is less suitable for larger turtles in particular who may damage it. While gravel can be included, it will make the tank harder to clean,

although it is essential for soft-shelled turtles who will burrow into it. There must be easy access from the water on to an area of dry land where the turtles can bask under a spotlight. A fluorescent lighting tube here is also important. Using a power filter in the

aquarium will help to keep the water clean, and adding a dechlorinating product to the water is recommended before filling the tank. There is really no point in adding any plants, even if you put in gravel, because the turtle will dig them up as it swims.

◆ ABOVE LEFT
Any aquatic plants growing in the aquarium substrate are likely to be uprooted by terrapins as they swim. Floating plants can be used for basking purposes.

◆ ABOVE RIGHT
Some terrapins, such as this red-eared, will spend long periods sunning themselves on land. This activity helps to ensure a healthy bone and shell structure.

◆ LEFT
A secure run will be essential to prevent tortoises disappearing in, or escaping from, the garden. A retreat and a water bowl must be included in the enclosed area.

FEEDING

There are a number of different prepared diets on the market in the form of pellets and foodsticks but, especially in the case of tortoises, it is important not to change their diets suddenly. This is because tortoises are very dependent on beneficial bacteria and other microbes in their digestive system to digest their food, and any sudden dramatic change can lead to a fatal diarrhoea. Introduce any new foods to your tortoise very gradually over a couple of months.

TORTOISE FOODS

The tortoises covered in this book are primarily herbivorous in their feeding habits but, in general, fruit should not be offered to them. Instead, provide a wide variety of vegetable matter, including wild plants, such as dandelion leaves and flowers, or chickweed and cultivated crops, such as alfalfa, tomatoes and cabbage. While ordinary lettuce contains little other than water, the red varieties of lettuce have a much higher nutritional content.

Always provide the food for tortoises on a low-sided tray, such as those used as plant stands, to prevent it being dragged around the vivarium and contaminated on the substrate. It will also be easier to remove uneaten

◆ LEFT
Tortoises can prove to be quite clumsy when feeding, and a heavy-weight food bowl that they will not be able to tip over easily is to be recommended.

◆ BELOW LEFT
Variety is important in the diet of these reptiles, but bear in mind that although some tortoises are mainly herbivorous, those from tropical forests must have fruit.

food before it can start to turn mouldy. Tortoises generally need feeding on a daily basis as they are browsers, eating throughout the day, and then resting before feeding again. If you are relying on a diet consisting of fresh food, then the use of a special vitamin and mineral mix will be essential as a supplement, especially for young tortoises.

Should you decide to use a complete food, it will not be necessary for you to add a supplement as well – indeed, this could even be harmful. Always read the instructions on the food carefully and, if in doubt, contact the manufacturers directly or ask your vet for advice. The palatability of dry foods can be improved by soaking them in a little water to soften the texture. Any leftovers will then need to be removed at the end of the day. You will soon be able to estimate quite accurately how much food your new tortoise needs on a daily basis, and this will help to prevent wastage. A heavyweight bowl of drinking water should be accessible in the vivarium at all times, but ensure that the design

of the bowl is such that the tortoise cannot fall in and drown. In older tortoises, particularly if they are eating mainly soft food, the edges of the jaws can become overgrown, and this will require veterinary treatment.

TERRAPIN FOODS

A prepared diet is essential to keep terrapins in good health. In the past, owners were forced to rely on raw meat and similar items which, aside from being nutritionally unbalanced, are likely to be a possible source of *Salmonella* infection for the terrapin. Complete diets have a further advantage over meat in that they do not pollute the water after each feed. Match the amount of food offered to the turtle's appetite to avoid wastage. Although turtles, generally, will not

feed on land, it is quite possible to persuade them to feed from the hand in water. Always take care not to be bitten: while chelonians do not have teeth in their mouths, they do have sharp edges to their jaws which can inflict a painful nip on a finger.

◆ A B O V E
A wide range of prepared diets are available in pellet form for both tortoises and turtles; particularly with tortoises, be sure to offer them plenty of fresh vegetable matter as well, although avoid feeding fresh fruit to most tortoise species.

◆ RIGHT AND INSET ABOVE
Fresh vegetables and other plants help to provide the necessary bulk and fibre in a tortoise's diet. A vitamin and mineral supplement will help to increase the nutritional value of the food.

GENERAL CARE

Chelonians are not particularly difficult to handle; you can pick them up placing your fingers on either side of the shell, but take care to avoid their feet, which may scratch you. The claws of turtles, as well as young tortoises, are sharp because they have not yet been worn down by contact with the ground, as in the case of older tortoises.

A vivarium needs daily cleaning, along with the feeding tray and water bowl, which should be both washed and rinsed. A terrapin tank should have its water changed once or even twice a week. Wear rubber gloves when doing this as there is always a slight risk of harmful bacteria, such as *Salmonella*, entering the body through minor cuts on your hands. It is vital to switch off the heating system before placing your hands in the water, and always leave a heaterstat to cool down for a few minutes before lifting it out of the water. Tortoises, terrapins and turtles can be transferred to a reasonably spacious temporary, plastic container – which they should not be able to climb out of – while their quarters are being cleaned.

CLEANING THE TANK

Never try to empty the tank by sucking water through a length of rubber tubing. If you want to use a siphoning method, fill the tube with tap water, and place one end in the tank, keeping your finger in place over the other, before releasing this and triggering the flow into a bucket. Alternatively, you can obtain a special aquatic siphon for this purpose. Rinse the cartridge of the power filter in this tap water as well, squeezing the foam out to remove the debris which will have been sucked in here. In the case of a small tank, you may be able simply to tip the water straight down a drain. Never use the kitchen sink for this purpose because of the risk of introducing harmful bacteria. When filling the tank again, check the water temperature with a thermometer first, ensuring that it is at the correct temperature before allowing the turtles back into the tank.

In the summer it will be beneficial, particularly as they grow bigger, to allow turtles outside on warm days. Rocks, for basking purposes, should again be included in an outdoor tank.

◆ A B O V E
Handling a chelonian safely. Beware, as they do have strong feet and sharp claws.

Although it may seem a nice idea to allow the turtles into an outdoor pond, this will need to be escape proof around the edges, preferably with a central island where they can emerge on to land. The turtles should always be brought inside again at night.

HIBERNATION

In temperate areas, Eurasian tortoises will instinctively want to hibernate as the days become shorter. It is important that they are in satisfactory health for this purpose, and have put on enough weight over the summer months to sustain them through their winter fast. A veterinary examination may be advisable to estabish their condition. The two key measurements are the tortoise's weight, which can be gauged simply by placing it carefully

SIPHONING THE TANK

1 Fill the tube with water. You will also need a bucket within easy reach. Ideally, you should wear protective gloves for this task.

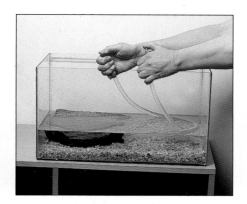

2 Use your thumbs to cover both ends of the tube. One end must be below the water level, with the other extending into the bucket.

3 Release the thumb over the end in the tank first, and then take your thumb away from the other end to start the water flow.

✦ BELOW
The southern toad is a North American species.
A period of cooling over the winter months is
thus likely to encourage spawning activity in
the springtime.

✦ BELOW
The American green tree frog, originating from
the south-eastern part of the United States,
is a very attractive species that does well in
a tall-sided, planted vivarium.

✦ BELOW
The marine or cane toad is the largest toad in
the world, growing to approximately 20 cm
(8 in) in size. It will feed on small vertebrates
such as pinkies.

water for breeding purposes. They are
insectivorous by nature, and some of
the largest species may even prey on
small rodents and young birds. It will
therefore be necessary to provide
them with invertebrates, although
on the whole, frogs and toads are
not expensive to keep.

Breeding of anurans is achieved
quite easily, often by cooling them
down for a period during the winter
months, in the case of those species
found in more temperate areas.
The breeding cues in those from the
tropics are more complex, which often
necessitates keeping them in drier
surroundings for a period of time,
before the start of the rainy period.

Females lay jelly-like eggs, in the
form of threads in the case of toads,
with frogs' eggs being clumped. The

✦ ABOVE
This Spurrell's leaf
gliding frog originates
in the tropical forests
of Costa Rica.

young frog or toad starts to develop in
the centre of the egg, emerging in due
course as a tadpole with feathery gills
on the sides of the head, which serve
to extract oxygen from the water.

Gradually, the tadpoles start to
grow legs, their tails become shorter
and their gills start to disappear as
they are transformed into miniature
anurans. They will spend longer at the
water surface, often resting on rocks
as they start to breathe atmospheric
air, before finally emerging on to land.
Young toads in particular may have
a long lifespan in front of them – over
20 years in some cases.

✦ LEFT
The spring peeper, so-called because
of its calls at spawning time, is
another North American species. It
is hardy, grows to over 2.5 cm (1 in)
long and has a call like a whistle.

✦ RIGHT
The bony-headed tree frog, like
others of its kind, can use all its
limbs to maintain its balance. Flies
are a useful food for tree frogs,
which do not hunt on the ground.

◆ BELOW
Requiring similar conditions to tropical fish,
dwarf clawed frogs make very attractive
occupants of a small heated aquarium, often
spawning in these surroundings.

SPECIES

It is important to match the type
of set-up carefully to the type of
frog that you are keeping, as their
requirements can be quite different.

DWARF CLAWED FROG

This frog (*Hymenochirus boettgeri*) is
an ideal choice if you are looking for
an aquatic species. The small size of
these frogs, which average about
3.5 cm (1½ in) long, means that
they can be accommodated easily,
compared with their larger relatives
known as African clawed frogs
(*Xenopus laevis*). These can reach
a size of 13 cm (5 in) or more and
are far more disruptive within an
aquarium, with their flattened body
shape and powerful legs meaning that
they will uproot any planted decor.

The water in the aquarium needs to
be heated to 24°C (75°F), and should
be relatively shallow. An undergravel
filtration system is recommended,
along with decor, such as bogwood to
provide retreats for the frogs. Java

◆ BELOW LEFT
The markings of grey tree frogs differ between
individuals, so that once a pair have spawned,
you should be able to recognize the male and
female. They grow to about 5 cm (2 in) long.

◆ BELOW RIGHT
The camouflage provided by the grey tree frog's
patterning is very effective. Decorate a vivarium
for them with cork bark, branches and other
decorative vegetation.

moss (*Vesticularia dubyana*), growing
on the wood, and floating plants at the
surface should be included. Male frogs
have large glands behind the front legs
and they call loudly when in breeding
condition. The eggs must be removed
from the aquarium, and will hatch
after five days. Tadpoles will change
into frogs after about two months.

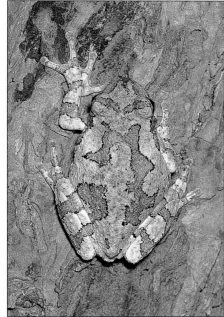

✦ LEFT
The stunning appearance of the red-eyed tree frog. Tropical tree frogs are more demanding in their requirements than those from temperate areas. It measures 7.5 cm (3 in) in length.

WHITE'S TREE FROG

The White's tree frog (*Litoria caerulea*) is an easier proposition to care for, although its large size means that it should be housed in a vivarium with stout-leaved plants, which will support its weight. Again, heated surroundings are essential, although this tree frog requires slightly lower levels of humidity – around 80 per cent – compared with the red-eyed species. The coloration of the White's tree frog is typically green, sometimes with a bluish hue, although piebald individuals, with green and prominent areas of white are also known. These are bold, lively frogs and they can become quite tame. Adults will eat larger invertebrates and pinkies. For breeding, reduce the humidity in their quarters to 70 per cent for one month before raising it again.

An attractive albino form of the dwarf clawed frog has also been bred and is quite widely available. It will require identical care.

GREY TREE FROG

There are a number of tree frogs available, and it is important to determine where they originate from, as not all are of tropical origin. The grey tree frog (*Hyla versicolor*) is a species found in the United States, and this needs slightly cooler and less humid conditions than its tropical cousins. The mottled grey coloration varies between individuals, with orange areas usually apparent on the thighs and a small cream-coloured area below the eyes. A tall aquarium set-up, incorporating cork bark as well as stout plants for climbing purposes, will be needed for these frogs.

RED-EYED TREE FROG

This frog (*Agalychnis moreletii*) is one of the most striking of all the tropical species, thanks to the stunning coloration of its eyes, offset against its bright green body colours. The fact that these frogs are nocturnal in their habits means that they are not as conspicuous as some frogs. Their care is also more specialized: include a small waterfall operated by an aquarium pump in their quarters to maintain the humidity level. Adult males are smaller than females.

✦ BELOW
White's tree frogs can reach 11.5 cm (4½ in) long. Females may lay up to 300 eggs twice a year, with tadpoles leaving the water at five weeks.

HORNED FROG

It is definitely not a good idea to house frogs or toads of different sizes together, because the smaller individuals may be eaten by their larger companions. While this is the case for most species of frogs and toads, some are more cannibalistic than others, with the horned frog (*Ceratophrys* species) being one of the worst offenders. In spite of this, the cute appearance of horned frogs means that they have become popular as vivarium pets.

The horns from which the species takes its name are actually enlarged areas above the eyes. These frogs are easy to accommodate. They require a vivarium with a thick layer of moss on the floor in which to bury themselves, remaining here for long periods, with just their faces evident, and snapping at any invertebrate within reach.

Breeding these frogs presents more of a challenge. The males are identified by darker markings on their throats. The temperature in their vivarium

◆ ABOVE AND INSET
The predatory nature of the horned frog is reflected by its very large mouth. It spends much of its time on the floor of the vivarium, partially hidden from view, and grows up to 12 cm (5 in).

◆ BELOW LEFT
Golden mantellas vary in terms of their coloration, from a reddish shade to orange.

should be reduced to approximately 20°C (68°F) for a maximum period of three months, before increasing the humidity level. Providing an area of water may also encourage spawning.

GOLDEN MANTELLA

The popular and attractive golden mantella (*Mantella aurantiaca*), which originates from Madagascar, can vary in appearance from shades of yellowish-orange through to reddish-orange. These are small frogs, measuring about 3 cm (1¼ in) when adult, and they should be housed in a vivarium with damp moss on the floor and plenty of hiding places.

◆ RIGHT
The Oriental fire-bellied toad is an attractive species that can be easily maintained. Males grip the females by their hind legs when spawning is occurring. They grow to 5 cm (2 in) long.

The golden mantella is an example of a species that should be housed together with other frogs if spawning is to take place – sexing these frogs by sight is difficult as their coloration is not a reliable indicator. A cave with water in it should be provided as it is here that the mantellas will spawn. Their eggs are sensitive to light and need to be kept in darkness until the tadpoles have hatched. The tadpoles metamorphose in about six weeks. Females lay several times throughout the year, with relatively small clutches, comprising fewer than a dozen eggs.

FIRE-BELLIED TOAD

The fire-bellied toad (*Bombina orientalis*) is an easy species to keep and breed, and is an ideal choice for someone who has not kept anurans before. These toads are hardy and they do not require artificial heat in the home, orginating as they do from the temperate areas of Asia. In fact, allowing the temperature in their quarters to drop to 10°C (50°F) in winter will stimulate breeding behaviour the following spring. These toads benefit from an aqua-terrarium with an accessible area of water. They enjoy foraging on land, and will feed on invertebrates out of the water. Males call loudly at the start of the breeding period, while females increase in size due to their eggs.

GREEN TOAD

A number of toads make popular vivarium subjects and can become quite tame. These include the green toad (*Bufo viridis*), which is not to be confused with the American green toad (*B. debilis*). Their patterning is green and reddish rather than the green and black of their African cousin.

Toads require a spacious terrestrial environment with a moss floor, as well as retreats and an area of water. Provide an aquatic set-up for breeding. Males are smaller than females, and can be distinguished by their croaking calls in the springtime. A female may lay thousands of eggs, and cannibalism is common among tadpoles. Even when the young toads have emerged on to land, it is a good idea to keep larger and smaller individuals separate for this reason.

◆ RIGHT
The variable markings of the Eurasian green toad can be seen by comparing two individuals. Their care in vivarium surroundings is straightforward, and they will eat a range of invertebrates. They are larger than their American counterpart, growing to about 15 cm (6 in) when adult.

HOUSING

The same type of basic equipment used for reptiles can be useful for amphibians as well. If possible, however, it is better to use acrylic containers rather than those made of glass or other materials because these are easier to move and clean. In some cases, however, especially with tree frogs, you may have little choice because these enclosures may have to be specially constructed, using sheets of glass stuck together with an aquarium sealant. Most herptile shops can offer this type of service.

The sensitive nature of the skin of these creatures, coupled with the fact that they generally require much lower temperatures than reptiles, means that

✦ ABOVE
Heater pads in various sizes to correspond to that of the tank are invaluable for a set-up for tropical amphibians. The heat output can be controlled thermostatically.

✦ BELOW
Not all frogs are tiny, as shown by this tree frog. The vivarium needs to correspond to the natural habitat in which the species occurs.

spotlights in their quarters will not be required. Instead, heat pads are used to a much greater extent for frogs and toads, even in the case of aquatic species. It is not a good idea to use a standard aquarium heaterstat, which could burn the amphibian's sensitive skin, while the relative low water level in the vivarium means that siting the unit would also create problems, as it has to be kept submerged. In addition, a heat pad is more versatile, serving to warm both the water and the air, operating under thermostatic control.

Both frogs and toads are quite secretive creatures by nature, and they should not be exposed to unnecessarily bright lighting. In fact, there have been suggestions that protracted exposure to ultraviolet light may be harmful to them, while tungsten bulbs will emit a relatively large amount of heat, and this too can be damaging. The best solution will be to use a full-spectrum fluorescent tube, which has a maximum output of no more than two per cent UV light. This should be sufficient to meet the requirements of those frogs and toads that are active during the day and may benefit from some exposure to this type of light, as well as helping you to have a clear view

◆ BELOW
A beautiful mantella frog found only on the island of Madagascar. A number of these species are now well established in collections, breeding regularly in vivaria.

Plastic substitutes can be used for decoration, and these will not damp off and turn mouldy, as can often happen with their living counterparts, especially if the ventilation within the enclosure is poor.

It is vital to fit the vivarium with a ventilated cover – which will often be included as part of an acrylic set-up although they do not include any areas for the attachment of lights. Frogs and toads can not only jump well in most cases, but they are also able to climb up the corners of their quarters – particularly in a vivarium set-up – and then slip out through the roof area, so a secure hood will be essential for their safety.

of the vivarium occupants without having to raise the temperature within the enclosure.

Great care needs to be taken, however, to ensure that water does not come into direct contact with the electrics when it is vital to spray the substrate to maintain the relative humidity level. Therefore, the type of lighting set-up recommended for aquaria is very important in this case.

Take care when siting the vivarium in the room, bearing in mind that the temperature within is likely to rise rapidly if it is placed close to a window when the sun is shining. A secure side table, near a power point, is the best locality, away from a radiator, which could also affect the temperature within the tank.

You can buy a range of items from herptile shops, including retreats and containers suitable for use as water receptacles, and different substrates. Bark, in various grades, and moss are most suitable for use as

substrates, while a plant sprayer can be used for misting the vivarium. You may want to include living plants such as ferns, which are most likely to thrive in this type of environment.

◆ BELOW
The stunning golden mantella is considered to be one of the most attractive of all amphibians, but its bright coloration gives a warning about its toxic skin secretions.

FEEDING

The feeding requirements of frogs and toads differ through their life-cycle, with tadpoles being partly vegetarian in their feeding habits. Adult animals, in contrast, require a variety of invertebrates to form the basis of a nutritional diet, with some of the larger toads being capable of eating small vertebrates.

INVERTEBRATES

You can purchase a suitable selection of invertebrates from pet stores or by mail order, from suppliers listed at the back of specialist publications. Crickets are especially useful for frogs and toads. They are available in a range of sizes and can be fed to the amphibians in one size or another as they grow larger. The crickets can be dusted with a nutritional balancer to improve their feeding value.

The movement of crickets also means that they will attract the attention of a frog or toad readily, and the fact that they will jump and climb (unlike mealworms) means that they are also ideal for tree frogs, which may otherwise be reluctant to descend to the ground in order to hunt for food. The only other way to feed frogs and toads is to place a shelf on the side of their quarters within easy reach, placing other food items on it for them to eat.

It is a good idea to offer some variety in the amphibian's diet to allow you to provide them with other items on occasion. Worms are often favoured by toads although if you dig these up in the garden, collect them from ground that has not been treated in any way with chemicals. The worms should be left to empty

their intestinal tract for a couple of days, in damp grass, before being offered to the vivarium occupants. In the case of the smaller species, you can offer green aphids as a change, brushing these off garden or wild plants with a clean paintbrush.

If you are keeping more than one frog or toad in the same enclosure, it is important to check that all of them have adequate opportunity to feed properly, and that the dominant individual is not taking all the food. Avoid overfeeding as this can be very harmful, with toads in particular becoming obese over a period of time. Amphibians should be eager to feed, although the amount of food that they need will vary, depending on their size and the time of year. Temperate species, for example, will have larger appetites when they first emerge from a period of winter inactivity, needing to replace the stores of body fat that they will have lost over this time.

SMALL VERTEBRATES

When offering dead day-old mice, known as pinkies and sold in frozen form by specialist suppliers, make sure they have thawed out thoroughly; simply dipping them in hot water may not be sufficient for this purpose, and you should allow adequate time for defrosting. You will need to persuade the amphibian to take the inert prey: waving the mouse slightly to one side of the amphibian's face should be sufficient to encourage it to strike, but take care to keep your fingers out of the way. Although amphibians do not have teeth they can inflict a painful nip and, once attached to a finger with their jaws, they will usually be reluctant to let go.

✦ BELOW
It is not a good idea to keep large and small specimens of the same species together, because in the case of amphibians, such as these toads, the smaller individual may fall victim to its larger companion.

◆ BELOW
Mealworms can be purchased in a variety of sizes, with mini-mealworms being valuable for smaller herptiles. Keeping them cool will slow their development.

◆ BELOW
Giant mealworms may be too large for some herptiles, but they are often favoured by bigger species. Their nutritional value can be improved by feeding them special foods.

◆ BELOW
Waxmoth larvae are especially useful for herptiles that may not be in top condition – after illness, for example – as they provide excellent nutrition.

COLLECTING LIVEFOODS

You can usefully augment the diet of your amphibians by collecting invertebrates if you have access to a garden or woodland, and if you are sure they have not been exposed to harmful chemicals. Greenfly can be dusted off roses, for example, and they are very valuable for recently-metamorphosed amphibians. Earthworms, too, are easy to acquire, and these are often favoured by toads, as well as axolotls and adult salamanders. If the ground is dry, watering a patch of earth will attract the worms back to the surface.

◆ BELOW
Choose your pet's food according to its particular species, and always ask the advice of the breeder from whom you bought your pet if you are unsure about its nutritional needs.

◆ ABOVE
Crickets can be obtained in a variety of sizes. Matching the size of crickets to that of the herptiles is important, particularly when prey is being swallowed whole.

GENERAL CARE

Frogs and toads generally require relatively little care, although it is important to change the water in their quarters regularly. Use a water conditioner to remove the chlorine-based chemicals present in fresh tap water, as these might be harmful to the amphibians. In the case of aquatic species especially, be sure that the temperature of the new water is similar to that of the water removed from the tank, using an aquatic thermometer for this purpose. There is no need to remove all the water under these circumstances because of the presence of the undergravel filter. Instead, take out about one quarter of the total volume.

Every month or so, it will be a good idea to replace the substrate in the quarters of the more terrestrial species and, in order to do this, you will need to catch the vivarium occupants. As a result, it is worthwhile keeping the plastic containers in which you brought your pets home, as these will make useful escape-proof, temporary accommodation while you

◆ LEFT
Always handle frogs and toads with disposable gloves, especially if you have any cuts on your hands. The yellow-bellied toad, seen here, is a close relative of the fire-bellied toad and needs similar care.

◆ LEFT
Always bear in mind that frogs and toads are surprisingly agile and can leap out of their quarters when the lid is off. They can also climb up the sides, so always open the lid with care.

◆ BELOW LEFT
The strawberry poison dart frog is beautiful to our eyes, but its bright coloration serves as a natural warning that its skin contains potent toxins.

clean their quarters. Wear disposable rubber gloves for this task, just in case you have any cuts on your hand, which could be irritated by the amphibians' skin secretions. Generally, however, it will not be necessary to handle them directly as you can usually shepherd them into the plastic containers with your hands.

Try to match the quantity of invertebrates you are offering as food to the amount the amphibians will eat within half an hour. It is not a good idea to leave invertebrates for any length of time, as they may escape into the room, with aphids then infesting

◆ LEFT
Fire-bellied toads will benefit from being maintained at a lower temperature over winter, to encourage breeding the following spring.

◆ BELOW
In the case of frogs or toads in the water, the simplest way to catch them is by scooping them up with a fish net of suitable dimensions.

◆ BOTTOM
You may also be able to use a net to catch frogs or toads on land, but it is often simpler to persuade them to hop into a container.

household plants, while crickets are likely to drown in large numbers in the water bowl. It is better to remove the bowl, or to cover it with a small sheet of perspex (Plexiglas) while you are feeding the amphibians, to prevent the invertebrates gaining access to it.

If you do need to catch small frogs in particular, then a net as sold for catching aquarium fish will be useful. Dip it into the water first, to prevent the risk of causing injury to the mucus covering on the amphibians' skin when you catch them. Again, it is better to persuade them to hop into the net than to pick them up by hand, although in the water you can scoop them up safely with the net.

There will be times when you may see the skin of a frog in the water. Frogs will shed their skins at irregular intervals, and it is a normal process. In some cases, the discarded skins may be eaten by the frogs themselves.

When spraying the vivarium, use only dechlorinated water. You may need to wipe over the vivarium glass if it starts to develop algal growth, caused by the high humidity in tropical set-ups. Never be tempted to use commercial spray to clean the glass, or in the room housing the vivarium, because these can be potentially fatal to amphibians.

BREEDING

Although it is theoretically possible to sex frogs and toads on the basis of their size, this is actually harder in practice, unless you can be sure that that they are of roughly the same age. Otherwise, one could simply be a younger individual of the same sex. As the breeding season approaches, so it becomes easier to distinguish the sexes. Males develop what are known as nuptial pads – swollen areas present on the forelegs, and often on the digits. Wrinkled, more darkly pigmented skin over the throat area is another indicator of a male anuran, with the loose skin here being inflated as part of the courtship display when the amphibians are calling.

Just having a pair, however, is no guarantee that they will breed. Conditioning is vital for this purpose. In the wild, there are a number of changes that occur in the amphibians' natural environment, and these stimulate the breeding process. In the case of species found in temperate parts of the world, temperature is an important trigger,

and reducing this in their quarters in the winter will serve this purpose. The reproductive triggers for anurans from tropical areas, where the temperature is constant throughout the year, are related more to changes in humidity rather than temperature. Making the

vivarium slightly drier for several weeks of the year and then raising the humidity level, again, should trigger reproductive behaviour, although it is obviously important that the amphibians themselves are in good health. In some cases, artificial

✦ **LEFT**
Calling is a natural prelude to mating in the case of frogs and toads. This oak toad is inflating his vocal sac.

✦ **BELOW LEFT**
The characteristic embrace when frogs or toads pair off is called amplexus, with the male fertilizing the eggs as they are laid by the female, who is often larger in size.

✦ **BELOW RIGHT**
The calls of frogs, such as this squirrel tree frog, are most likely to be heard in springtime, after rain and at dusk.

◆ LEFT
The prolific spawning of many frogs and toads reflects the fact that in the wild only a small percentage of the resulting tadpoles will survive to breeding age themselves.

hormones have been used to condition frogs and toads for breeding purposes, although these should always be used with care.

When the time for egg-laying is near, most frogs and toads will spend longer in water, where the female will lay her eggs. The eggs are normally fertilized by the male externally as they are laid, with the male clasping the female with his legs in an embrace described as amplexus. A few species lay their eggs on land. In the case of the red-eyed tree frog, the eggs are attached to a leaf overhanging water so that, when the tadpoles wriggle free, they will fall into the water where they can continue their development.

The number of eggs varies greatly, from just ten or more in some cases through to thousands in others, where only a small proportion of the offspring will survive.

The transparent, jelly-like material around the egg helps to protect the developing tadpole from fungi until it hatches, although infertile eggs often suffer fungal attack while among those that are developing normally. It is not usually necessary to treat the eggs, but once the tadpoles have hatched, the remaining eggs should be removed. At first, the tadpoles will be inert, using up the remains of their yolk sacs, but within a few days, they start to swim and feed on tiny particles in the water.

It is important to provide tadpoles with plenty of space as they grow, partly to reduce the likelihood of cannibalism; tadpoles become more carnivorous as they grow larger. Powdered fish flake is a valuable addition to their diet at this stage, and will be less likely to pollute the water than pieces of raw meat. Water quality is vital, and partial water changes must be carried out as the tadpoles grow.

Gradually, the legs of tadpoles will start to develop, along with their body shape, and the tail starts to shrink. Provide an area, in the form of a rock in their quarters, where the young amphibians can emerge on to land as their lungs start to function. Soon afterwards, they can be transferred to an aqua-terrarium to roam on land, with an area of water also accessible. Small invertebrates should now form the basis of their diet.

◆ BELOW LEFT
Male frogs develop nuptial pads on their forelegs. This can help to distinguish the sexes.

◆ BELOW RIGHT
A metamorphosing Trinidad leaf frog tadpole. The strong legs and frog-like body shape have already developed by this stage.

NEWTS AND SALAMANDERS

This group of amphibians are distinguished from frogs and toads by the fact that they have tails. They are rather shy and secretive creatures in most cases, whose environmental needs centre around water. Most show the amphibian cycle of reproduction, laying eggs which hatch into tadpoles and metamorphose into miniature adults. Some give birth to live offspring. Others display a remarkable degree of parental care by guarding their eggs.

INTRODUCTION

◆ BELOW
A smooth newt on a rock. These amphibians return to water to breed in the springtime.

This group of amphibians include the biggest members of the group, which are the endangered giant salamanders found in parts of China and Japan. They can reach at least 1.5 m (5 ft) in length, but are not likely to be seen outside zoological collections. Others are much smaller in size, rarely exceeding more than 30 cm (12 in) in length.

It can be difficult to distinguish between newts and salamanders since there are no clear differences between them. In general terms, however, newts are more dependent on water than salamanders, especially for breeding purposes. Both groups have a wide distribution in cooler parts of the world, being rather secretive and shy by nature. The brilliant skin coloration of many salamanders is, again, an indication of their highly toxic skin secretions.

◆ BELOW LEFT
A brightly coloured European fire salamander. The bright coloration serves as a warning to predators about the toxic skin secretions produced by these amphibians.

◆ BELOW RIGHT
A marbled salamander. Although the basic colour scheme of these amphibians is the same, it is possible to identify individuals quite easily by their skin markings.

◆ BELOW
An adult red-spotted newt. Males develop a
broad tail fin rather than a crest at the start of
the breeding period. Also, unlike most newts,
pairs grip together when mating.

◆ BELOW
A young red-spotted newt, which has recently
emerged on to land. It is highly colourful at this
stage, often being described as a red eft. Its
appearance gradually changes as it matures.

An unusual phenomenon associated with salamanders is that of neoteny. Like other amphibians, their life-cycle begins with an egg which hatches into a larva or tadpole. The larvae then develop and lose their gills, emerging on to land as miniature adults. In the case of the axolotl, the larvae do not metamorphose into adult salamanders but continue to grow, with the result that they can then breed in the larval state. This can be related to a shortage of iodine in the diet, which is necessary for the manufacture of the thyroid hormones that help to trigger the change into the adult form. Often, however, if the water level is allowed to drop back, then the axolotl will transform into an adult salamander, and will breed in this state.

The reproductive behaviour of the salamander is generally less dependent on water than is the case with many other amphibians. Some populations of the fire salamander, for example, give birth to live tadpoles rather than lay eggs.

All newts and salamanders are predatory in their feeding habits, catching their prey both on land and in water. The care of most salamanders and newts is very straightforward and,

in some cases, it is possible to keep them in outdoor vivaria for at least part of the year. If you decide on this approach, however, you need to ensure that their quarters are escape-proof, because allowing non-native species to escape is not only likely to be illegal but could also have serious effects on local wildlife if the escapees establish themselves in your neighbourhood.

However, it may be possible to hatch the eggs of any newts which you find in the part of the country where you live, and allow these to build up a population in your garden. There may

be restrictions on transferring wild newts or salamanders to new environments, however, so check on this beforehand. It is also possible to obtain eggs of such amphibians from breeders who have surplus stocks. Most breeders with regular stock on offer will advertise in the specialist herpetological magazines. A local newt society may also be able to help.

◆ BELOW
The yellow phase of the fire salamander is more common than the orange variety shown opposite, although both colour forms can result from a single spawning.

◆ BELOW
The variance in markings seen in the fire
salamander is reflected by these two individuals.
This species is widely kept, and can be bred
quite easily.

SALAMANDER SPECIES

FIRE SALAMANDER

Variability in appearance is a feature
of the fire salamander (*Salamandra
salamandra*), which is found over a
wide area of mainland Europe in the
wild. Some populations display yellow
spots, set against a black background,
whereas others have yellow stripes and
some even have fiery orange, rather
than yellow, markings. There is also
some variability in size, and individuals
can range from 20–30 cm (8–12 in) in
length when adult. Fire salamanders
are easy to house in a spacious
vivarium, with plenty of retreats.

Perhaps surprisingly, fire
salamanders cannot swim at all well,
and the water container in their
quarters must be not only shallow,
but must allow easy access both in and
out of the water. A cool environment
is another important consideration,
particularly during the summer
months when the temperature indoors
can rise rapidly; fire salamanders
should be kept at a maximum of 20°C
(68°F). It may, therefore, be necessary
to move the salamanders outdoors
to a vivarium in a shaded corner of
the garden, out of direct sunlight.

◆ LEFT
An example of the
fire salamander,
found in the
Cantabrian region
of Spain. This is
one of the
populations where
the discontinuous
spots have merged
to create stripes
running down the
sides of the body.

MARBLED SALAMANDER

The marbled salamander (*Ambystoma
opacum*) is found in eastern parts of
the United States. This species can
be kept outdoors during the warmer
summer months. It grows to a
maximum size of 11 cm (4¼ in) and is
black in colour, with silvery markings,
which are whiter and brighter in the
males. Mating is unusual in that it
takes place on land in the autumn.
The eggs are laid in a dried-up pool,
and the female stays with them over
the winter until they hatch.

◆ LEFT
Spaghnum moss
makes an ideal
substrate for
salamanders like the
marbled seen here.
Spray the moss as
necessary, using
dechlorinated water,
to prevent it from
drying out.

◆ RIGHT
A black axolotl.
These salamanders
are unusual in that
they remain and
breed in larval form.

SPOTTED SALAMANDER

The range of the spotted salamander
(*A. maculatum*) extends down the
eastern part of North America, from
southern Canada. These salamanders
are recognizable by the clearly defined
pattern of yellow or yellowish-orange
spots extending down their bodies in
two distinctive rows. They grow to a
size of about 20 cm (8 in) in total, and
require moist surroundings compared
with the marbled salamander. An
outdoor enclosure will suit them well,
although they are shy by nature and
will be hard to spot outdoors.

AXOLOTL

The axolotl (*Ambystoma mexicanum*)
ranks as one of the most bizarre and
distinctive of all amphibian species.
It can grow up to 30 cm (12 in) in
length, and is confined in the wild to
two Mexican lakes, although it has
been bred for many generations in
private collections, in spite of its
endangered status. Only the dark
brown form occurs in the wild; the
albino mutation has been developed
from captive stock. There are also
piebald variants, which have black and
white coloration, plus rarer individuals
which are a golden shade.

As tadpoles, axolotls must be kept
in aquatic surroundings, thriving in
water kept at room temperature.
They are inactive by nature, but if kept
together they may fight, sometimes

even to the extent of biting off a
companion's limbs. Remarkably,
however, this may regenerate to
form a completely functional limb,
providing the water is clean and
fungus does not attack the wound.

It is possible to encourage axolotls
to change into adult salamanders by
allowing the water in their tank to fall.
Their gills will then start to recede as
a result, to the extent that they will
disappear altogether; if the water level
is topped up again, then the gills will
grow back in due course. As a result,
the axolotl is sometimes known as the
"Peter Pan of the amphibian world".
Females may lay as many as 300 eggs
at a single spawning, draping these
around aquatic plants. Hatching will
usually take about two weeks.

◆ ABOVE AND INSET RIGHT
The popular albino axolotl. Note the prominent
feathery gills, which enable these large tadpoles
to extract sufficient oxygen from the water.

◆ BELOW
When in breeding condition, a male Alpine
newt has blue areas on the flanks and a low crest
on the back. His underparts are also brighter
than those of the female.

NEWT SPECIES

JAPANESE FIRE-BELLIED NEWT
Part of the reason for the popularity
of the Japanese fire-bellied newt
(*Cynops pyrrhogaster*) is the fact that
it is almost entirely aquatic, and can be
housed in an aquarium with unheated
water throughout the year. These
newts grow up to 12 cm (4½ in), and
take their name from their fiery red
underparts, with black markings.

To encourage breeding, allow the
water temperature in the aquarium
to fall in the late winter. This species
will distribute its eggs in true newt
fashion, carefully attaching each egg to
the underside of the leaves of aquatic
plants. The young should be reared in
more terrestrial surroundings, once
they have lost their gills, until the age
of about six months, when they can be
returned to an aquatic set-up.

ALPINE NEWT
The Alpine newt (*T. alpestris*), as
its name suggests, is found in
mountainous areas of Europe, and

◆ BELOW
A young marbled newt. Both juveniles and
females of this species display the orangish
vertebral stripe down the back, whereas
breeding males develop a crest.

some forms are more aquatic by
nature than others. They are
sufficiently hardy to be kept in
outdoor enclosures throughout the
year, although the enclosure must
incorporate land areas. Growing
to a length of about 13 cm (5 in),
these newts rank among the most
colourful European species, with
males in particular developing a much
more vibrant shade of blue on their
backs and sides than females, while
their underparts are a rich shade of
pure orange. Females are easy to
distinguish by the brown coloration
on their upperparts.

MARBLED NEWT
Another colourful species is the
marbled newt (*T. marmoratus*), which
originates from south-west Europe.
This species is terrestrial in its habits,
and this needs to be reflected in the

+ BELOW
The red eft – the immature form of the
red-spotted newt – may not return to water
for several years, although it will stay in damp
surroundings, growing to 12 cm (5 in) overall.

+ BELOW
A smooth newt tadpole hatches from its egg.
The gills at the sides of the head allow young
amphibians to take oxygen from the water
until their lungs develop.

design of its vivarium. The set-up should comprise an area of sphagnum moss lining the floor, with adequate retreats, as well as a shallow dish of water that is accessible to the newts. Following a period of winter dormancy, the newts require an aquarium of water for spawning, before returning to their terrestrial lifestyle. They may grow to 17 cm (7 in) in length.

RED-SPOTTED NEWT

The red-spotted newt *(Notophthalmus viridescens)* is one of the most striking of the North American species, and is extensively found on the eastern side of the continent. There are slight variations in appearance between individuals, as there are three distinctive types among their wide range. Even so, the distinctive red spots, highlighted by black circles on the sides of their bodies, are clearly apparent in all cases. The number of spots varies, depending on the individual, and the remainder of the upperparts are brownish with tiny black spots in adults, who have yellower underparts.

The newly metamorphosed red-spotted newts are the most dramatically coloured, and are known as red efts. As well as displaying the distinctive spotted appearance of adults, they also have a body colour which varies from bright orange to red. They retain their colour for the time that they remain on land, which can be up to three years before they switch back to an aquatic lifestyle to breed, acquiring their adult coloration at this stage. The female is likely to lay up to 200 eggs, in small batches, over a period of three weeks or so.

+ BELOW
A crested newt tadpole, with its feathery gills and legs clearly evident. It will now be preying on a variety of small water creatures.

HOUSING

The set-up required by newts and salamanders is not only influenced by the species which you are keeping, but also by the time of year. Salamanders by nature are more terrestrial in their habits, and so they will benefit from an enclosure which has a large floor area, compared with its height. It needs to be lined predominantly with damp moss. There are acrylic enclosures of this type available, which come complete with a ventilated and secure roof covering, incorporating a feeding hatch.

Unfortunately, the moss is unlikely to grow in these surroundings, and ultimately will need to be replaced. Suitable retreats will be essential in the enclosure, as salamanders often like to burrow away under logs. These should always be lifted carefully as a result, to avoid any risk of injuring amphibians which may be hiding there. A dish of water which allows the salamanders to submerge themselves is also important, with a rim that merges with the surrounding substrate. Smooth pebbles which allow the amphibians to climb back out again are essential, but these must be firmly supported in the tank.

When filling the water container, it helps to use a large jug (pitcher) for the purpose. Fill this with water from the cold tap, which must then be left to stand for at least 24 hours to remove any chlorine-based chemicals; alternatively, you could use a dechlorinator. This also applies in the case of water that is used to spray the moss. Since the water will need to be changed regularly, try to position the container so that you can lift it out easily without causing a major disturbance in the vivarium.

You may want to add a couple of sprigs of water plants to the container. Elodea or Canadian pondweed (*Elodea canadiensis*) is a good choice for this purpose, particularly if there is a likelihood of the vivarium occupants breeding as it is popular for egg-laying purposes, especially with female newts. Living plants in the substrate are harder to establish, although small ferns in pots may thrive in these surroundings. They can also give an indication of poor ventilation if they start damping off and turning mouldy, which is likely to have an adverse effect on the amphibians' health.

Axolotls need an entirely aquatic set-up if they are to remain in a larval state. Their housing needs are very basic, however, and they can be kept in a large acrylic tank or a standard glass aquarium. They are unlikely to climb out of their quarters so a cover may not be essential, but it will protect

the axolotl from falling prey to a determined cat, and should help to stop potentially harmful chemicals from wafting in. In the interests of cleanliness, and as axolotls require a meat-based diet, it is better not to include any gravel on the floor of their aquarium, to make it easier to keep their environment clean.

Newts will need to be transferred to aquatic surroundings in the springtime for breeding. An aqua-terrarium, divided in two by means of a partition, is ideal for this purpose but check that the top of the partition is smooth and will not damage the newt's skin. There must be easy access in and out of the water by means of rocks which are securely supported to prevent them falling over and injuring the newts. An undergravel filter will maintain the water quality. Plants set in gravel are essential for spawning purposes.

SETTING UP A VIVARIUM

1 It is important to create a humid yet well ventilated set-up. Cork bark provides an attractive backdrop, with the plant providing cover.

2 Place the plant towards the back of the tank, where it will be possible to disguise the pot more easily, while still allowing you to see the occupants.

3 A plastic water container is very important to allow the vivarium occupants to bathe and, hopefully, spawn. Use bark chips as the substrate.

4 The moss should be kept damp by regular spraying, as the amphibians will often retreat here. Only use dechlorinated water in the vivarium.

FEEDING

Newts and salamanders eat livefoods but it may be possible to persuade them to eat small goldfish pellets when they are living in water. This is a safer option than other aquatic livefoods available from fish-keeping outlets. Tubifex worms, for example, are likely to introduce unpleasant bacteria into the water, while daphnia, or "water fleas", may bring parasites or even predatory insects with them, and these could attack tadpoles. The best option when providing livefood is to breed your own.

Although daphnia can be cultured in a water tank outdoors, there will be less risk of disease if you use terrestrial livefoods such as whiteworm (*Enchytrae* species). These can be bred at home with little effort, and can be used when these amphibians are both on land or in water. You cannot buy supplies of whiteworm in the same way as other livefoods, such as mealworms, but you can usually acquire starter kits.

To cultivate whiteworms you will need a clean plastic container with a lid, such as an empty margarine tub. Half fill the tub with a peat substitute

and then, with a pencil, dab some holes in the peat. The holes should be partly filled with damp bread, which has been moistened in milk and will act as nourishment for the worms. Divide the culture up and cover the worms, placing the lid on top to prevent it drying out too quickly. If kept at a temperature of 20°C (68°F) it should be possible to harvest from the culture after about one month. Lift out the worms with tweezers and drop them into a saucer of dechlorinated water, which will keep them apart from the substrate, and offer them to the amphibians. Whiteworms are a very nutritious food and are especially valuable for young amphibians.

For a supply of uncontaminated aquatic livefood, leave a bucket of water outdoors in the summer. This should attract a variety of gnats and similar creatures to lay their eggs in it, which will soon hatch into larvae. These can then be sieved out with a tea strainer and transferred to the tank. Avoid offering more food than the amphibians will eat or you may find your house becomes invaded by gnats.

Larger salamanders, in particular, require bigger prey, and worms of various types are suitable for this purpose. These are available from livefood suppliers, and represent no danger to the amphibians' health, compared with garden worms.

Species such as fire salamanders may even be persuaded to eat pinkies (dead day-old mice), but since it is the movement of their food which attracts them to it, you will have to offer the mouse by hand. Avoid using forceps, particularly sharp-ended ones, as these can cause injury if the amphibian snatches at its food.

Axolotls are often fed on raw meat but this pollutes the water rapidly, and it soon starts to smell unpleasant. Persuade them to eat other foods, such as mealworms, since these are less of a pollutant, and are cheap enough to keep in good supply.

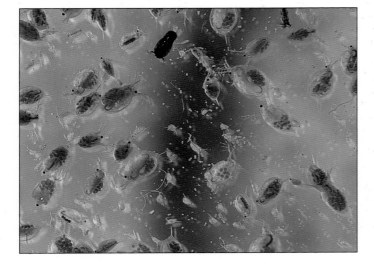

◆ LEFT
Daphnia, also called water fleas because of their shape, are a valuable food for aquatic amphibians. They can be cultured in a pond or large aquarium, and are caught easily with a sieve or fine net.

BREEDING

◆ LEFT
The appearance of male newts alters at the start of the mating season. In many species, the male will develop prominent crests, which are only visible at this time of the year.

Distinguishing between male and female newts and salamanders is the first step towards successful breeding, and this is most easily accomplished in the spring, when the differences between the sexes will be more pronounced. Male newts, for example, will generally become much more colourful at this stage and will often develop prominent crests along their backs. Females swell with eggs and start to look rather stocky, compared to their mates.

Examining them from beneath in a clear container can also be valuable at this time to highlight the difference in the appearance of the cloacal region, which becomes far more swollen in the case of males. Male salamanders often display swellings on the front feet, rather like the nuptial pads seen in frogs and toads.

A range of display behaviour is likely to be seen in the spring, with the male newt following the female closely, often fanning the water with his tail. This releases a scent which encourages her to mate. He releases a packet of spermatozoa, known as a spermatophore, which the female picks up and takes into her cloaca. The eggs are laid in among aquatic vegetation, and after she has done this the female will take no further interest in them. Remove the eggs at this stage, before they hatch, or the tadpoles may be eaten by the adult newts.

Salamanders as a group do show more varied breeding behaviour than newts. Some species, for example, mate directly, and a number display

parental care towards their eggs, with the female staying with them until they hatch. Although most salamanders lay in the water, some will produce their eggs on land. Check on the individual breeding habits of your chosen species.

It is again possible to watch the development of the tadpoles through the eggs. The young hatch with feathery gills which allow them to take oxygen from the water. With eggs of newts being laid over the course of several weeks, it is important to keep the young in groups of similar size to reduce the likelihood of cannibalism. Good water conditions are vital.

Change 25 per cent of the volume of the water in their quarters each week, replacing it with dechlorinated water which has been standing for a day to reach room temperature. Small livefoods are needed to rear the young.

As they start to resemble miniature adults, lower the water level and allow them on to land. A platform is useful, and a damp, mossy substrate is an ideal hiding place for the young amphibians when they first emerge. They can then be offered small terrestrial livefoods, and should grow rapidly. For axolotls there is no need to make these changes, but you must allow them more space as they grow larger in size.

◆ RIGHT
Some newts are more aquatic in terms of their lifestyles, but all species will return to the water at the beginning of the breeding season.

GENERAL CARE

Salamanders, in particular, need to be handled with care because their bright coloration is actually a warning sign that they produce toxic skin secretions, which could enter through a cut in your hands and make you feel unwell. It is not a good idea to handle them anyway, however, because you are likely to damage their delicate skin, and this will predispose them to skin infections. A net, as used for aquarium fish, will make it easy to catch them in the water but, on land, wet the net first in the water container, again to protect the amphibian's sensitive skin.

The secretive nature of this group of amphibians may mean that often they are not easily seen, especially when housed in an terrarium rather than an aquatic setting. Even so, you should inspect their quarters carefully each day to ensure that nothing is amiss if you cannot see the amphibians moving around. Try to establish a

♦ ABOVE
Although they like to remain close to water, most amphibians require a largely terrestrial set-up. Different surroundings will often be needed for breeding purposes.

♦ LEFT
Catching a fire salamander with a fish net. Place your hand over the top of the net to prevent the salamander from climbing out and, possibly, falling on the floor.

routine, as far as possible, by feeding them in the evening after spraying their quarters. This is most likely to bring the amphibians out in to the open to seek their food.

When a group are being housed together in the same accommodation, it is important to ensure that they are all receiving an adequate supply of food. If you are feeding them in the water, aim to separate the amphibians as far as possible using a net because, otherwise, there is a possibility that one will seize the limb of another in a feeding frenzy, confusing it with its prey, and could bite it off.

Some species need to be allowed to overwinter at a relatively low temperature if they are to breed in the following spring. Only those which

◆ BELOW
Adding a dechlorinator to water for amphibians. Products of this type sold for fish-keeping purposes will be necessary. Always take care to measure out the correct volume.

are healthy and well fed should be allowed to have a period of winter dormancy for a couple of months. Reduce the amount of food offered beforehand so their guts can empty. A dense layer of moss should be provided in the vivarium, allowing them to burrow down into the substrate of their quarters. It is preferable to lower the temperature gradually, rather than plunging them suddenly into a cold environment.

Overwintering can usually be accomplished more easily in an outdoor set-up, which has suitable areas for hibernation purposes. It is important that the enclosure here is escape-proof, and there is an area of higher ground within so that there is no risk of heavy wintertime rain flooding the amphibian's quarters.

◆ BELOW
An Alpine newt walks over lichen. Mosses are often used on the floor of an amphibian set-up and will only require regular spraying with water to remain in good condition.

In the event of heavy rains, you may need to bale out the pond at intervals, to prevent it from overflowing.

In the spring, the amphibians will gradually emerge from their sleeping places and should then make their way back to the water. In the case of newts, spawning will occur soon after their return to the pond.

Very little is required in the way of maintainance for an outdoor enclosure for newts and salamanders. The grass can be allowed to grow quite long although, if you do decide to cut it back, you must take great care not to harm the vivarium occupants. You must also be very careful about using horticulatural chemicals nearby in the garden. If these filter through the soil into the pond water, they could prove deadly for the amphibians.

INVERTEBRATES

The invertebrates, meaning creatures without backbones, represent the largest group on the planet. They come in many weird and wonderful forms, some of which are highly colourful, whereas others, such as stick insects, blend very effectively into the background. A number are predatory, and can give painful, even fatal, stings and bites, while many live on a vegetarian diet, sometimes having evolved powerful mouthparts for this purpose.

INTRODUCTION

Many people use the terms "insects" and "invertebrates" as if they are the same. In fact, insects are just one of the groups within the invertebrate category. They are distinguished by their three pairs of legs, whereas the arachnids, incorporating spiders and scorpions, have a different body structure with four pairs of legs. Invertebrates are distinguished from all the other groups covered in this book by the lack of a backbone. This has not prevented them from becoming the most numerous category of creatures on the planet, however, colonizing virtually every available habitat. As a group, invertebrates are exceedingly diverse in both lifestyle and appearance and, although they will not become tame in the same sense as many other pets, their behaviour is fascinating and keeping them can be highly rewarding.

◆ LEFT
Invertebrates such as the praying mantis are effective hunters, grabbing their prey with their forelegs.

◆ BELOW LEFT
Invertebrates have evolved to blend with their surroundings as shown by this leaf-mimic katydid from Malaysia.

◆ BELOW RIGHT
Another leaf katydid, from Costa Rica. Note the difference in its appearance.

Some invertebrates, such as leaf-cutter ants, are social by nature, living in tightly structured communities, but the sheer size of such groups means that they are very difficult to accommodate satisfactorily in the home. Others, by contrast, are highly aggressive by nature, and need to be kept on their own. Introducing two praying mantis, for example, is likely to end with one being decapitated.

Tarantulas, one of the most popular group of invertebrate pets today, are also highly aggressive towards each other. They have venom that allows them to overcome their prey, and they may also bite if you try to pick them up unexpectedly. These spiders also have irritating hairs on their bodies, which can stick into the skin or even enter the eyes if you hold them too close to your face. Coupled with the

The ability to use
vegetation for their
camouflage is seen
in a wide range
of invertebrates.
This example is a
leaf-mimic moth.

fact that tarantulas are extremely
delicate creatures by nature – their
bodies can rupture easily as the result
of a fall – you can see why they are
not pets to be handled regularly, but
are better admired from outside their
quarters. Scorpions also possess a
painful and dangerous sting, and
they are not to be recommended as
childrens' pets for this reason.

Stick insects, better known in the
United States and Canada as "walking
sticks", are a much better choice for
children. These creatures are entirely
herbivorous in their feeding habits and
can be handled quite safely, especially
in the case of the larger species,
although some do have protective
spines on their bodies. The only
drawback, perhaps, is that, as with
other invertebrates, the reproductive
rate of stick insects is such that you
will very soon be overrun with eggs.

The prolific nature of these
invertebrates is a reflection of the
fact that, in the wild, they have a very
precarious life and, out of many
hundreds of eggs, just a handful of
the resulting young invertebrates
will themselves survive for long
enough to breed.

The potential for invertebrates
to reproduce rapidly, under suitable
conditions, and build up a population
of plague proportions means that

keeping certain species may be
outlawed in some countries. This is
the case with the giant land snail.

Not all invertebrates live on land.
There are some species that are found
in freshwater ponds and lakes and
even in the sea. These species tend
to be kept less often as pets because
of the difficulties of accommodating

them successfully in the home.
However, some of those that live
partly out of the water, such as various
crabs, are occasionally seen for sale in
larger pet stores. As with any other
pet, so long as you are aware of their
needs and can provide the necessary
habitat, there is no reason why you
should not consider keeping them.

◆ TOP RIGHT
Mantids are
generally coloured
to blend in with
their surroundings,
but their shapes can
differ, as shown by
these Costa Rican
leaf mantids.

◆ LEFT
Leaf insects are
quite commonly
kept. They have
evolved on different
lines compared with
stick insects, but still
rely on their shape
and coloration to
remain concealed.

STICK INSECT AND LEAF INSECT SPECIES

These insects are sometimes described collectively as phasmids. This name comes from the ancient name for a ghost, and refers to the amazing powers of mimicry of these creatures. In the same way that stick insects are named after the tree branches that they resemble, leaf insects get their name from tree and plant leaves. The similarity is such that blowing gently on a stick insect will cause it to rock back and forth, just as a twig would sway in a breeze. Phasmids have a wide distribution around the world, with the greatest concentration being in warmer climates.

INDIAN STICK INSECT

The most commonly kept member of the phasmid group is the Indian or laboratory stick insect (*Carausius morosus*), which grows to a length of about 10 cm (4 in). If you intend to breed your stick insects, there is no need to worry about sexing them – males of this species are extremely rare, and females lay fertile eggs without mating. It is possible to recognize males by the red coloration of their middle body segment, called the thorax. Indian stick insects have a life expectancy of about one year.

◆ LEFT
The Indian stick insect is very easy to cater for in the home, and will almost inevitably produce fertile eggs without mating. The young hatch as miniature adults, growing through a series of moults.

◆ BELOW
Asian stick insects can be maintained successfully like most other species on bramble leaves. The safest way to pick up adults is by placing fingers each side of the body.

GIANT PRICKLY STICK INSECT
A much larger species is the giant prickly stick insect (*Extatosoma tiaratum*), which originates from Australia. Mature females grow up to 20 cm (8 in) long, while males are smaller, at 15 cm (6 in), and less bulky with functional wings, although they rarely fly. Females can be handled easily, but they must have stout

◆ BELOW
A pair of giant prickly stick insects, with the large green female on the right and her smaller partner on the left. The wings of the male are folded along his back.

◆ LEFT
A giant spiny stick insect. This is the only commonly kept species that spends much of its time on the ground, so include a cork bark retreat in its quarters.

branches of bramble to support their weight. In this case, it is possible to distinguish young females by the presence of spikes on their abdomen. Once mature, they lay hundreds of eggs in small numbers, expelling them with considerable force from their abdomens.

GIANT SPINY STICK INSECT

Occurring on New Guinea and neighbouring islands, the giant spiny stick insect (*Eurycantha calarata*) differs significantly from the previous species, since it is terrestrial in its habits – a fact that must be reflected in the layout of its accommodation. A large floor area, rather than height, is important in this case. Males grow to about 12.5 cm (5 in) long, being slightly smaller than females, and can be distinguished by the presence of a long spine of the upper part of their hind legs. In contrast to other species, giant spiny stick insects will often eat fresh grass. They must have a shallow container of drinking water on the floor of their enclosure. The females will bury their eggs in the substrate, with the nymphs, which are miniatures of the adults but green in colour, emerging five months later.

PINK-WINGED STICK INSECT

The pink-winged stick insect (*Sipyloidea sipylus*) is a delicate species that is able to glide long distances. The wings, as with other stick insects, are usually kept furled up, but it is a good idea to cut off sharp thorns from bramble that is provided for food, to reduce the likelihood of damaging the wings. Adult females are slightly larger than the males, and will grow to about 10 cm (4 in) in length. Rather than scattering their eggs in their quarters, they stick them around carefully, with the small nymphs emerging about 40 days later.

JAVANESE LEAF INSECT

The Javanese leaf insect (*Phyllium bioculatum*) is a typical example of the leaf insect group, which should all be kept at a temperature of 24°C (75°F). High humidity is essential, and bramble is used for feeding purposes.

◆ ABOVE
An immature giant prickly stick insect, described as a nymph. Given their relatively short lifespan, it is better to obtain pet stick insects as nymphs, although these are one of the longer-lived species, with a life expectancy of around two years.

◆ LEFT
A leaf insect on bramble. Their requirements are very similar to those of stick insects from tropical areas. A heat pad can be used to provide them with warmth.

TARANTULA AND BABOON SPIDER SPECIES

MEXICAN RED-KNEE TARANTULA

The large spiders called tarantulas are found in the warmer parts of the world. The Mexican red-knee tarantula (*Brachypelma smithi*) is the best known of this group. It is recognizable by the orange-red coloration at the top of its legs, which is offset against its predominantly black body colour. The sexes are alike in coloration, but males can be distinguished by the

◆ RIGHT
The Mexican red-knee is a particularly striking tarantula. Young captive-bred spiderlings of this species are readily available, although it will take several years for them to attain maturity. When adult, their bodies measure about 6 cm (2½ in) – about 2.5 cm (1 in) bigger than the other tarantulas shown here.

◆ LEFT
Tarantulas differ in terms of their temperament, although they are not pets to be handled. The Chilean rose has proved to have a relatively placid disposition.

on account of its attractive pinkish coloration and its relatively docile temperament, which has helped to ensure successful breeding. Males of the species may have slightly larger legs than females when mature. Aim for a relative humidity of about 75 per cent in the terrarium for this tarantula; the temperature should be maintained at around 25°C (77°F).

◆ BELOW
Not all tarantulas live on the ground. The pink-toed is an arboreal species, found in tropical forests of South America. Its housing must be designed accordingly.

presence of their palpal bulbs, which look like miniature boxing gloves on the end of the palps near the mouth. It is a burrowing species and this must be reflected in its accommodation, with a suitable retreat being provided.

CHILEAN ROSE TARANTULA
Originating from further south in the Americas, the Chilean rose (*Grammostola cala*) has become a popular species over recent years,

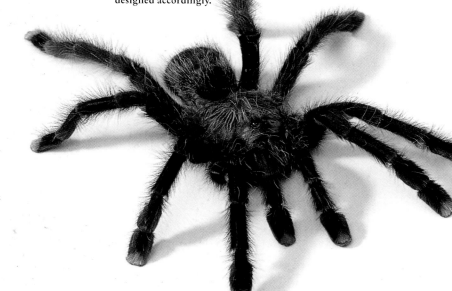

PINK-TOED TARANTULA

The pink-toed tarantula (*Avicularia avicularia*) occurs in the Amazon region of South America, and so it will require a slightly higher temperature and a humidity of about 80 per cent in its quarters. A humid environment is vital to the well-being of these spiders. The pink-toed is also an arboreal species, at home in the treetops rather than burrowing on the ground. A tall, well ventilated enclosure will be needed for these spiders, with branches for climbing purposes. Males are smaller in size than females, and are coloured black overall, apart from the tips of their legs, which are pinkish-white. There is also a yellow-toed tarantula (*Avicularia juruensis*), although this is far less commonly available. It requires similar care.

INDIAN BLACK AND WHITE TARANTULA

There has been increased interest in Asiatic tarantulas over recent years, thanks to their impressive markings. The Indian black and white tarantula (*Poecilotheria regalis*) has become a popular member of the group, in spite of the fact that its sting is more potent than almost any other tarantula. The Indian black and white requires a relative humidity of 75 per cent and a temperature of 25°C (77°F) in its quarters. Breeding these spiders is not especially difficult. Males are smaller, without the females' rounded form.

BABOON SPIDER

These spiders originate from Africa, and have a reputation for being aggressive, rearing up when they feel threatened, and biting if given the opportunity. They can also move very

quickly and it is important not to allow them an opportunity to escape while you are attending to them. As with similar species, the baboon spider has a potent venom, and you should avoid handling it. Always wear gloves when handling is required.

♦ LEFT
Baboon spiders are of African origin, often occurring in arid grassland areas. Provide water at all times, however, as dehydration can be a major insidious killer of pet tarantulas.

♦ BELOW
The Indian black and white tarantula, and related Asiatic species, have become popular over recent years. They do have an unpleasant bite, and will need to be handled with particular care.

Many baboon spiders originate from grassland areas rather than tropical forests, and they do not require high humidity. The substrate can include dried grass, with a water container included. The temperature should be as for other tarantulas.

OTHER INVERTEBRATE SPECIES

SCORPIONS

These close relatives of the tarantula have a painful, if not deadly, sting on their tails, and they need to be handled with extreme care. In fact, these arachnids are best left in their quarters, with special forceps being recommended for moving them safely. Those that are kept as pets are

◆ LEFT
A praying mantis. During courtship, a male is at risk of being decapitated by his larger female partner. Feeding her well beforehand can help to protect him. They reach about 10 cm (4 in) long.

Scorpions often originate from hot, dry areas of the world but the imperial is a rainforest species and must have a warm, humid environment if it is to thrive. The substrate in the imperial's quarters must also be loose, to allow it to burrow. Retreats, provided by cork bark, are also important. A secure ventilated lid over the terrarium is vital for all species, although lighting is not important – scorpions are nocturnal and are most likely to emerge from their hiding places when the light level is low. Scorpions feed on invertebrates.

PRAYING MANTIS

Another predatory invertebrate kept as a pet is the praying mantis (*Mantis* species). There are a number of

species, and it can often be difficult to distinguish between them. Their common name comes from the way in which they rest, with their front legs folded as if in prayer. The legs grab at passing prey at lightening speed, while the mantis remains immobile, relying on its camouflage for disguise. Crickets can be used as a food. Mantids must be housed on their own because of their predatory habits. The female has six segments on the underside of the abdomen, while the male has eight.

GIANT MILLIPEDES

Giant millipedes belong to the family Sphaerotheriidae. These creatures can produce toxic secretions to protect themselves, which they squirt from pores on their bodies, and because of

generally larger members of the group, such as the imperial scorpion (*Pandinus imperator*), which originates from West Africa. Their appearance is impressive because of their large pincers; large pincers are an indication that the sting is less potent than that of scorpions with smaller pincers.

◆ ABOVE
Giant millipedes may look inoffensive, but they do need to be handled with care.

◆ OPPOSITE BOTTOM
Rainbow crabs can be housed in an aquarium with a shallow area of water. Check the salt concentration needed.

◆ LEFT
Giant land snail are among the easiest of all
invertebrates to keep as pets. They will feed
on a wide selection of vegetation and have a
very high rate of reproduction.

this they must be handled with care; it is always preferable to wear gloves when handling them. The tropical millipedes that are popular as pets can grow to over 25 cm (10 in) long. These millipedes are inhabitants of tropical rainforests, and this climate must be reflected in their accommodation. Millipedes feed on vegetable matter.

GIANT LAND SNAIL

Another large species that is widely kept in Europe – but is illegal in the United States and Canada because of fears that it could become established in warmer areas there – is the giant land snail (*Achatina fulica*). This snail is a native of Africa. It can grow to a length of more than 20 cm (8 in), and is easy to cater for, with a heated propagator often being used as accommodation. Assorted vegetable matter will form the basis of the diet for these snails, but they should also be offered cuttlefish bone as an additional source of calcium for their shells. Since they are hermaphrodite, keeping two snails together will invariably result in fertile eggs being laid. The eggs can be found stuck on to the sides of the snails' quarters.

LAND HERMIT CRABS

Various types of crab can be kept as pets, particularly land hermit crabs (*Coenobita clypeatus*), which are found on the sea shoreline rather than in deep water. These crabs need a covered terrarium since they are able to climb well, in spite of the bulk of their shell. Their surroundings must be kept humid with a container of shallow salt water, using sea salt as used in marine aquaria. As they grow, these crabs abandon their shells in search of new ones, leaving them scattered around the floor. Hermit crabs are natural scavengers, and will eat animal rather than vegetable foods; formulated foods are also available. Other crabs may require a more aquatic home, with dilute salt water provided, to mimic their estuarine habitat. The water level should be low to allow them access to dry areas in the tank. A temperature of 25°C (77°F) will be necessary.

HOUSING

Most of the popular invertebrates kept as pets require heated surroundings as they originate from tropical parts of the world. This can be accomplished in various ways, using equipment developed for use in other fields, such as an electric propagator or heat pads under thermostatic control, with the temperature in the vivarium monitored with a thermometer. The shape of the enclosure is a very important feature, and is influenced by the lifestyle of the invertebrate as well as by its size.

The majority of invertebrates are not especially active by nature, often displaying a tendency to remain inert and avoid the attention of predators. In the case of stick insects, which

generally live off the ground, a tall vivarium will be the most appropriate for their needs. While smaller nymphs can be housed in temporary accommodation – such as glass jars with ventilated, screw-top lids – they will need to be transferred to permanent surroundings as they grow larger.

Although not aggressive by nature, stick insects will often nibble at the legs of their companions if their quarters become overcrowded. This can, ultimately, have fatal consequences because stick insects rely heavily on their legs to support themselves as they climb around in the branches. In the case of a young nymph, the loss of a leg will not necessarily be catastrophic as it is likely to grow back at the next moult. A wide selection of acrylic containers, in a range of sizes and

◆ ABOVE
Various lightweight plastic containers can be used both to transport and house a range of herptiles. They are suitable for both aquatic and terrestrial species.

◆ LEFT
Height can be an important consideration in the design of vivaria for terrestrial invertebrates, including some tarantulas. Special sizes can be constructed quite easily.

◆ BELOW
The heat output in a vivarium should always be under thermostatic control. Modern thermostats can be easily adjusted.

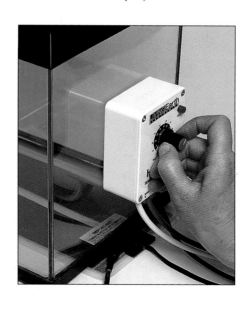

◆ BELOW
Some vivaria can incorporate living plants, making them an attractive focal point in the home. Lighting and ventilation are important for successful plant growth.

shapes, can be used for housing invertebrates. The substrate used will depend very much on the occupant and its particular requirements. A moisture-retentive substrate, such as vermiculite, may be useful for cases where high humidity is required. Nevertheless, the vermiculite needs to be damp but not soaked to the extent that stale water accumulates in the substrate. This is not only likely to be harmful for the occupant but can also result in an unpleasant odour being associated with the vivarium.

Many invertebrates will burrow into the substrate and, for these species, a thick layer of bark may be needed in their enclosure. The decor is also important to provide retreats for terrestrial species. In the case of burrowing tarantulas, a plastic flower pot cut and angled well down in the substrate is recommended; this will be disguised by the substrate above. Tarantula species that are arboreal will also appreciate retreats rather than being left exposed on the bark. Use cork that is curled, so that the spider can retreat round under the curve of the trunk.

Decor to match the creature's natural environment will enhance the appeal of the vivarium as a focal point in the room. A sandy base, made using sand sold for reptile vivaria, is recommended for land hermit crabs. The sand can mimic a beach and, if decorated with small pieces of driftwood and scattered shells, it will create an interesting view.

You will need to be careful when lighting enclosures for invertebrates, however, because many are shy and will not emerge under these conditions.

With a tungsten bulb in particular, there is also a real possibility that the additional heat will not only cause the vivarium temperature to rise, but will also cause the relative humidity to fall back. This can be very harmful to the occupants. If you are using a converted aquarium, the best compromise is to choose a fluorescent tube that simulates natural daylight. This will be out of reach of the occupants in a sealed unit, and it is unlikely to affect the temperature in the vivarium.

FEEDING

Invertebrates vary widely in their feeding habits, with some being vegetarian while others are active predators. In most cases, you will need to provide the food yourself as there are very few prepared foods sold commercially for this group of pets. It is therefore important to make adequate provision in advance, particularly for those, such as stick insects, which are quite specific in their feeding habits. Thankfully, most stick insects will eat bramble readily and this can be collected quite easily, even in urban locations, or else it can be cultivated without difficulty.

PREPARING BRAMBLE
To cultivate bramble at home, simply dig up some wild bramble roots and plant them in a suitable container of

◆ ABOVE
A giant millipede and its food. Provide only a small quantity, which the millipede can eat before the food starts to turn mouldy.

soil, keeping them moist. The shoots will grow rapidly, particularly in the spring, and it can be useful to transfer the container directly into the stick insects' quarters once the shoots are well developed. When the insects have eaten the leaves, the plant can be replaced with another and, especially if pruned back, it will soon sprout again.

◆ LEFT
Crickets taking moisture from the cut surfaces of a carrot. Crickets will often drown in open containers of water.

This method means that it is not necessary to cut fresh bramble every few days, as would otherwise be necessary. This can prove to be difficult during the winter when the leaves often shrivel up and become brown around the edges. If you do provide bramble, place it in a narrow-necked container of water, stuffing the sides with tin foil to prevent the stick insects from falling in and drowning. Similar arrangements work well for leaf insects. Should bramble become impossible to obtain, then privet may make a suitable substitute.

FRUIT AND VEGETABLES
Giant millipedes will prefer to feed on fresh fruit and this can be sprinkled lightly with a herptile vitamin and mineral supplement to improve its nutritional value. Chop fruit into small chunks and provide it in an

◆ OPPOSITE TOP
A commercially produced vivarium for stick insects. The bramble serves not just as a food source, but it also allows them to climb. Note the ventilation panel in the roof.

◆ ABOVE
During the winter months, it can be hard to find bramble with fresh leaves. Trim back brown edges to make the green areas more accessible.

◆ ABOVE
Prolong the life of bramble shoots by keeping them in a jar of water. Cover the neck of the jar, to prevent the stick insects from drowning.

live for long in a tarantula's enclosure because they require different conditions. You will quickly learn how much food is needed but start off cautiously and feed according to the invertebrate's appetite.

Since crickets have to be purchased in quantity, it will be useful to have a separate set-up where they can be maintained until required. A typical acrylic set-up, with grass and flour as food, should be provided. It needs to be kept reasonably warm, with a shallow container of water, lined with a sponge to prevent the crickets from drowning, being included.

Mealworms are even easier to look after and will require only a container lined with chicken meal, with a few slices of apple on the surface of the food to provide them with moisture. Keep the worms cool to delay their change into pupae and then mealworm beetles. Once they do become mealworm beetles, they are likely to lay eggs, and these will hatch into another generation of mealworms.

easily accessible container, wedged firmly into the substrate. Be prepared to change the contents every day, before the fruit can turn mouldy.

Giant land snails are far less demanding in terms of their feeding requirements, as they will eat almost anything that is of vegetable origin. Peelings and discarded leaves from household vegetables can therefore be offered to them, with vegetables being

preferable for this purpose. Cabbage is often a favourite. You can even grow suitable foods, such as bean sprouts, at home to guarantee a fresh supply of food every day.

In the case of those invertebrates that prey on others, then crickets or mealworms should be offered, depending on their size. It is important not to provide too much food – for example, crickets will not

PREPARING BRAMBLES IN A BOTTLE

1 Start with a narrow-necked bottle, which will help to keep the stems in a relatively upright position. This will ensure the stems always remain below the water line.

2 Foil is ideal for wrapping around the stems and using to form a cover over the top of the bottle. Beware of catching your fingers on any sharp thorns at this stage.

3 This bramble is now ready to be transferred into the stick insects' quarters. The foil helps to hold the stems in place and prevents the insects from falling into the bottle.

GENERAL CARE

Tarantulas can inflict a painful bite, possessing fangs on the underside of the body which they use to overcome their prey. These spiders need to be handled very carefully.

Invertebrates are pets to be admired from a distance rather than handled regularly, not just because of the toxins produced by some groups, but also because their bodies are frail, especially in the case of young individuals. It is often much cheaper to start out with young individuals, particularly in the case of tarantulas, where spiderlings sell for a fraction of the price of a mature individual.

In the case of some invertebrates, such as stick insects, you may even purchase eggs that you can hatch at home. In terms of handling hatchlings though, you should not attempt to pick them up directly as you can damage them very easily. Instead, use a clean paintbrush, as used for picture painting. It is usually quite easy to persuade a young stick insect nymph to step on to the end of the brush so that you can move it elsewhere.

◆ BELOW
A Mexican blonde tarantula. In spite of their large size, all tarantulas are quite fragile creatures and they can be easily killed as the result of a fall.

With stick insects, it will help to line the floor of their quarters with newspaper, with the vessel or pot containing bramble standing on top. You can then change the floor covering very easily, once or twice a week. Relying on newspaper rather than a loose substrate also means that as the stick insects mature, you will be able to spot their eggs more easily.

The accommodation for tarantulas and scorpions needs very little attention. In contrast, giant land snails need to have their quarters cleaned out frequently, and their food replaced each day. Much depends on the size and the number of individuals being housed.

The environment outside the invertebrates' quarters can also be hazardous for them, even though they are not roaming here. You must take particular care not to use any sprays that could be harmful if particles of chemicals are wafted on air currents into their quarters. Fly sprays are one of the more obvious hazards, but other preparations, such as flea treatments for dogs and cats, can be equally dangerous. Take care to treat other pets elsewhere.

The moulting period can be difficult for invertebrates, especially if they have not been kept in ideal surroundings. In the case of stick insects, for example, they need to be able to hang off branches to their full length so they can split their skin easily and wiggle free. This is why a

◆ BELOW
An East African tree millipede. This is an arboreal species and its quarters need to be designed accordingly, with suitable branches being provided for climbing.

◆ BELOW
A pill millipede. As is obvious from this individual, millipedes do not have a thousand legs, as their name suggests. They can be kept quite easily.

tall container is especially important for stick insects, particularly as they grow bigger.

Increasing the relative humidity in the vivarium as the time for moulting approaches can be helpful. For tarantulas, the most obvious sign of an imminent moult is that the spider loses its appetite, its body colour becomes darker and it may spin a web, called a moulting cradle. The spider

will then lie on its back in its web, and the skin will start to split, enabling the tarantula to free itself from its previous skin. At this stage, the new skin will be soft but it soon hardens, and the spider will regain its appetite. Young tarantulas are likely to moult every three months or so, up to the age of about two years old, after which time they can be expected to moult about twice a year.

◆ BELOW LEFT
A large tropical millipede. Beware of holding millipedes in your hands because they may produce toxic skin secretions. These are highly secretive creatures by nature.

◆ BELOW RIGHT
An emperor scorpion. This species relies more on its powerful claws rather than its venom to defend itself. Extreme care is needed when handling any type of scorpion.

◆ BELOW
A young pink-toed tarantula. Invertebrates,
including tarantulas, will usually produce large
numbers of offspring, and you will need
adequate space for rearing them.

BREEDING

While it is highly unlikely that invertebrates such as crabs will breed successfully in the vivarium, the prolific nature of other species, such as stick insects and tarantulas, means that, potentially, you could be faced with hundreds of offspring. In the case of the Indian stick insect, it is impossible to avoid having eggs laid, even if you have just one individual. This is because of a remarkable phenomenon known as parthenogenesis. Females lay eggs that are effectively clones of themselves, without the need to mate. Some other stick insects also display this feature although, generally, eggs produced as a result of mating have a higher hatchability rate, and the nymphs will hatch more quickly from the eggs.

Stick insect eggs are usually scattered randomly around their quarters and resemble seeds in

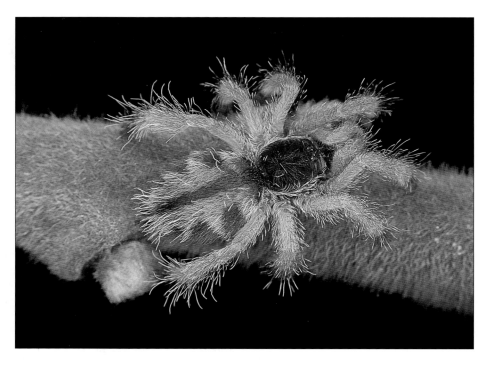

◆ BELOW
Young spiderlings bear a strong resemblance
to adults, as shown by this four-month-old
tarantula. The young will often have a more
feathery appearance than their elders.

appearance. The eggs can be easily collected if newspaper is used to line the floor of their quarters because, unlike the droppings, the eggs will roll off the paper into a container such as a clean margarine tub. Attach a plastic bag with some air holes punched into it at the top, holding it in place with an elastic band. Keep the eggs out of direct sunlight and away from a radiator while they complete their development. It can take anything from a few weeks to a year or more for the eggs to hatch. There is no set period, and the eggs will often hatch over a long period of time. The young nymphs are miniature adults and, as they hatch, they should be transferred carefully to accommodation where bramble is readily accessible to them.

Giant land snails also breed readily, although these do need to mate. Since they have both male and female sex organs in their bodies, keeping two snails together will invariably result in

◆ BELOW
Scorpions display a remarkable degree of
parental care, with the female carrying her
offspring around with her on her back for
the first week or so of their lives.

eggs, which are laid in a jelly-like substance stuck around their quarters. The young snails are tiny replicas of the adults when they hatch, and their individual shell markings will soon become apparent.

Breeding tarantulas is a more involved process but, potentially, it can result in a large number of offspring. It is usual to introduce the male briefly to the female's quarters for mating purposes. This needs to be supervised as it could develop into an aggressive encounter. She may not lay for several months – if she moults beforehand, then she will no longer be fertile, as the seminal pouch where the

sperm is stored will be lost as well. If mating is successful, the female produces her eggs in an egg sac of silk, and she will guard this structure containing her young ferociously.

The young hatch after an interval that is likely to extend over nine weeks or more. They are often whitish but recognizable as miniature spiders at this stage. The female must then be transferred elsewhere as she is likely to prey on her young. Tiny livefood, such as wingless fruit flies and microcrickets, can be used for rearing the young spiders, which will also need to be separated from each other to prevent cannibalism.

The male praying mantis suffers a grisly fate when he mates – his partner is likely to rip off his head – but this does not stop the process. The female produces an egg sac, and this may contain as many as 500 young. These need to be reared in a similar way to young tarantulas.

Female scorpions are dedicated parents, with the female giving birth to live offspring two to eight months after mating. These are white and helpless when born, and will be carried on their mother's back for the first week of life. Once they are moving around on their own, separate them from their mother.

HEALTH CARE

Veterinary knowledge of herptiles and invertebrates has grown significantly over recent years, thanks in part to the increasing popularity of this group of creatures as pets. Those illnesses which are most often seen can frequently be linked to nutritional deficiencies or environmental shortcomings, such as inadequate lighting or incorrect relative humidity in the creature's quarters. The good news is that these factors are easily corrected.

REPTILE HEALTH

It is not always easy to determine when a reptile is sick, but perhaps the most significant indicator is a loss of appetite.This, in turn, could be a reflection of the creature being kept at a sub-optimal temperature, or it might be a sign of bullying by a companion, as often happens with male lizards. Weight loss and lack of interest in its surroundings are other signs that all is not well with a reptile.

Diagnosis of the exact problem will usually require the assistance of an experienced herptile vet and, probably, some laboratory tests as well. In many cases, ill-health in reptiles has a parasitic involvement, with unicellular protozoa in the digestive tract often being responsible for severe, if not fatal, illnesses, particularly in snakes and tortoises. Digestive problems can usually be detected from faecal samples, with appropriate treatment then given. This sampling should also detect any sign of *Salmonella*, which can be acquired by human beings from reptiles.

COMMON DISORDERS
A reptile's loss of appetite may result from mouth rot, which is especially common in tortoises that have recently emerged from hibernation, and also in snakes. In extreme cases, it may be necessary to anaesthetize the reptile, so that the mouth can be cleaned and the treatment given.

✦ ABOVE
Dullness, depression and loss of appetite are common indicators of illness with these species.

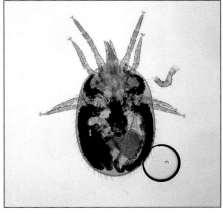

✦ ABOVE
Snake mites can easily become established in a vivarium, resulting in progressive debility.

External parasites can also present a problem, with the small size of snake mites making them very difficult to spot. Worse still is the fact that these parasites can survive for months within a vivarium, and so a number of snakes can be infected in sequence. The risk of infection is often far greater in pet stores selling these reptiles than in home vivaria. Provided that the cause is recognized, then a treatment to kill the parasites safely can be obtained from your vet.

Ticks are much larger than snake mites, and they swell up as they penetrate beneath the scales and feed

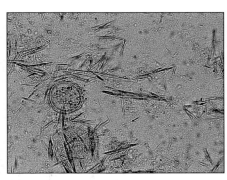

✦ ABOVE
Round unicellular microbes, called protozoa, are parasites commonly found in the intestinal tract of reptiles. They can cause illness or death.

✦ ABOVE
Mouth rot often develops in reptiles which are already debilitated. Urgent treatment is needed to make the individual feed normally.

on the snake's body fluid. Ticks can spread microscopic blood parasites when feeding in this way. As a result of their complex life-cycles, ticks cannot be spread directly from snake to snake, and they are most likely to be encountered in recently imported individuals. Treatment is straight-forward. The ticks can be persuaded to drop off by smothering them with petroleum jelly, which will block their breathing hole. Ticks can also sometimes be a problem in tortoises, congregating in the soft tissue beneath the shell.

Fungal infections are most likely to afflict terrapins. These infections develop most commonly at the site of wounds, but they can usually be treated effectively using veterinary medication. Nutritional problems also sometimes afflict terrapins, and these will cause swollen eyes and soft shells. Making changes to the diet – boosting the Vitamin A level in the case of eye inflammation, and checking on the Vitamin D3 and calcium : phosphorus ratio – will be necessary to ensure a healthy shell. On occasion, a tortoise may fall and injure its shell. This may bleed, and there can be a deeper fracture within. Repair of this type of injury is possible, but healing will be slow and the shell is likely to show signs of permanent damage.

Snakes and lizards may suffer from moulting problems, especially when newly rehomed. In the case of snakes, the spectacles that cover the eyes may be retained. If this occurs, it is important to seek specialist help from a herptile vet, with careful bathing and the use of forceps being required to remove the spectacles.

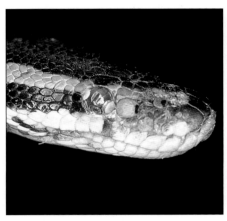

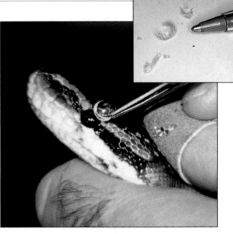

◆ A B O V E
A snake tick anchored to the head. These parasites swell in size as they feed and there is a danger they will transmit microbes to the snake.

◆ A B O V E   A N D   I N S E T
A retained spectacle – the transparent covering over the eyes – being removed. This problem occurs when the snake hasn't moulted properly.

TREATING A TORTOISE SHELL INJURY

1 This is a case of shell rot in a Hermann's tortoise. The diseased tissue is being removed while the tortoise is anaesthetized, and then the repair work can begin.

2 The areas which have had to be removed are now filled in with calcium hydroxide. A similar technique can also be used in cases of shell damage on tortoises, turtles and terrapins.

3 *(right)* In the final stage of the shell repair process, the treated area is then covered with a synthetic hoof material, which will provide a tough outer casing.

◆ BELOW
Poor environmental conditions will predispose amphibians to illness. They must be kept in damp surroundings, with the humidity being maintained by regularly spraying with water.

AMPHIBIAN HEALTH

Amphibians are very easy to maintain in good health, and when cases of illness do occur their cause can often be traced back to something that is wrong in the way they are being kept.

FUNGAL INFECTIONS

Since they spend much of their time close to or in water, they are very vulnerable to fungal infections, particularly following an injury to their bodies. This may not even be evident in some cases – rough handling, which strips away the protective covering of mucus on their bodies, can be sufficient to allow fungal microbes to invade.

The signs of a fungal infection of this type will be most apparent when the amphibian is in the water. Depending on the type of fungus, it may create a halo effect at the site of infection, or a more obvious cotton wool- (cotton ball-) type growth. Fungi spread rapidly, especially in the case of an amphibian that is already weakened, and so rapid treatment will be necessary.

A specific anti-fungal cream, available from your vet, which can be applied to the affected area, will

◆ BELOW
Poor environmental conditions will predispose amphibians to illness. They must be kept in damp surroundings, with the humidity being maintained by regularly spraying with water.

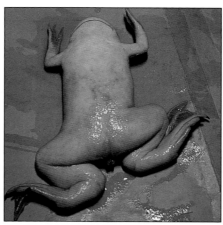

◆ ABOVE
Red leg is a bacterial illness especially common in frogs. It usually creates a reddish, inflamed appearance, and is worse under the hind leg.

be useful for treatment. It will also help if the amphibian is temporarily transferred to a slightly drier environment, although this will not be possible with axolotls, which cannot be transferred out of water.

In such cases, one of the fungal treatments sold for tropical fish, often based on dyes such as methylene blue, may be helpful if added to the water. Simply changing the water in the aquarium can be beneficial as this will reduce the number of fungal organisms present in the water, and will improve your pet's chances of making a recovery.

◆ ABOVE
Jagged rocks and dirty conditions in an aquatic vivarium can damage the sensitive skin of frogs, causing soreness, which can become infected.

◆ ABOVE
An amphibian may have to be confined to a small bath if the treatment involves it being immersed in a medicated solution.

◆ ABOVE
The most common problems associated with amphibians such as this alpine newt are caused by unsuitable housing conditions.

Breeders may use this approach if they find that amphibian eggs are being killed by a fungus before they can hatch, but this is unusual. Eggs are normally protected by a natural immunity and it is only those that are infertile that will be affected by fungi. Even so, once the young tadpoles have hatched it is a good idea to transfer them to a tank away from the other eggs, to lessen the risk of them developing fungus. Do not place them in newly dechlorinated water, as this will not contain the microscopic food particles present in water that has been allowed to stand and is showing signs of algal growth.

When catching or moving sick amphibians, remember that microbes will be transferred on the net, so that dipping this in a solution of aquarium disinfectant is recommended. Always clean out and disinfect the tank, even if any other amphibians present are unaffected by signs of illness.

RED LEG

It is not just fungal infections which can strike when an amphibian's sensitive skin is damaged. Frogs are especially susceptible to a condition described as "red leg", owing to the signs of reddish inflammation which become evident on their hind limbs. This is usually caused by insanitary surroundings, and a complete water change will serve to protect any other frogs that are sharing the same accommodation. The substrate should also be replaced entirely. The treatment of red leg is difficult, but sometimes the use of antibiotics in a bath for affected individuals can lead to a recovery.

◆ LEFT
Injuries caused by sharp branches or rocks in your pet amphibian's set-up will often cause skin infections, so be sure the furnishings in the vivarium are safe.

INVERTEBRATE HEALTH

It may seem that there is little that can be done to assist a sick invertebrate but it is possible to correct even life-threatening problems in some species, especially in the case of tarantulas. This is significant because, although most people think that invertebrates only have a very short lifespan, this is not always the case – female tarantulas can live for more than half a century if housed in suitable conditions.

TARANTULAS

The main enemy of tarantulas in the home is dessication. Although a number of these spiders come from arid areas of the world, dew forms at the entrance to their burrows each day, raising the humidity level and providing the spiders with drops of water. It is essential to provide a shallow container of water in the terrarium of all tarantulas.

The biggest threat of injury to tarantulas is incorrect handling.

TREATING DEHYDRATION IN A TARANTULA

1 Dehydration is a major killer of tarantulas. This individual is in poor condition, being shrivelled and emaciated and showing signs of hair loss on the abdomen.

In the worst cases, this can result in the spider falling to the floor and rupturing its body, which in turn can lead to the seepage of haemolymph, which is the spider's blood. This is a life-threatening situation.

Applying a plaster is not a viable option because of the hairs on the spider's body, but some success at stemming the flow of haemolymph

2 In serious cases like this, your vet may be forced to try to rehydrate the spider by administering fluid directly into its body, using a syringe and needle, as shown here.

has been claimed from sprinkling the wound with flour and applying rice paper over the damaged area. More permanent sealing of the wound can be achieved with dental cement. Spiders that have been injured in this way may then encounter more difficulty at their subsequent moult, however, and further assistance from the vet may be required at this stage.

◆   A B O V E
Healthy tarantulas have a good covering of hairs on their bodies. Any bald patches, notably over the abdomen, may be an indication of rough handling or old age.

◆   L E F T
Stick insects may sometimes lose a leg as the result of an injury or overcrowding, with a companion nibbling off another's leg. The leg should regrow at the next moult, however.

It can be difficult to provide treatment to some invertebrates, since so little is known about their illnesses. In general, however, millipedes prove to be quite healthy creatures.

Tarantulas sometimes lose their limbs, like stick insects. This is far less serious as the joints of the limbs seal off effectively, rather like when a lizard sheds part of its tail. The limb may regrow at the next moult. The same applies if a tarantula has a bald area on its abdomen, and new hairs will regrow.

On occasion, particularly with recently acquired tarantulas, the spider may encounter difficulties in shedding its skin, and it will need help if it is to survive. The best way to resolve the situation is to prepare a solution of glycerine, made using 15 ml (1 tbsp) added to 150 ml (⅔ cup) of water at room temperature. Then, with a dropper, drizzle this mixture over the spider; take care to avoid the book lungs – the hairless patches on the underside of its body, which enable it to breathe.

The glycerine will soften the spider's exoskeleton so that it should have freed itself several hours later. You need to be extremely careful about trying to interfere directly in these circumstances. Do not prise the old body casing off, because you could very easily damage the new skin beneath, causing a fatal loss of haemolymph. Even when the spider has moulted, do not handle it for two weeks, to avoid the risk of injury.

LAND HERMIT CRABS

These can become dessicated easily, and if you have one that appears to be less active than normal, it could be that it is dehydrated. If this is the case, it will benefit from a series of salt water baths. Normally, a healthy individual will withdraw rapidly into its shell if touched, and you should take note if it does not.

◆ LEFT
Body posture can help to indicate an invertebrate's state of health, as in the case of this giant millipede. Curling up in this way suggests that it is quite healthy.

◆ BELOW
A plump body, bright coloration and a full complement of legs are signs of health in tarantulas. Yet these spiders may appear off-colour just prior to the moult.

FISH

Fish are found in a wide range of aquatic environments, having adapted successfully to live in both fresh and saltwater. They survive in these habitats by very different mechanisms, since in fresh water, there is a risk that vital body salts will pass out of the body into the less concentrated water around them.

As a result, freshwater fish produce a large volume of urine, with salts being absorbed from the kidneys to minimize losses from their bodies. Marine species, however, face the problem of losing fresh water from their bodies into their environment. Because of this their urine is very concentrated, to retain fresh water in their bodies.

All fish generally require a stable environment if they are to thrive, although some species are more resourceful than others. Guppies, for example, are far more adaptable in their needs than fish that live on tropical reefs. This in turn is reflected in their care in aquarium surroundings, with guppies being among the easiest tropical freshwater fish to keep and breed here.

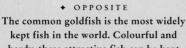

◆ OPPOSITE
The common goldfish is the most widely kept fish in the world. Colourful and hardy, these attractive fish can be kept in the home in an aquarium or outdoors in a pond.

◆ LEFT
A tuxedo rainbow delta guppy – just one of the many highly distinctive and colourful ornamental strains of this free-breeding tropical fish which exist in aquaria today.

GOLDFISH AND OTHER COLDWATER FISH

GOLDFISH

The goldfish, in its many forms, is the most commonly kept fish in the world, partly because of its versatility, as it can be housed in both garden ponds and indoor aquaria. All goldfish are descended from dull green carp living in southern China. The earliest records of these fish acquiring golden coloration date back to about AD 400, after which the local people started to breed them selectively. Goldfish were introduced to Europe in the 1600s and they now exist in a range of varieties.

It is not just their coloration which has changed, but also their body shape, as well as the shape of the fins in some cases. The common goldfish is a sleek, orange fish, frequently growing to 20 cm (8 in) or more, especially in pond surroundings. These are hardy fish, as are the shubunkins which have a distinctive mottled blue coloration, broken with black and gold areas. The London shubunkin has a more angular tail fin than its Bristol counterpart. The comet is another sleek variety, which is often red and white in colour, with a pointed tail. Its active nature means that it is more suited to life in a pond than an aquarium, particularly in the case of larger individuals.

✦ ABOVE
Long-bodied and sleek, the comet is an active goldfish originating from the United States.

✦ ABOVE
A red and white lionhead, so-called because of the fleshy swellings on its head.

✦ ABOVE
A Bristol shubunkin. These attractive fish can be exhibited, as can most other goldfish varieties.

✦ ABOVE
A chocolate oranda. These goldfish have a hood on their head and a recognizable dorsal fin.

✦ ABOVE
A butterfly moor. Matt-black coloration serves to distinguish these goldfish.

◆ BELOW
A golden orfe. These fish can ultimately grow up to 50 cm (20 in) in large ponds. Young fish often have dark markings on their heads, which disappear with age.

◆ BELOW
Easy to keep in a spacious pond, ornamental carp are very popular fish. This individual has what are known as mirror scales on the sides of its body, which look reflective.

◆ BELOW
Koi come in many different recognized varieties, and are frequently described under their traditional Japanese names. This is an impressive silver ogon.

The so-called fancy goldfish are far more suitable as aquarium pets since they are not especially hardy. They can be recognized by their more corpulent body shape. It is important when buying these goldfish to check that they are swimming properly and are not lying at an abnormal angle in the water, which is indicative of a swim bladder disorder. Examples of fancy goldfish include the moor, which is instantly recognizable by its black coloration. Pearlscales, too, have become more popular over recent years, with raised scales resembling tiny pearls on their bodies.

Changes to the shape of the tail fin have given rise to varieties such as the fantail, while the lionhead actually has no tail on its back. This feature serves to distinguish it from the oranda, with both these types of fancy goldfish having raspberry-like swellings on their heads, called hoods, which develop to their maximum extent over the course of several years. These two fish are bred in a variety of colours, including blue and chocolate, while red-capped orandas with white bodies are also very popular.

Other commonly available coldwater fish, such as the golden orfe (*Leuciscus idus*), are generally more suited to outdoor life in ponds. These are active fish that need well aerated

water and thrive best in groups. Blue as well as silver variants are also sometimes available.

KOI
These ornamental carp can grow up to 90 cm (3 ft) in suitable surroundings. They have been kept for centuries as a food source, initially in China and then in Japan, where the first colour sports occurred in the 19th century. Today, they are no longer eaten.

The term "koi" is an abbreviation of their full name "nishikigoi", which literally means "colourful carp". Koi varieties are described under their native Japanese name, with some varieties such as the ogon being a single colour – golden in this case –

whereas others, like the kohaku, are patterned, with this variety being reddish-orange and white.

Although prize-winning koi can sell for huge amounts of money, koi fish at much more reasonable prices are widely available. These will grow very rapidly and they need to be kept in large ponds, equipped with a filtration system to deal with their corresponding high output of waste. They are quite hardy, provided they can overwinter in a deep area of a pond where the water will not freeze.

◆ BELOW
The barbels, which distinguish koi from goldfish, can be seen hanging down from the sides of the mouth of this gold ghost koi. Barbels are used for finding food.

CARE IN AN AQUARIUM

Setting up a suitable aquarium for a goldfish is very straightforward, but it is still a good idea to include a filtration system of some kind, as this will help to maintain the water quality. Although you can use a power filter, you may prefer to use an undergravel filter, which will be less obtrusive. The decision of what type of filter to use will be influenced to some extent by the choice of tank, since in order to be effective, this type of filter needs to cover the entire floor area. Most undergravel filters are, therefore, rectangular in shape, but they can be cut down in size, if necessary, to fit a particular area.

It is important to choose a large aquarium at the outset, so that there will be space for the goldfish as they grow. This will be particularly important if you intend to keep more than one fish together. Do not be tempted by circular designs, modelled on the old-style goldfish bowl, because, although these may be satisfactory for a single small individual, they are soon likely to be outgrown.

If you obtain a glass tank, do not forget to stand this on a level surface, on a sheet of polystyrene, to eliminate any unevenness in the surface which could put pressure on the glass and cause the tank to spring a leak. Lay the filter plate in place and then prepare the gravel. This should be reasonably coarse, with a particle size of about 5 mm (¼ in), as it is between the pieces of gravel that the beneficial bacteria which break down the goldfish's waste will develop. You can use ordinary gravel, but there are a number of more striking alternatives now available, although these need to be chosen carefully. White gravel will enhance the appearance of most goldfish, even the moor, but avoid blue gravel as this effectively drains the colour from these fish.

Allow on average about 1 kg per 4.5 litres (2¼ lb per imperial gallon), as you need to build up a covering of gravel to a depth of approximately 7.5 cm (3 in) above the undergravel filter. Wash the gravel thoroughly in batches, using a colander, since it will inevitably be dirty even if it is prewashed. Otherwise, if tipped into the tank in this state, an unsightly scum, which will be hard to eliminate, will form on the water once the tank is filled. You may want to include some decorations but, generally, try to leave an uncluttered area where the fish can swim. In terms of planting, you can include some sprigs of Canadian pondweed (*Elodea canadensis*), the ends of which simply need to be weighed down in the gravel, although there is a chance these may be dug up by the fish.

A calibrated watercan will be useful for filling the aquarium as you will need to add a water conditioner, which will neutralize chlorine-based chemicals present in tapwater that are toxic to fish. These products also help the fish to settle in their new environment, protecting the delicate covering over their gills.

The addition of a biologically active product, containing beneficial bacteria, to seed the filter bed is also recommended. The other piece of equipment which will be required is an air pump of a suitable size for the aquarium. This sits outside the tank and needs to be set up so that water cannot be inadvertently sucked into it once it is operating.

Special goldfish food should be offered to the fish, once they are settled in their quarters. Feed small quantities about three times a day to avoid polluting the tank. On average, about a quarter of the volume of water in the aquarium should be changed every week or so, certainly for the first two months until the undergravel filter is fully established. After this, the interval between water changes can be shifted to once per fortnight.

ASSEMBLING AN AQUARIUM

1 The undergravel filter needs to be fitted first, lying directly on the bottom of the tank, and covering the entire area here. The air uplift, attaching to the filter plate, is on the left.

2 Positioning the rockwork is important not just so that it looks attractive, but also so that it is safe and will not topple over. Some fish will spawn on rocks such as slate.

3 The gravel must be thoroughly washed before being added to the tank, as dirty gravel will cause a scum to form on the surface of the water once the water is added.

4 Bogwood is a feature of some aquaria, especially those containing fish from the Amazon region. It serves to provide hiding places, and these are favoured by catfish in particular.

5 The air feed runs to the air pump. Be sure to fit a non-return valve near the pump outlet, to prevent any risk of water running back into the pump along this tubing.

6 Once the basics are in place, the next stage is to add water. Using a bowl, as shown, will ensure that the gravel is not disturbed when you pour in the water.

7 It is easier to put the plants in place once the tank is filled, but do not connect and switch on the heaterstat while your hands are in the water. This could be dangerous.

8 You can buy collections of plants recommended for aquaria of specific sizes. Always aim to include the smaller plants at the front, with larger ones at the back.

9 Fitting a splash shield reduces the risk of water coming into contact with the electrics, or causing corrosion. It also helps to prevent evaporation of water.

CARE IN A POND

Setting up an outdoor pond, especially for koi, is likely to be a costly and time-consuming exercise. Even so, the availability of new materials and particularly butyl liners, with a life expectancy of perhaps 50 years or more, means that this task is now considerably easier, and the results more durable than in the past. The major advantage of creating a liner pond is that you can make this to a suitable size for the fish, whereas many of the pre-formed ponds on the market are simply too small, and not deep enough for overwintering fish, where a minimum depth of approximately 1.2 m (4 ft) should be the aim.

If you have a young family, however, great thought needs to be given to the design of the pond: toddlers can drown in just a few inches of water. It may well be better to construct a raised pond, built above ground level, which young children will not be able to fall into without climbing up on top of the structure first. As an additional precaution you can cover the top with a removable mesh-clad framework.

When siting the pond, it is obviously pleasant if it can be easily seen from inside your home, but it must not be overhung by trees, as the leaves are likely to pollute the water when they fall. Tree roots can also potentially damage the liner, even to the extent of causing a leak by perforating it. This can be a problem with some aquatic plants too, which is why those on the floor of the pond are best grown in containers.

When it comes to working out the amount of liner required, there is a very simple formula for this purpose. You need to take twice the maximum depth figure and add this to both the width and length figures, to give you the dimensions needed for the liner. You will also need an underlay to place in the hole under the liner, having removed any protruding sharp stones or roots from this area first. It also helps to bed moulded

Pond filtration system

Goldfish flakes

Fish pellets

Frozen pond food

ponds down on an underlay of some sort, as they should not move at all. Always check, using a spirit level and a plank of wood, that the shell is level in the ground before starting to fill it with water.

Allow the pond at least a week or two to settle down before adding any fish. This will also allow plants an opportunity to start growing if you construct the pond in the spring. Koi are often destructive towards vegetation, and so only a few waterlilies are usually recommended for their ponds, particularly if the fish are quite large. These fish are usually kept in clear water, and a pond filter, of the appropriate turnover relative to the volume of the pond, will be essential for them.

In the case of goldfish, however, oxygenators such as Canadian pondweed (*Elodea canadensis*) can be included in weighted bundles, along with some marginals which can add colour and interest in the shallower area around the side of the pond. If you want to add a fountain, this will benefit the fish by improving the oxygenation of the water, but keep it away from waterlilies, which will grow better in a part of the pond where the water is calm and still rather than splashing.

The appetites of pond fish can be directly related to the temperature of the water. As this falls with the approach of winter, so a change to an easily digested, low temperature food is recommended. This can be used in the spring as the fish start to eat again after their winter fast. Floating pellets are a good choice, because this will attract the fish up to the surface for their food, and koi in particular can be tamed to feed from the hand.

◆ ABOVE LEFT
Plants are not only decorative in a pond, but can also be beneficial to the fish, providing cover as here or spawning localities. Not all waterlilies are hardy.

◆ ABOVE RIGHT
A group of koi being fed by hand. A fish's appetite varies through the year in temperate areas, and special easily digested foods are recommended when the weather turns colder.

◆ BELOW
An outdoor pond offers tremendous scope from a decorative standpoint, depending on the size of your garden.

BREEDING COLDWATER FISH

It can be very difficult to sex these fish easily, particularly when they are small and also when they are out of breeding condition. Mature male goldfish can be distinguished by the tiny white pimples which develop on their gill plates behind the eyes, extending along the adjacent pectoral fins on each side of the body. These should not be confused with the parasitic disease, known as white spot, which covers the entire body. As the time for spawning approaches, so the males will start to chase females relentlessly, which in turn will have become swollen with their spawn.

Mating is likely to occur during the morning, once the early rays of the sun have started to warm the pond water. The eggs will be scattered around the pond, falling down into the weed. This can be very important, because the pond growth helps to conceal the eggs from the fish, which are otherwise likely to eat them, as well as providing protection for the tiny fry when they first hatch. This

◆ LEFT
Breeders choose the so-called "brood stock" of particular varieties of goldfish with care, to ensure the best examples are paired together, rather than allowing them to breed at random. This increases the chances of producing quality offspring.

◆ BELOW LEFT
Keeping goldfish well fed will encourage breeding activity. Females often spawn several times during the late spring, extending through the summer months.

can take a week or so, depending on the temperature of the water. Although hundreds of eggs may be produced at a single spawning, only a very small number of young fish are likely to survive in the pond.

If you want to rear a larger number of fish successfully, then you will need to transfer them to an aquarium filled with pond water. This is important because it contains micronutrients, called infusoria, which the young fry will eat as their first food. There are also commercial substitutes available, after which the small fish can be introduced to powdered flake food as they grow larger. Immediately after

◆ RIGHT
Male goldfish in spawning condition can be
distinguished by the appearance of white spots,
which are evident on the gills and along the
edges of the pectoral fins.

hatching, however, they digest the
remains of the yolk sacs attached to
the undersides of their bodies before
they become free-swimming.

Young goldfish tend to be greenish-
bronze at first, resembling their wild
ancestors in colour; it is only later that
they acquire their distinctive golden
hue. This change may not occur until
the fish are over a year old, and a few
individuals may never actually alter in
colour during their lifespan, which can
be 20 years or more.

Koi are difficult to sex visually until
they grow to about 23 cm (9 in) long,
by which stage the ovaries of the
female fish give their bodies a more
rounded appearance. Again, rising
water temperature in the spring serves
as an important breeding trigger.
Rather than allowing the eggs to be
scattered so they fall to the bottom of
the pond – where they will be hard to
collect and are likely to end up in the
filtration system – special spawning
mops, made from nylon, are dropped
into the pond at this stage, with the
eggs sticking to them.

These mops are then removed
elsewhere, with the young koi
swimming freely about 10 days later.
The young koi can be reared in aquaria
at first, but groups must be divided
up to prevent overcrowding as the fish
grow bigger. Their potential lifespan
is even longer than that of goldfish;
koi will frequently live for 80 years
or more. When it comes to breeding
those koi where bodily markings are
significant, there is no guarantee that
even a top-quality pair of fish will
produce a high percentage of similar
offspring. This is what helps to sustain
the high prices paid for the best
examples of these fish.

◆ ABOVE
A shubunkin male
driving the female.
She will release her
eggs for the male
to fertilize. It is an
exhausting process
for both fish.

◆ LEFT
These shubunkin fry
hatched 48 hours after
spawning. They absorb
the remains of their
yolk sacs before
swimming free.

TROPICAL FRESHWATER FISH

Many people like to keep a community aquarium, housing a number of different tropical fish together, but it is vital to check at the outset that the fish which you are thinking of buying will be compatible with each other. Some shops operate the so-called "traffic light system", which helps to identify fish that are likely to be aggressive, indicating these on tanks with a red dot. Those which are recommended for community set-ups are indicated in green, and those which may have special requirements are shown in orange.

It is not just a matter of whether the fish will agree well with each other which needs to be considered, though, because different species may have widely differing needs in terms of water chemistry, making them incompatible on this basis. Tetras, for example, living in rivers swollen by rain, require soft, acidic waters, whereas cichlids, from the Rift Valley region in eastern Africa, need hard water to mimic that of their native surroundings. The growth rate of the fish may also be significant in

✦ ABOVE
Tiger barbs should be kept in shoals. They can be disruptive, and must not be mixed with long-finned companions, as they may nip their fins.

✦ BELOW LEFT
The panther catfish is a member of the *Pimelodus* group. These catfish are active and predatory by nature, so should not be mixed with smaller companions.

✦ BELOW RIGHT
The knife-edge livebearer produces live offspring rather than eggs. These fish will thrive in a community tank.

determining their compatibility. It is sometimes suggested not to house angelfish (*Pterophyllum* species) in a set-up alongside barbs and similar fish. The trailing fins of the angelfish are likely to be nipped by the barbs while they are small, but the rapid growth of angelfish means that they may turn on their tormentors in due course. It is also worth bearing in mind that fish do differ in temperament, to the

extent that some individuals may prove to be more aggressive than others of the same species.

There is also the possibility that, although they may be quite amenable towards different species, they will not agree well with others of their own kind. This applies in the case of the red-tailed black shark (*Labeo bicolor*), which is a very popular occupant of the community tank, provided that only one such fish is kept in the group. Outbreaks of aggression are most likely to develop not when you first set up the aquarium but subsequently, once the fish are

established and their territorial instincts are coming into play. Any overcrowding at this stage will worsen the situation, and it is not just the number of the fish which is significant in this respect but the area of the tank which they inhabit.

In a community tank, aim to include a selection of fish which live close to the surface and on the bottom, as well as mid-level occupants. This will lessen the risk of bullying as the fish will space themselves out naturally. Including fish, such as catfish, that are likely to be active after dark rather than during the daytime will also help.

Some aquarium fish, especially those which grow large such as the oscar (*Astronotus ocellatus*), need to be housed on their own, partly because keeping a group together is impractical in terms of the space required. Be prepared to invest in a large aquarium with an efficient filtration system at the outset. This is likely to prove cheaper in the long term than purchasing a series of aquaria as these fish increase rapidly in size. Housing such fish will inevitably work out as being more expensive than setting up a community aquarium.

♦ ABOVE
The neon tetra is one of the most popular tropical fish. It is suitable for a mixed aquarium, and looks impressive when kept in shoals.

♦ RIGHT
The glowlight tetra requires similar conditions to the neon. Females have a more rounded body shape than males and are slightly larger.

A SELECTION OF TROPICAL FRESHWATER FISH

In terms of a community aquarium, it is a good idea to group fish which come from the same part of the world so that you will be able to match them in terms of water quality. Fish that originate from the freshwater rivers of the Amazon region are very popular in this respect.

TETRA

There are many different types of tetra suitable for the community aquarium but, undoubtedly, the most colourful is the cardinal tetra (*Paracheirodon axelrodi*). It can be distinguished easily from the brightly coloured neon tetra (*P. innesi*) since the red stripe extends along the full length of the lower side of its body, rather than being confined to the rear. These fish should be kept in shoals, which should also mean that you have pairs for spawning purposes. Sexing is relatively difficult, however, although the females tend to have slightly broader bodies.

◆ ABOVE
A Myer's hatchetfish. The upturned mouth and flat top to the body indicate these fish live close to the surface, with their narrow bodies minimizing water resistance.

◆ BELOW
A corydoras catfish. These catfish are found near the bottom, as suggested by their down-pointing mouths, allowing them to feed here, as well as by their flat underparts.

GUPPY

Guppies (*Poecilia reticulata*) and their relatives, such as platies and swordtails (*Xiphophorus* species), are also popular fish for a community aquarium. They have been bred in a dazzling array of colour varieties, and sexing is quite straightforward since females are larger and duller in coloration than males. The breeding habits of these fish are unusual, in that they are livebearers rather than egg-layers, which increases the chances of at least some offspring surviving in a densely planted aquarium. It may be better to keep them in a group on their own, however, as they often prefer slightly brackish water conditions, particularly the black molly (*P. sphenops*).

CATFISH

Although many catfish grow too large, or are unsuitable for a typical community aquarium, the corydoras group will usually thrive in these surroundings. They are quite small, typically averaging around 7.5 cm (3 in) in size, and will spend most of their time on or near the floor of the

(*Brachydanio albolineatus*) are another social fish from this part of the world. They display an attractive violet sheen on their bodies, with males being more brightly coloured than females.

Members of the group to avoid include the tinfoil barb (*Barbus schwanenfeldi*), because it will rapidly outgrow a community aquarium, and the tiger barb (*B. tetrazona*), as this will nip at trailing fins, such as on the Siamese fighting fish (*Betta splendens*). These fish belong to the anabantoid group, also known as bubblenest breeders because they construct a nest of bubbles where the female lays her eggs. Another fish that is suitable for mixed housing is the dwarf gourami (*Colisa lalia*). Some gouramis are too large for a community tank, however, and may fight with small companions.

◆ BELOW
Catfish with long barbels, like this beautiful tiger shovelnose, usually have predatory natures and will not make good aquarium mates.

aquarium, frequently resting on wood or slate here. Female corydoras can sometimes be recognized by their slightly larger size and, for breeding purposes, it is better to keep them in smaller groups consisting of a male and two females. The bronze corydoras (*Corydoras aeneus*) is one of the most commonly kept species in the world.

OTHER SPECIES
There are a number of cyprinids from Asia which are popular aquarium occupants, including the rosy barb (*Barbus conchonius*). These are an attractive reddish shade overall, with females being recognizable by their transparent fins. Pearl danios

SETTING UP A TANK

A tropical freshwater tank will need to be set up in a similar way to that recommended previously for goldfish, with an undergravel filter and a layer of gravel on top. In addition, however, a heaterstat will be required in order to maintain the water temperature at around 25ºC (77ºF) for the fish. These differ in their power output, with about 100 watts being needed in an environment at room temperature for every 100 litres (22 imperial gallons) of water in the tank. You can work out the volume of the aquarium easily: multiply the length, depth and width measurements together in millimetres, and then divide by 1000 to give a figure in litres, from which you should subtract approximately 10 per cent to allow for the volume occupied by decor such as rockwork.

In addition to the undergravel filter, a small power filter can also be recommended, partly to assist with the circulation of water in the tank. It has a foam cartridge, drawing particulate matter into the unit. This will then be trapped in the filter and broken down by the bacteria which will become established here. There are also other

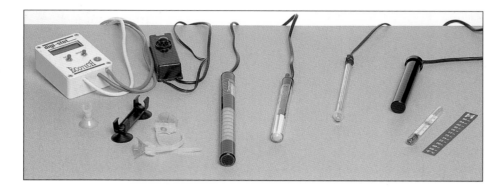

types of filter which can be used, but always check on the cost of the filtration media as these may work out to be expensive if they need to be changed regularly.

Items are available to decorate the aquarium and these can help to create an attractive aquascape, especially if you add a decorative sheet outside at the back of the aquarium, which will emphasize the natural setting. A selection of plants can be grown in a tropical aquarium, and it is important to follow a planting scheme to create the best effect. Leave an unplanted area at the front of the aquarium where the fish can swim and will be clearly visible.

You can place a large impressive plant in the centre, with smaller plants around the sides. Put these in place when the tank is half-full, otherwise they are likely to be displaced as you add the water. It may be better to keep them in pots, disguised by the gravel and the decor in the tank, so that their roots will not block the undergravel filter bed. Floating plants can be added once the tank is full.

If you choose living rather than plastic plants, then good lighting in the tank will be essential. Lighting should be set in a hood so there is no risk of condensation affecting the contacts. Lights, which help the growth of the plants and also enhance the colour of the fish, are available from aquatic outlets.

◆ BELOW
The choice of gravel is important, not only for the correct functioning of an undergravel filter, but also because it could affect the water chemistry.

CLEANING A FILTER

1 When cleaning out a filter, have a bucket to hand, where you can tip out the water. The filter media may sometimes need replacing, so remember to check for this.

2 If possible, it is better to wash out the foam cartridge rather than discarding it, because you will be throwing away the beneficial bacteria here at the same time.

3 Should you replace the foam, then it will take time for a new bacterial population to become established on the new cartridge, and this is likely to affect the filter's efficiency.

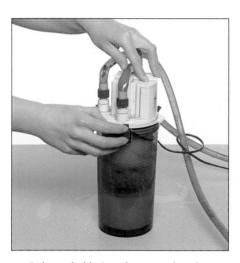

4 Only use dechlorinated water, such as that removed from the tank, to wash the parts of the filter, because the chlorine in tapwater will kill the beneficial bacteria.

Suitable safe rockwork, obtainable from an aquatic shop, can be included. It needs to be free from calcium, which will otherwise dissolve in the water and affect the water chemistry. Bogwood is also available, and can be used to add further retreats for the fish. It must be prepared by being soaked in a bucket of water, with the contents being changed regularly to remove the tannins which will leach out of the wood and turn the water a brownish colour. Alternatively, there are synthetic substitutes available, designed to resemble bogwood in appearance.

When you fill the tank pour the water in carefully, preferably on to a saucer placed on the gravel, so that it will cause less disturbance to the substrate. It must be treated with a water conditioner to remove harmful chlorine-based chemicals and help the fish to settle in their new environment. Special bacteria added to the tank to seed the filter bed will also be helpful. These can be bought from good fish suppliers and simply need to be sprinkled into the water.

CHANGING THE WATER IN A FRESHWATER TANK

1 A gravel cleaner plus a bucket will be needed. Fill the tube with dechlorinated water, keeping a finger over each end, and placing one end in the bucket with the other in the aquarium.

2 By releasing your finger from the lower end of the tube last, water will flow into the bucket with the gravel cleaner stirring up the mulm, which is removed in the water.

3 When topping up the aquarium, be sure the water is at the same temperature as that already in the tank, and add a water conditioner, before pouring it in carefully.

GENERAL CARE AND FEEDING

♦ BOTTOM AND BELOW
There are now specialist diets available (*bottom*) for particular groups of fish, as well as foods to improve coloration (*below*), and rearing foods.

If possible, always allow a new aquarium to settle down for a few days before adding any fish. This will give you an opportunity to monitor the temperature of the water, ensuring that the heating system is working correctly (a digital thermometer is usually attached to the outside of the tank for this purpose).

SETTLING IN

When you acquire the fish, take them home as quickly as possible, and allow the bags in which they have travelled to float on the surface of the aquarium water for 15 minutes, to allow the temperature to rise again. This will make it less stressful for the fish when you release them into their new home.

It is not a good idea simply to pour the fish and water in the bags into the aquarium, as this can introduce parasites, such as white spot, which may be present in the bag water. Instead, net the fish from the bags

and transfer them directly into the aquarium, disposing of the bag water. Nets in a range of sizes are available from aquatic stores. When using a net, scoop the fish up from beneath, as this is usually the easiest way to catch them.

As a precaution, place your hand over the top of the net to prevent the fish jumping out, before lowering the net back into the water. It will be easier and safer to catch the fish individually. When releasing them

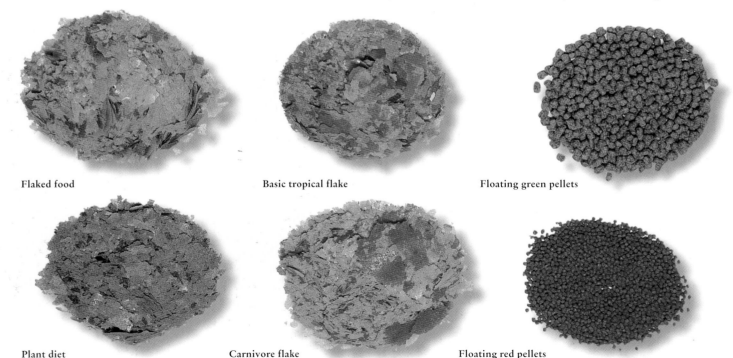

Flaked food

Basic tropical flake

Floating green pellets

Plant diet

Carnivore flake

Floating red pellets

into the aquarium, allow them to find their own way out of the net. Some, such as loaches can have spines which may occasionally catch in the mesh. They will usually free themselves easily by wriggling in the water, but you can help by inverting the net so that the fish sinks out of it. Avoid handling fish directly, certainly with dry hands, because you may damage the mucus covering their bodies.

Keep the lights off at first and allow the fish to settle overnight. You can then start feeding them the next day.

SUITABLE FOODS

A wide range of commercial diets are now produced for tropical fish, with specialist foods, such as catfish pellets, available for specific varieties. Pelleted foods sink to the bottom of the tank, whereas flake foods float on the surface, which makes them especially valuable for surface-feeding fish.

Although these foods will keep the fish in excellent health, it does help to vary their diet. The provision of livefoods will help to trigger breeding behaviour. Although aquatic livefoods such as tubifex worms can be provided, there is a risk that they will introduce disease. It is safer to feed livefoods such as tubifex in a

◆ RIGHT
Frozen and freeze-dried foods are a safe and convenient way to feed livefoods.

◆ TOP LEFT
Catfish often feed at the bottom of the tank, and are regarded as scavengers for this reason.

◆ TOP RIGHT
Corydoras can be given catfish pellets, which sink readily to the floor of the aquarium.

◆ ABOVE
Beware of wasteful overfeeding as decomposing food can affect the fish's health badly.

freeze-dried state; food prepared in this way can also be stored for longer. Alternatively, you can purchase frozen fresh livefoods, which should be defrosted before being fed to the fish. Never overfeed with this food because it will quickly decay in the aquarium if left uneaten.

If you need to be away from home, there are slow-release food blocks that can be left in the aquarium without polluting the water. If you will be away for long, it is better to arrange for someone to check the aquarium daily, in case the fish fall ill or the equipment fails in your absence.

Freeze-dried bloodworms (*top*) and tubifex worms (*below*).

Frozen food

BREEDING

One of the fascinations of keeping tropical fish is the possibility of being able to breed them successfully in the home aquarium. Fish will display a remarkable range of breeding behaviour and, although many species simply lay large numbers of eggs and take no further interest in them – even eating them in some cases – others display remarkable parental concern, brooding the eggs in their mouth and providing a refuge here for the young fish once they hatch.

Perhaps not surprisingly, it is the livebearers such as the guppy which generally prove the easiest to breed successfully in aquarium surroundings. The eggs, in this case, are retained within the body of the female fish, and develop up to the point of hatching, with the young fish bursting out of their egg cases just as they emerge from their mother's body. Unfortunately, they are at risk of being cannibalized by larger fish in the aquarium, and it will be essential for

the aquarium to be densely planted if the young fish are to survive the critical early weeks of life.

The other alternative is to move the pregnant female into a separate tank, housing her in what is known as a breeding trap. This will keep her confined while her young can swim

off into an annexed tank. Once she has produced her brood, the female can then be returned to the main tank, leaving the young to be reared on their own. Livebearers generally produce fewer offspring than egglayers, with a typical guppy brood consisting of about 100 young fish.

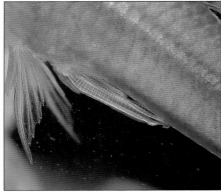

◆ ABOVE
In the case of livebearers, the anal fin is modified into a copulatory organ, called the gonopodium, which helps to separate the sexes.

◆ LEFT
Selective breeding has resulted in stunning strains of livebearers, especially guppies. These fish are blonde cobra guppies.

These may be guarded by the adult fish for a time but, ultimately, it will be necessary to remove the eggs so they can be hatched elsewhere.

Hatching typically only takes a day or two, and the young fish will then rest for a few days, absorbing the remains of their yolk sacs before they start to swim freely around the aquarium. A special fry food intended for the young of egg-laying species can then be offered to them, followed by larger food such as brine shrimp as they grow older. A gentle foam filter will be important to keep the water in good condition, with regular partial water changes, along with the use of a water conditioner, which at this stage is necessary for the well-being of the young fish. They will need to be separated into smaller groups as they grow larger, to prevent overcrowding.

Sexing livebearers is usually very straightforward, because males are invariably smaller and often more colourful than females. If possible, choose the biggest females on offer, because they will produce the largest number of offspring, but if you are particularly interested in breeding your own guppies, for example, you will need to start out with young females. This is because these fish only need to mate once in order to remain fertile for their entire lives.

It can be harder to distinguish between the sexes in the case of egg-laying fish, but the differences often become clearer as the time for spawning approaches. Males often become more colourful, while females swell with spawn at this stage. A separate spawning tank will give the greatest likelihood of success, with the adult fish being transferred back to the main aquarium once they have finished spawning.

The design of the spawning set-up depends on the fish themselves. A stack of marbles used as a floor covering will allow the eggs to fall down between them where they will be out of reach of the fish. Alternatively, plastic mesh of the appropriate size, draped over the sides of the tank and trailing into the water, with the edges held in place with masking tape, can be used to protect the eggs as they are laid. Some fish, such as catfish, will spawn on rockwork and other tank decor.

MARINE FISH

Setting up a marine aquarium is more complex and costly than most fresh-water aquaria but, thanks to modern technology, it is quite straightforward to maintain fish in these surroundings. Most marine aquaria feature coral reef fish from the warmer parts of the world, such as the Red Sea and the Caribbean. These are often brightly coloured and sometimes bizarrely shaped, which adds to their appeal but, again, it is important to ensure that they are compatible, because some can prove to be aggressive.

ANEMONES

The anemone fish, also called clown fish because of their appearance, are one of the easier groups to care for in a marine aquarium, and they can also be bred successfully. The coloration of anemone fish can vary – there are a number of similar species which are mainly orange with white stripes, while others, such as the chocolate or yellow-tailed anemone fish (*Amphiprion clarkii*), are a darker shade. These fish have a close relationship with the Radianthus group of sea anemones, and it is important to include one of these

◆ ABOVE
A regal tang swims past a fanworm. Keeping invertebrates alongside fish in the aquarium can be difficult because they are likely to be eaten.

◆ ABOVE
A striking orange anemone fish. In this case, the fish will benefit from being housed with a sea anemone, with which they normally associate in the wild.

◆ LEFT
A yellowhead wrasse. Some wrasses change dramatically in appearance from juveniles to adults.

invertebrates alongside them. The fish will retreat within the stinging tentacles of the invertebrate for protection if danger threatens.

The damsels are closely related to anemone fish. They are predominantly blue in colour and relatively hardy, and they are often recommended for introducing to a marine aquarium in the early stages. It is not easy to sex them, and take care not to overcrowd them because males, especially, are territorial by nature.

TANGS AND SURGEONS

These fish, so-called because of the sharp spines which can be raised on each side of the base of the tail, have a flattened, yet tall, body shape. They are often beautifully coloured but they can be aggressive towards each other, and it may be better to house them separately. The yellow tang (*Zebrasoma flavescens*) can be kept in a small group in a large aquarium, but the powder blue surgeon (*Acanthurus leucosternon*), which can potentially

grow to 25 cm (10 in) long, is far less social. These fish are primarily vegetarian in their feeding habits, browsing on marine algae and vegetable foods, although young individuals may also eat livefoods.

TRIGGER FISH

This is another boldly-coloured group which reaches a similar size to tangs and surgeons. Trigger fish have powerful jaws and must not be housed with marine invertebrates, which they will eat in the wild. The clown trigger fish (*Balistoides conspicillum*), with its bold white spots and mainly brown and yellow body colour, is popular, as is the Picasso trigger (*Rhinecanthus aculeatus*), with its markings and coloration recalling the artist's work.

OTHER SPECIES

Puffer fish have similar feeding habits to trigger fish, and while some species will live in brackish water, inhabiting estuaries in the wild, others live in the ocean. Their bodies are often covered in spines. Other fish with a similar compact body shape include box fish, which can be dangerous if stressed as they can release a toxin into the water which poisons the other inhabitants.

One of the most popular members of this group is the long-horned cow fish (*Lactoria cornuta*), with bony projections on its head that resemble horns. Their slow swimming style means that they may not be able to keep up with faster tankmates when obtaining food, so check that they receive their share.

Avoid keeping the cleaner wrasse (*Labroides dimidiatus*) with puffer fish because it may harass them, causing them to release their deadly toxin. Wrasses, in general, are colourful fish and are relatively easy to maintain in a tropical marine aquarium.

One of the most appealing of all tank occupants is the seahorse, with its unique breeding habits. Males brood their young in a pouch on the front of their bodies. Seahorses feed mainly on live brine shrimps. Their slow, inoffensive nature means that they are best housed as part of a mainly invertebrate set-up.

◆ ABOVE
A seahorse, revealing its ability to merge into its background, anchors on to coral here.

◆ RIGHT
A yellow dogface puffer, showing its powerful jaws. Its teeth can give a painful nip.

SETTING UP A MARINE TANK

It is vital that all equipment used in a marine aquarium is made of glass or plastic, rather than metal, which is likely to be corroded by the salt water in the tank.

TANK DECOR

In contrast to freshwater set-ups, a marine tank looks rather bare. An undergravel filtration system is to be recommended, however, but with a thick layer of cockleshell serving as the filter bed, often with a covering of coral sand on top. Suitable decor to provide retreats for the fish will again be required, and these can support a range of invertebrates in tanks where they will not be harmed by the fish. It is often recommended to add "living rock" to a marine aquarium, consisting of rockwork which features a range of established invertebrates. This, too, should only be put in place once the system is running properly.

When planning the aquarium, ensure that you have a good view of the fish, with decorations being concentrated towards the back and around the sides of the tank. Aside from living rock, you can incorporate tufa rock which, with its loose structure, provides plenty of nooks and crannies where small invertebrates can establish themselves. Check that

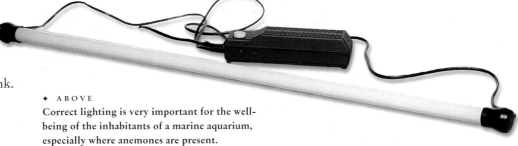

✦ ABOVE
Correct lighting is very important for the well-being of the inhabitants of a marine aquarium, especially where anemones are present.

the rocks will not affect the pH reading of the water, which should be on the alkaline side of the scale, between 8.0 and 8.4.

WATER

Once the decor is in place, you can fill the tank with water. Only use water from the cold supply to avoid the risk of copper being introduced to the aquarium, as this can be toxic, especially to invertebrates. Add a set volume of water to a plastic bucket before stirring in the recommended quantity of sea salt, bought from specialist suppliers, and ensure that the salt dissolves completely before pouring the solution into the tank.

Once the tank is full, switch on the air pump, to ensure that the salt has dissolved, because this will assist in circulating the water, as well as the heating system. Check on the concentration of salts in the water by measuring the specific gravity figure

with a hydrometer. This needs to be set against the water temperature to give a reading; the temperature needs to rise to approximately 25°C (77°F). The reading should be approximately 1.023, but it may take several days to stabilize when the tank is first set up. This is why it is important not to add fish to a marine aquarium immediately, but to allow the system time to settle down for perhaps a week beforehand.

LIGHTING

If you are including invertebrates such as corals and sea anemones, the lighting above the tank will be very important. These invertebrates often have living algae present in their bodies, and they will only thrive if there is adequate light in order to photosynthesize and produce their own nutrients. Special high intensity lights are available from aquatic stores for this purpose – try to locate a specialist fish supplier for the best selection – and these will need to be suspended over the water. Their light output, for maximum benefit to the invertebrates, should be towards the blue end of the light spectrum.

✦ LEFT
Coral sand (*far left*) is the favoured substrate for marine aquaria, but coarser crushed tufa rock (*left*) may be used as a base. The coral sand can then be added over a gravel tidy to create the impression of a sandy base.

SETTING UP A MARINE TANK

1 Fitting a decorative back sheet will greatly enhance the overall natural effect of the finished tank. These seets are obtainable in various lengths and designs to suit different tanks.

2 The undergravel filter must cover the entire base of the floor of the tank if it is to function effectively. These can be purchased to fit various sizes of aquarium and can be cut if necessary.

3 The substrate chosen, which in this case is coral sand, should then be tipped in to the tank and spread out evenly over the filter, where it will serve as the filter bed.

4 Choose suitable rocks to decorate the tank and provide hiding places for the fish. Ensure that these are chemically safe, like tufa rock, and cannot be dislodged because this could have catastrophic results.

5 You can infill between the rockwork with additional substrate if required. Plants are not a feature of marine tanks, so the decor may appear to be rather sparse, although you will be able to see the fish more clearly.

6 If you want to add extra colour and interest in the tank, then it is possible to obtain items such as pieces of coral for this purpose. These should be cleaned as necessary beforehand.

FEEDING AND GENERAL CARE

Your marine aquarium will need occasional maintenance to ensure the welfare of the fish, but as long as the set-up is adequate and a good care routine is established, you should not encounter many problems.

MARINE DIETS

The range of specialist foods now available makes feeding marine fish straightforward. Formulated foods are available for some marine invertebrates. It is important that the food matches the dietary needs of your fish. You may need to use different types if you have vegetarian and more omnivorous species sharing the tank.

Feeding small quantities, several times a day, is recommended to prevent food being wasted and polluting the water. In some cases, as with seahorses, you will need to set up a brine shrimp hatchery to maintain a constant supply of food. Brine shrimp are obtainable in the form of eggs, which are then hatched in a well aerated aquarium of heated water.

WATER CONDITION

It takes time for the filtration system to reach maximum efficiency, so restrict the number of fish for the first

✦ LEFT AND RIGHT
Obviously, living freshwater plants cannot be kept in marine aquaria, but plastic substitutes can be used if required.

✦ BELOW
Air pumps and related equipment are important for the successful functioning of the marine aquarium.

✦ LEFT
Visiting an aquatic outlet specializing in marine fish and invertebrates is the best way to obtain suitable decor for your aquarium.

✦ ABOVE
A selection of processed foods now available for marine fish from fish-keeping stores.

✦ LEFT
A marine cleaner shrimp. These small invertebrates can be added to the tank.

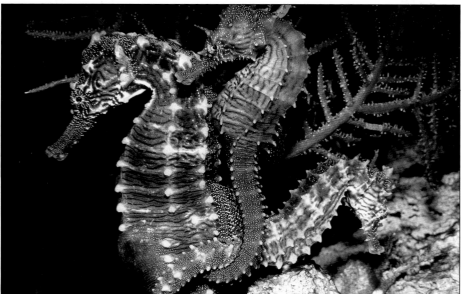

A family of seahorses. The breeding of marine fish is now becoming more commonplace, thanks to a growing understanding of their reproductive needs.

two months to nitrite-tolerant species. This is because the level of nitrite may rise higher at this stage, until the bacteria are present to convert this chemical to nitrate as part of the nitrogen cycle. If you overfeed the fish, then the level of pollution caused by the breakdown of the uneaten food will rise as well.

Since a coral reef is such a stable environment, marine fish from these areas of the world must be kept in similar water conditions. Partly as a result of the heat of the lighting, however, water will evaporate from the tank, leaving the salt behind and

therefore increasing its concentration. Regular hydrometer checks are very important, with dechlorinated water being added to the tank to correct the concentration as necessary.

WATER TESTING

Checks on other aspects of water chemistry, such as the nitrite level and pH, will also be required. Use a pipette to extract water samples from the aquarium. Using a test kit, you can compare the colour change in your water sample to an accompanying chart to determine the result. Should the pH fall below 8.0, then you will

need to replace a quarter of the volume of water, checking the specific gravity as well.

The nitrite level will give a good indication of the efficiency of the filtration system, and a filter maturation product is helpful for this purpose. It will peak at a figure of about 15 parts per million (ppm) and should then fall back to zero to confirm that the chemical is being converted to nitrate. Watch the fish first introduced to the tank, as they will be vulnerable to developing signs of the parasitic illness known as velvet disease, which may be triggered by relatively high nitrite levels.

BREEDING

The likelihood of breeding marine species within an aquarium is less than with tropical freshwater species, but a range of species, from clown fish to seahorses, are now being spawned increasingly successfully. There are recommendations for each species – an increase in the duration of lighting can help with clown fish, for example.

USING A WATER TEST KIT

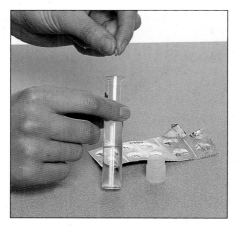

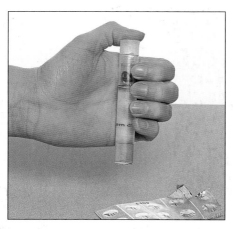

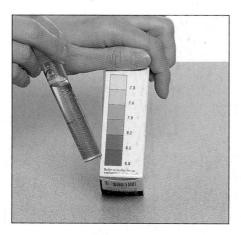

1 Test kits of this type are easy to use and reliable, giving trustworthy readings of water chemistry. The first step usually entails adding water and then the reagent.

2 Place the cap on the tube, and then wait for the reaction to take place. You may have to shake the tube several times, turning it up and down, to mix the solution.

3 In most cases, the result is easily read by comparing the colour of the solution in the tube with that on the accompanying chart. Regular checks are advisable.

HEALTH CARE

Since fish are normally housed in groups rather than individually, it is important to transfer any sick individual to separate quarters with a view to safeguarding the health of the other fish as far as possible. Effective treatment for many fish ailments can be obtained from aquatic and specialist fish-keeping stores. These products can be used at home, but be sure to use them strictly in accordance with the manufacturer's instructions.

FISH HEALTH

◆ BELOW
A typical tank set-up which can be used for treating sick fish. Note the bare base to the tank.

Many of the common diseases that affect fish can be traced back to poor water quality, which leaves them vulnerable to developing infections.

Recently acquired fish are the most at risk, particularly if they have suffered any damage to their scales or fins during the move, as this will make it easier for fungi and other harmful microbes to penetrate the body. Since it is possible to introduce diseases into the established aquarium when new fish are added (for example, if the water in their previous tank was contaminated) it is worthwhile using an isolation tank for a couple of weeks, to check the new arrivals are in good health and feeding well. Many of the formulated fish foods now available contain Vitamin C, and this may help to boost the immune system of the fish at this stage.

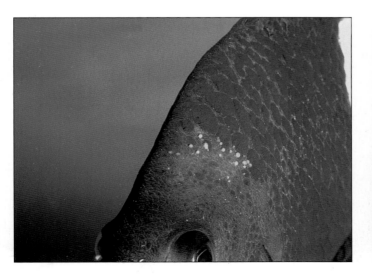

◆ BELOW LEFT
If fish are not isolated before being introduced to the aquarium, they can introduce parasites such as white spot, which will quickly affect other fish and will be harder to control.

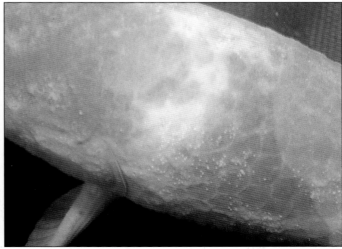

◆ BELOW RIGHT
Another case of white spot, this time of the freshwater variety, in a koi. Diseases in pond fish are hard to spot until they are well-advanced – by which time it could be too late.

◆ ABOVE
A very severe case of fungus smothering a black moor goldfish. Fungus in fish is often linked to the more superficial injuries.

◆ ABOVE
Fin rot which has spread from the tail up the caudal peduncle of a young koi. Poor water conditions often result in this type of infection.

An isolation tank can be converted easily into a treatment tank, should a fish fall ill. A sick fish should be removed at the earliest opportunity from the main aquarium to avoid infecting the others and to improve its chances of recovery. Signs of illness will vary according to the specific condition but loss of colour and appetite are typical, along with a difficulty in swimming.

In the case of many parasitic diseases there may be obvious signs. Fish leeches and anchor worms stick to the fish's body, often causing irritation so that the fish rubs against rockwork. They should not be pulled off directly from the body because this increases the likelihood that the resulting wound will be infected by fungus. These particular parasites are especially common in coldwater fish.

The parasite commonly known as white spot or "ich" (as a result of its scientific name, *Ichthyophthirius multifiliis*) can strike any fish, and spreads very rapidly within an aquarium, thanks to the fact that each individual white spot can contain thousands of the microscopic tomites which are released into the water of the aquarium or pond. These are the intermediate stage in the life-cycle, so removing a fish at this stage should

lessen the likelihood of the infection spreading. Treatments can be used to kill off the free-swimming stage in the life-cycle before the tomites are able to bore into the fish's body.

A similar parasite encountered in marine fish is Oodinium, which causes velvet disease. Outbreaks are often precipitated in this case by a high level of nitrite in the aquarium. If left untreated, the fish will become weak and succumb to fungus, particularly in the case of freshwater species, with the fungal spores being ever-present in the water. Under normal circumstances, the fish will have sufficient resistance to fight the infection, but beware of those which may have suffered fin damage – for example, coldwater fish

in ponds outdoors – for their immune system will not function as well during spells of cold weather.

Signs of an infection of this type depend not only on the part of the body affected, but also the type of fungus. There may be a halo-like effect in some cases, or the fungal growth may appear like strands of cotton wool (cotton balls). Treatment should be carried out in a separate tank, using a proprietary remedy. It is important to use a sponge filter rather than a box-type design, as any carbon here may inactivate the remedy. It is also vital to take care when treating fish in tanks containing invertebrates, as copper-based remedies may assist the fish but are likely to kill their companions.

◆ LEFT
The cause of some parasitic illnesses in fish can be clearly seen, such as anchor worm, which is affecting this goldfish. Always try to check new fish for such parasites.

COMMON ILLNESSES

DROPSY

It is not always possible to treat fish ailments successfully, and the illness known as dropsy is particularly hard to counter. It is often seen in goldfish, with infected individuals suffering from a swollen abdomen which causes them to have difficulty in swimming. Not all cases seem to have infectious origins, but affected fish lose their appetites and, in the case of infectious dropsy, death will follow rapidly. Dropsy is often the result of a bacterial disease, although the illness does not seem to be highly infectious, and it rarely reaches epidemic proportions.

PISCINE TUBERCULOSIS

This is probably the most serious bacterial illness encountered in fish, and it can be spread to people. There are no clear-cut symptoms, but bulging eyes, loss of weight and widespread mortality in a tank can

◆ LEFT
The raised scales seen in the case of this ten-year-old koi are indicative of dropsy, which is often known as "pine cone disease" because of its appearance. The cause in this case was a liver tumour.

be indicative of an outbreak, which can only be confirmed by an autopsy. As a general precautionary measure, it is always sensible to wear rubber gloves when attending to the fish's needs, and this will give effective protection against piscine TB as well. This disease causes a unpleasant skin infection in human beings, usually on the hands where they have been in the water, although it can be treated.

OTHER DISORDERS

Bulging eyes are a feature of some fish, and are often associated with some varieties of goldfish, such as the moor. In other cases, bulging eyes can be a sign of illness or injury, particularly if just one eye is affected. There is usually nothing that can be done to correct a problem of this type, and it is often fatal. The same applies in the case of a swim bladder disorder, which will cause the fish to have difficulty in swimming properly. Fancy goldfish are particularly vulnerable to this condition, which causes them to lose their buoyancy. In the case of tropical fish, swim bladder disorder is often linked with old age.

A less serious disorder, however, is constipation. This is often identified by a long strand of droppings, rather like a length of cotton thread, trailing down from the underside of the fish. Constipation in fish may be related to the feeding of dry food only. Offering a more varied diet, and including livefoods in a suitable form for the type of fish, should help to resolve the problem naturally, as may the addition of fresh greenstuff to the diet of vegetarian species.

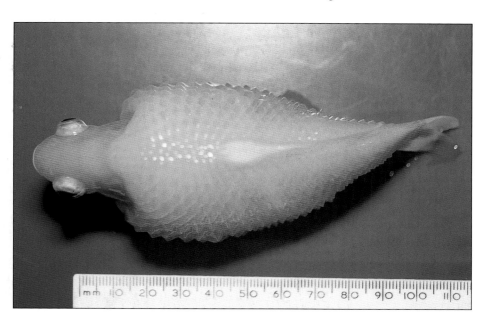

◆ ABOVE
A goldfish displaying signs of dropsy and pop-eye (exophthalmos), which causes the eyes to bulge abnormally. The symptoms in this case were the result of kidney disease.

Pop-eye is not a specific disease but a symptom which can have a number of causes. In the case of this Oscar, it was caused by an infection inside the eye.

A goldfish suffering from swim bladder disorder, preventing it from maintaining its position in the water. This problem is most common in goldfish with round bodies.

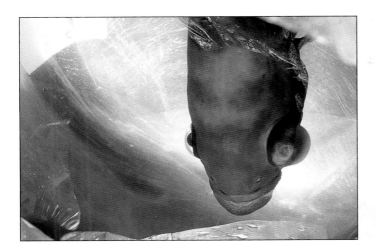

SUDDEN DEATH

One of the most worrying situations is when most, if not all, of the tank occupants are suddenly found dead. This may be due to an environmental factor rather than an outbreak of illness. Check the water chemistry for signs of a sudden shift in the chemical concentration. In any event, change up to a quarter of the volume of water without delay to stabilize the condition of any remaining fish.

Check the functioning of the tank equipment, as it could be that the filtration system has failed or the heaterstat has stopped working. The heater may have continued to warm the water, and this should be obvious by checking the thermometer. A drop in the water temperature, perhaps as the result of a power cut, is far less severe. Once the power is switched back on, the water temperature will gradually rise again.

Poisoning from a source outside the tank is another possibility. A number of common household products, including insecticides which may be sprayed on to houseplants, and flea preparations for other pets, can be deadly for fish. These could be drawn into the water via the air pump. Never be tempted to use such products in a part of the home, or next to a pond, where they could indirectly cause harm to the fish.

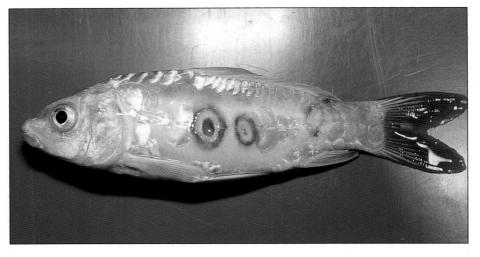

◆ LEFT
Some fish are more susceptible to certain ailments than others. Discus are especially at risk from the parasitic illness known as "hole in the head" disease.

◆ ABOVE
Ulcers caused by bacterial infections can be common in young koi. Look for such signs prior to purchasing these fish, checking both sides of their bodies.

ACKNOWLEDGEMENTS

The author, photographer and publisher would like to thank the following for their help and co-operation in making this book: Ian Abercrombie, John Ainley, J. Ansley, Harriet Bartholomew & Flora, Jonathan Bartholomew, Stephen Bartholomew, S. L. Bond, Jane Burton, William Church, Ian Cinderby, M. Clark, Peter Curry, P. J. Daniels, Carley Deanus, Lauren Deanus, Dawn Deanus, Vanessa Dyer, Jill Fagg, Sue Fisher, Emma Freeman, Dr M. Hackelsberger, V. A. Harris, Alison Hay, James Hay, Debra Hodson, Duane Joy, A. E. Kensit, Simon Gardner, Jo King, Graham Knott, Simon Langdale, Jenny Lavender, Rosie Lowen, Jeanette Marina, M. J. McLellan, Mary Rodriguez, Jackie Roswell, Steve Rudd, Kevin Stevens, Wendy Stevens, Antonia Swierzy, N. P. Tabony, Anne Terry, B. Terry, J. Ward, Angela Warrell, Stuart Worth. Thanks are also due to the Sherfield family, John and staff at Pampered Pets of Godalming, and Sue and family at Burntwood Kennels, Dunsfold.

PICTURE CREDITS

t=top; b=bottom; c=centre;
l=left; r=right

Dennis Avon: 94, 95, 96, 97t, 98t, 98c, 98b, 99t, 99c, 99b, 100t, 100bl, 101t, 101b, 107b, 108t, 109t, 111b, 112b, 114b, 122t, 122b, 123t, 123br, 125bl.

BBC Natural History Unit: Niall Benvie 2, 12t; **Bernard Castelein** 161tl; **John Cancalosi** 143tl; **Jim Clare** 76b; **Georgette Douwma** 160c; **Hanne and Jens Eriksen** 84b; **Jeff Foott** 189tl; **Jürgen Freund** 48c, 158t;

Andrew Harrington 13t; **Fabio Liverani** 184bl; **Vivek Menon** 161tr; **Steven David Miller** 85t, 85b; **Chris O'Reilly** 12b, 184t; **Pete Oxford** 76t, 77b, 133t, 174b; **Tony Phelps** 143tr; **Rico and Ruiz** 158c; **Doug Wechsler** 185tr; **David Welling** 161b; **Andrey Zvoznikov** 30br.

Bruce Coleman Collection: Ingo Arndt 155b; **Trevor Barrett** 225b; **Jen and Des Bartlett** 209bl; **Erwin and Peggy Bauer** 56t; **Jane Burton** 10, 30t, 42b, 43t, 74t, 75b, 78b, 79tl; 169t, 187bc, 187br, 190, 225tl, 236br, 238t; **John Cancalosi** 169b, 193b, 211; **Bruce Coleman Inc.** 226t; **Jeff Foott** 243t; **Sir Jeremy Grayson** 208t, 208tr; **Werner Layer** 78t, 187t, 226b; **Joe McDonald** 151bl; **Robert Maier** 47t, 57tr, 79tr, 188t; **Hans Reinhard** 66t, 66b, 75tl, 163tr, 220t, 237t; **Marie Read** 185tl, 194t; **Alan Stillwell** 210t, 210b; **Kim Taylor** 46b, 67t, 189tr, 189b, 208b, 209tl, 209br, 217c, 217b; **Uwe Walz** 224t; **Jörg and Petra Wegner** 33t, 34t, 34c, 34b, 35t, 35c, 35b,44t, 47b, 75tl, 88b; **Rod Williams** 159cl, 177t, 177b; **Günter Ziesler** 30bl.

Camfauna UK: 7, 153cl, 154bl, 154br, 155t, 156t, 157b, 165b, 165bl, 215tl, 215tr, 216cr, 217t.

John E. Cooper: 214c, 214bl, 214bc, 216tl, 216tr.

Cyril Laubscher: 97b, 100br, 102b, 103, 108b, 110t, 111t, 112t, 113t, 113b, 115t, 118t, 119t, 119b, 125tl.

W. G. V. Lewis MRCVS: 86br, 87tr.

Dermod Malley FRCVS: 86t, 86bl, 87tl, 87b, 88t, 88c, 89t, 90t, 90br, 91t, 92t, 93t, 121bl, 121br, 122tr, 122c, 123bl, 124t, 124b, 124bc, 125br, 212tc, 212tr, 212bc, 212br, 213tl, 213tc, 213tr, 213cl, 213cr, 213b.

Chris Mattison: 5, 6, 128b, 129c, 130c, 130bc, 131tc, 131tr, 131bl, 132tc, 132tr, 132c, 132br, 135tl, 135tc, 135bl, 135br, 136t, 137br, 139t, 140c, 141tl, 141tc, 141tr, 142tr, 143c, 143b, 144t, 145tl, 145c, 146tc, 146c, 147c, 148c, 148b, 149tr, 149cr, 150b, 152br, 154t, 154br, 156b, 157t, 159cr, 160t, 160b, 163tl, 163b, 164b, 165t,166t, 166bl, 166bc, 166br, 168t, 168b, 170b, 171tl, 171tc, 171tr, 171c, 171b, 172t, 172br, 173b, 175t, 176b, 179tr, 179b, 180b, 182t, 182bl, 183br, 183t, 183bl, 183br, 185b, 186c, 186b, 188b, 191tl, 191tr, 191bl, 191br, 192b, 193t, 196t, 196bl, 196br, 197t, 197tr, 197b, 198t, 198br, 199c, 201b, 203t, 204t, 204br, 205, 206t, 206c, 206b, 209tr, 217t.

Photomax: 218, 219, 220cr, 220bl, 220bc, 220br, 221tl, 221tc, 221tr, 221b, 225tr, 227t, 227c, 227b, 228t, 228bl, 228br, 229tl, 229tr, 229bl, 229br, 230t, 230b, 231t, 231b, 234t, 235tl, 235tr, 235c, 236t, 236bl, 237b, 238c, 238b, 239t, 239bl, 239br.

Warren Photographic: Jane Burton 11, 42tl, 42tr, 56b, 57tl, 57b, 60c, 60bl, 65tl, 65tr, 65cl, 65br, 79br, 83tc, 83tr, 83c, 83bl, 83br, 89b, 248.

William H. Wildgoose: 244c, 244bl, 244br, 245tl, 245tr, 245b, 246t, 246b, 247tl, 247tr, 247bl, 247br.